EASTERN & CENTRAL NORTH AMERICA

ALL ABOUT
BACKYARD
BIRDS

Cornell Lab of Ornithology
Illustrations by **Pedro Fernandes**

The**Cornell**Lab of Ornithology

EASTERN & CENTRAL NORTH AMERICA

ALL ABOUT BACKYARD BIRDS

The**Cornell**Lab of Ornithology

Northern Bobwhite
Photo by B. N. Singh

Editors: Hugh Powell, Brian Scott Sockin, and Laura Erickson
Designer: Patricia Mitter
Assistant editors: Kathi Borgmann, Diane Tessaglia-Hymes,
and Francesca Chu
Illustrator: Pedro Fernandes
Cover photos: Carolina Chickadee and Northern Cardinal by
B. N. Singh flickr.com/photos/bnsingh; American Goldfinch
by Keith Bowers; Eastern Bluebird by Alan Gutsell

ISBN: 978-1-943645-04-6

Printed in China

Library of Congress Cataloging-in-Publication Data
available.

10 9 8 7 6 5 4 3

The**Cornell**Lab
Publishing Group

Phoenix St. Claire Publishing, LLC
120A North Salem Street
Apex, NC 27502
www.cornelllabpg.com

CONTENTS

CONTENTS

Belted Kingfisher

Common Grackle

Of all this planet's living creatures, birds are the ones that draw our attention most insistently, year-round, with vivid plumage and myriad sounds. Their flight stirs our imagination; their song inspires our music. Birds are depicted on national emblems, postage stamps, and coins. In our imaginings, Pegasus and angels bear the feathered wings of birds.

Of all wildlife, birds are the most easily seen and heard, in wilderness, on farms, and in the heart of large cities. Birds are accessible everywhere and to almost everyone, a portal to the natural world. When we start paying attention, look and listen, we develop a familiarity with nature that enriches our time outdoors, whether in wild spaces or urban and suburban settings. Think of your home as your own personal "great outdoors" and start exploring the rich tapestry of visual and auditory wonder that surrounds you every day.

Of the roughly 10,000 bird species worldwide, some are iconic and easily recognizable, such as the Bald Eagle, the national symbol of the United States. Other species have inspired names of sports teams, such as the Northern Cardinal, the Common Raven, the Blue Jay, and the Baltimore Oriole. But many birds that surround us are less familiar, their songs woven into the background soundtrack of our everyday lives and the movies and TV shows we watch.

But how exactly do you go about identifying an unfamiliar wild creature likely to fly away before you can figure out what it is? When you notice any bird, pay attention to its size and shape, color pattern, behavior, and the habitat where you saw it. If you have a camera, take pictures, but make sure you're also noticing these features on the living, breathing bird. When you encounter a bird you already know, keep watching to improve your familiarity (e.g., many more people recognize robins hopping on lawns than flying overhead).

Great Blue Heron

All About Backyard Birds is based on the #1 birding website, *AllAboutBirds.org* from the Cornell Lab, used by more than 14 million people each year. In this book, you will find a treasure trove of information, best practices, and advice about backyard birding, whether you're just starting out or are a seasoned birder. You will also discover information about the Cornell Lab's vast online resources and learn about our free **Merlin**® Bird ID app, downloaded by more than one million people.

We've also included a special section about the Cornell Lab's "citizen science" projects—scientific studies driven by contributions from bird watchers just like you—including the Cornell Lab's Project FeederWatch, NestWatch, and Great Backyard Bird Count. Our largest citizen-science initiative is called **eBird**, which provides a free portal for you to create and keep your own bird lists. eBird is the preeminent bird recording tool, with which citizen scientists record more than 100 million bird sightings each year. These projects empower you to participate and contribute to important science while having fun.

Following these primers are pages for each of our 120 common eastern and central North American backyard birds, replete with gorgeous illustrations created for this book by science illustrator Pedro Fernandes.

All About Backyard Birds is the first Cornell Lab Publishing Group book to use our dedicated book companion app, **Bird QR**, which you can tap to scan symbols on each bird page to hear the sounds and calls of that species. You can also use Bird QR with other symbols throughout the book to directly link your smartphone browser to deeper content to learn more on *AllAboutBirds.org*, giving you an optional multimedia experience when you use this guide.

So, let's get started and have fun!

Brian Scott Sockin
CEO/Publisher
Cornell Lab Publishing Group

HOW TO USE
THIS BOOK

GETTING STARTED

All About Backyard Birds is an interactive field guide for new and developing birders, based on *allaboutbirds.org*, the #1 North American birding website from the Cornell Lab of Ornithology. The content you will find in this book was curated by some of the world's leading bird experts and is presented in a friendly, easy-to-understand manner, just like the All About Birds website.

The **first** section of this book is presented as "Birding 101," a primer for beginning and novice birders, but also a refresher for more advanced birders. You will learn how to identify birds with best practices, how to find, watch, and listen to birds, how to choose equipment, and how to take photos of birds (including how to "digiscope" with your smartphone).

The **second** section, "Attracting Birds to Your Backyard," shares some of our best advice and tools to help you "birdscape" or create bird-friendly habitat outside your home. We begin with the three essential elements that all birds need to thrive—food, water, and shelter—followed by descriptions of different types of bird feeders and information on bird food options and what to look for when buying or building nest boxes. We also equip you with the things you need to know to attract the birds you want to see at home, and how you can protect and keep them safe while enjoying them.

The **third** section, "Getting Involved," shares information about citizen science and how you can participate and contribute to important scientific studies at the Cornell Lab.

The **fourth** section is the bird field guide, covering 120 species of common backyard birds in eastern and central North America. Each species page features easy-to-use sections with graphics, cool facts, backyard tips, and more. The diagram on the following page will show you how to navigate the species field guide pages, including where you will use the **Bird QR** app to listen to bird sounds with your smartphone or tablet (you can also use Bird QR on other pages to connect you with content from All About Birds).

Instructions on how to download Bird QR free from Apple and Android stores can be found on page 14.

Group

Common and
scientific names

Photo

Food
preferences
and icon

Nesting
preferences
and icon

Habitat
preferences
and icon

Range
map

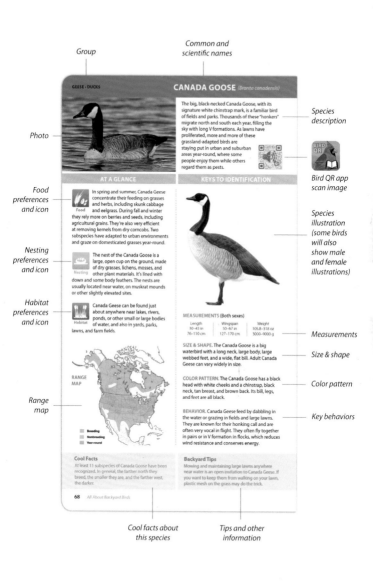

Species
description

Bird QR app
scan image

Species
illustration
(some birds
will also
show male
and female
illustrations)

Measurements

Size & shape

Color pattern

Key behaviors

GEESE · DUCKS

CANADA GOOSE (Branta canadensis)

The big, black-necked Canada Goose, with its signature white chinstrap mark, is a familiar bird of fields and parks. Thousands of these "honkers" migrate north and south each year, filling the sky with long V formations. As lawns have proliferated, more and more of these grassland-adapted birds are staying put in urban and suburban areas year-round, where some people enjoy them while others regard them as pests.

AT A GLANCE

Food In spring and summer, Canada Geese concentrate their feeding on grasses and herbs, including skunk cabbage and eelgrass. During fall and winter they rely more on berries and seeds, including agricultural grains. They're also very efficient at removing kernels from dry corncobs. Two subspecies have adapted to urban environments and graze on domesticated grasses year-round.

Nesting The nest of the Canada Goose is a large, open cup on the ground, made of dry grasses, lichens, mosses, and other plant materials. It's lined with down and some body feathers. The nests are usually located near water, on muskrat mounds or other slightly elevated sites.

Habitat Canada Geese can be found just about anywhere near lakes, rivers, ponds, or other small or large bodies of water, and also in yards, parks, lawns, and farm fields.

RANGE MAP

Breeding
Nonbreeding
Year-round

KEYS TO IDENTIFICATION

MEASUREMENTS (Both sexes)

Length	Wingspan	Weight
30–43 in	50–67 in	105.8–318 oz
76–110 cm	127–170 cm	3000–9000 g

SIZE & SHAPE. The Canada Goose is a big waterbird with a long neck, large body, large webbed feet, and a wide, flat bill. Adult Canada Geese can vary widely in size.

COLOR PATTERN. The Canada Goose has a black head with white cheeks and a chinstrap, black neck, tan breast, and brown back. Its bill, legs, and feet are all black.

BEHAVIOR. Canada Geese feed by dabbling in the water or grazing in fields and large lawns. They are known for their honking call and are often very vocal in flight. They often fly together in pairs or in V formation in flocks, which reduces wind resistance and conserves energy.

Cool Facts
At least 11 subspecies of Canada Goose have been recognized. In general, the farther north they breed, the smaller they are, and the farther west, the darker.

Backyard Tips
Mowing and maintaining large lawns anywhere near water is an open invitation to Canada Geese. If you want to keep them from walking on your lawn, plastic mesh on the grass may do the trick.

Cool facts about
this species

Tips and other
information

BIRD QR

BIRD QR is a dedicated book companion app that helps to bring *All About Backyard Birds* to life, created especially for this and other books from the Cornell Lab Publishing Group.

Visit the Apple or Android store to search "Bird QR" and download the app for free. Once downloaded, open the app and touch "Tap To Start," which will bring you to the main menu screen (shown bottom right). From there, you can start scanning symbols in the book by touching the "Scan Book QR Now" button or navigate to another page.

All About Backyard Birds features two kinds of color-coded scannable symbols for use with Bird QR:

 Listen to Bird Sounds. Each bird species page in this book has this symbol to listen to bird sounds on that page with Bird QR. Simply scan the symbol and choose the sounds you want to hear. They are also stored in "Scan History" for you to quickly pull up later on your smartphone.

 Open Website URL. When you see this symbol on a page in this book and scan with Bird QR, it will open your browser and take you to a specific URL page to learn more.

In Bird QR, you can also learn how to get the free Merlin® Bird ID app from the Cornell Lab, new Cornell Lab Publishing Group books that also work with Bird QR, and resources available from the Cornell Lab's All About Birds website (*AllAboutBirds.org*), from which this book was created.

 Look for new capabilities and functions of the Bird QR app such as video streaming in future updates.

BIRDING
101

BIRD IDENTIFICATION

4 **KEYS TO BIRD IDENTIFICATION:** To identify an unfamiliar bird, focus first on four keys to identification.

Eastern Bluebird

With more than 800 species of birds in the U.S. and Canada, it's easy for a beginning bird watcher to feel overwhelmed by possibilities. Field guides often look crammed with similar birds arranged in seemingly haphazard order. We can help you figure out where to begin.

First we share where *not* to start. Many ID tips focus on very specific details of plumage called field marks, such as the eyering of a Ruby-crowned Kinglet, or the double breast band of a Killdeer. While these tips are useful, they assume you've already narrowed down your search to just a few similar species.

Instead, start by learning how to recognize the group a mystery bird belongs to. You may still need to look at field marks to clinch some IDs. But these four keys—**Size and Shape, Color Pattern, Behavior,** and **Habitat**—will quickly get you to the right group of species, so you'll know exactly which field marks to look for.

1 SIZE AND SHAPE

Birds are built for what they do. Every part of the bird you're looking at is a clue to what it is.

The combination of size and shape is one of the most powerful tools to identification. Though you may be drawn to watching birds because of their wonderful colors or fascinating behavior, when it comes to making identifications, size and shape are the first pieces of information you should examine.

With just a little practice and observation, you'll find that differences in size and shape will jump out at you. The first steps are to learn typical bird silhouettes, find reliable ways to gauge the size of a bird, and notice differences in telltale parts of a bird such as the bill, wings, and tail.

Soon, you'll know the difference between Red-winged Blackbirds and European Starlings while they're still in flight, and be able to identify a Red-tailed Hawk or Turkey Vulture without taking your eyes off the road.

Become Familiar with Silhouettes

Often you don't need to see any color at all to know what kind of bird you're looking at.

Silhouettes quickly tell you a bird's size, proportions, and posture, and quickly rule out many groups of birds—even ones of nearly identical overall size.

HOUSE FINCH.
A small-bodied finch with a fairly large beak and somewhat long, flat head. The House Finch has a relatively shallow notch in its tail.

Beginning bird watchers often get sidetracked by a bird's bright colors, only to be frustrated when they search through their field guides. Finches, for example, can be red, yellow, blue, brown, or green, but they're still always shaped like finches. Learn silhouettes, and you'll always be close to an ID.

Judge Size Against Birds You Know Well

Size is trickier to judge than shape.

You never know how far away a bird is or how big that nearby rock or tree limb really is. Throw in fluffed-up or hunkered-down birds and it's easy to get fooled. But with a few tricks, you can still use size as an ID key.

Sometimes you need two reference birds for comparison. A crow is bigger than a robin but smaller than a goose.

Compare your mystery bird to a bird you know well. It helps just to know that your bird is larger or smaller than a sparrow, a robin, a crow, or a goose, and it may help you choose between two similar species, such as Downy and Hairy woodpeckers or Sharp-shinned and Cooper's hawks.

Judge Against Birds in the Same Field of View

Your estimate of size gets much more accurate if you can compare one bird directly against another.

When you find groups of different species, you can use the ones you recognize to sort out the ones you don't.

Use size and shape to find the full range of species hiding in a large flock. Amid these orange-billed Royal Terns are some smaller Sandwich Terns. You'll also notice a giant Herring Gull in the background, as well as several smaller Laughing Gulls to its right.

For instance, if you're looking at a gull you don't recognize, you can start by noticing that it's larger than a more familiar bird, such as a Ring-billed Gull, that's standing right next to it. For some groups of birds, including shorebirds, seabirds, and waterfowl, using a known bird as a ruler is a crucial identification technique.

Apply Your Size and Shape Skills to the Parts of a Bird

After you've taken note of a bird's overall size and shape, there's still plenty of room to hone your identification.

Turn your attention to the size and shape of individual body parts. Here you'll find clues to how the bird lives its life: what it eats, how it flies, and where it lives.

Start with the bill—that all-purpose tool that functions as a bird's hands, pliers, knitting needles, knife-and-fork, and bullhorn. A flycatcher's broad, flat, bug-snatching bill looks very different from the thick, conical nut-smasher of a finch. Notice the slightly downcurved bills of the Northern Flickers in your backyard. That's an unusual shape for a woodpecker's bill, but perfect for a bird that digs into the ground after ants, as flickers often do.

Bills are an invaluable clue to identification, but tail shape and wing shape are important, too. Even subtle differences in head shape, neck length, and body shape can all yield useful insights if you study them carefully.

Noticing details like these can help you avoid classic identification mistakes. For example, the Ovenbird is a common eastern warbler that has tricked many a bird watcher into thinking it's a thrush. The field marks are certainly thrushlike—warm brown above, strongly streaked below, even a crisp white eyering. But look at overall shape and size rather than field marks, and you'll see the body plan of a warbler—plump, compact body, short tail and wings, thin, pointed, insect-grabbing bill.

Measure the Bird Against Itself

This is the most powerful way to use a bird's size for identification.

It's hard to judge a lone bird's size, and an unusual posture can make shape hard to interpret. But you can always measure key body parts (e.g., wings, bill, tail, legs) against the bird itself.

Look for details such as how long the bird's bill is relative to the head. That's a great way to tell apart Downy and Hairy woodpeckers as well as Greater and Lesser yellowlegs, but it's useful with other confusing species, too. Judging how big the head is compared to the rest of the body helps separate Cooper's Hawks from Sharp-shinned Hawks in flight. Get in the habit of using the bird itself as a ruler, and you'll be amazed at how much information you can glean from each view. Good places to start include noting how long the legs are; how long the neck is; how far the tail extends past the body; and how far the primary feathers of the wing end compared to the tail.

2 COLOR PATTERN

When identifying a bird, focus on patterns instead of trying to match every feather.

A picture, even a fleeting glimpse, can be worth a thousand words. As soon as you spot a bird, your eyes take in the overall pattern of light and dark. And if the light allows, you'll probably

Painted Bunting

glimpse the main colors as well. This is all you need to start your identification.

Use these quick glimpses to build a hunch about what your mystery bird is, even if you just saw it flash across a path and vanish into the underbrush. Then, if the bird is kind enough to hop back into view, you'll know what else to look for to settle the identification.

Imagine that you're on vacation in Yosemite National Park. You see a small, bright-yellow bird flitting into the understory. Yellow immediately suggests a warbler (or the larger Western Tanager). Did you pick up a hint of grayness to the head? Or perhaps some glossy black? Just noticing that much can put you on track to identifying either a MacGillivray's Warbler or a Wilson's Warbler.

Some birds have very fine differences that take practice even to see at all. But don't start looking for those details until you've used overall patterns to let the bird remind you what it is. Read on for a few tips about noticing patches of light and dark, and the boldness or faintness of a bird's markings.

Light and Dark

When you're trying to make an ID, keep in mind that details can change, but overall patterns stay the same.

Remember that birds molt and their feathers wear. Their appearance can vary if the bird is old or young, or by how well it had been eating last time it molted. And of course, the light the bird is sitting in can have a huge effect on the colors you see.

At a distance and in very quick sightings, colors fade and all that's left are light and dark. It helps to familiarize yourself with common patterns. For example, American White Pelicans are large white birds with black trailing edges to their wings. Snow Geese are similarly shaped and colored, but the black in their wings is confined to the wingtips.

Ring-necked Ducks and scaup are dark ducks with a pale patch on the side; Northern Shovelers are the opposite: light-bodied ducks with a dark patch on the side.

Ring-necked Duck

Many birds are dark above and pale below—a widespread pattern in the animal world that helps avoid notice by predators. By reversing this pattern, male Bobolinks, with their dark underparts and light backs, look conspicuous even from all the way across a field.

Other birds seem to be trying to call attention to themselves by wearing bright patches of color in prominent places. Male Red-winged Blackbirds use their vivid shoulder patches to intimidate their rivals (notice how they cover up the patches when sneaking around off their territory). American Redstarts flick bright orange patches in their wings and tail, perhaps to scare insects out of their hiding places.

Many birds, including Dark-eyed Juncos, Spotted and Eastern towhees, American Robins, and several hummingbirds, flash white in the tail when they fly, possibly as a way of confusing predators. White flashes in the wings are common, too: look for them in Northern Mockingbirds; Acorn, Golden-fronted, and Red-bellied woodpeckers; Common and Lesser nighthawks; and Phainopeplas.

Bold and Faint

Notice strong and fine patterns.

There are some confusing bird species that sit side by side in your field guide, wearing what seems like the exact same markings and defying you to identify them. Experienced birders can find clues to these tricky identifications by noticing how boldly or finely patterned their bird is. These differences can take a trained eye to detect, but the good news is that there's a great trial case right outside at your backyard feeder.

House Finch

House Finches are common across most of North America. Much of the continent also gets visits from the very similar Purple Finch. Males of the two species are red on the head and chest and brown and streaky elsewhere. The females are both brown and streaky. So how do you tell them apart? Look at how strongly they're marked.

Male House Finches tend to be boldly streaked down the flanks, whereas male Purple Finches are much paler and more diffusely streaked. Even the red is more distinct, and more confined to the head and breast, in a male House Finch. Male Purple Finches look washed all over, even on the back, in a paler raspberry red.

The all-brown females of these two species are an even better way to build your skills. The streaks on female House Finches are indistinct, brown on brown, with little actual white showing through. If a female Purple Finch lands next to it, she'll stand out with crisply defined brown

Purple Finch

streaks against a white background, particularly on the head.

Once you've had some practice, these small differences can be very useful. Similar degrees in marking can be seen between the coarsely marked Song Sparrow and finely painted Lincoln's Sparrow, and between immature Sharp-shinned and Cooper's hawks.

3 BEHAVIOR

There's what birds wear, and then there's how they wear it. A bird's attitude goes a long way in identification.

Bird species don't just look unique, they have unique ways of acting, moving, sitting, and flying. When you learn these habits, you can recognize many birds the same way you notice a friend walking through a crowd of strangers.

Chances are you'll never see a Cedar Waxwing poking through the underbrush for seeds, or a Wood Thrush zigzagging over a summer pond catching insects. But similar-sized birds such as towhees and swallows do this all the time. Behavior is one key way these birds differ.

Because so much of a bird's identity is evident in how it acts, behavior can lead you to an ID in the blink of an eye, in bad light, or from a quarter-mile away. Before you even pick up your binoculars, notice how your bird is sitting, how it's feeding or moving, whether it's in a flock, and if it has any nervous habits such as flicking its wings or bobbing its tail.

And remember that to get good at recognizing birds by their behavior, you must spend time watching them. It's tempting to grab your field guide as soon as you see a field mark. Or, after identifying a common bird, you might feel rushed to move on and find something more unusual. Resist these urges. Relax and watch the bird for as long as it will let you. This is how you learn the way a bird acts, how you discover something new...and let's face it, it's probably why you went out bird watching in the first place.

Posture

The most basic aspect of behavior is posture, or how a bird presents itself.

You can learn to distinguish many similarly proportioned birds just from the poses they assume. It's a skill that includes recognizing a bird's size and shape, and adds in the impression of the bird's habits and attitude.

Warblers and flycatchers can be distinguished by posture.

*Warbler
Silhouette*

*Flycatcher
Silhouette*

For example, in the fall season, the small, drab-green Pine Warbler looks similar to the Acadian Flycatcher, right down to the two wingbars and the straight bill. But you're unlikely to confuse the two because their postures are so different. Pine Warblers hold their bodies horizontally and often seem to crouch. Flycatchers sit straight up and down, staying on alert for passing insects.

Horizontal versus vertical posture is the first step. Next, get an impression of the how the bird carries itself. Does it seem inquisitive like a chickadee or placid like a thrush? Does it lean forward, ready for mischief, like a crow? Or is it assertive and stiff, like a robin? Do the bird's eyes dart around after targets, like a flycatcher, or methodically scan the foliage like a vireo? Is the bird constantly on alert, like a finch in the open? Nervous and skittish like a kinglet?

Movement

As soon as a sitting bird starts to move, it gives you a new set of clues about what it is.

You'll not only see different parts of the bird and new postures, you'll sense more of the bird's attitude through the rhythm of its movements. There's a huge difference between the bold way a robin bounces up to a perch, a mockingbird's showy, fluttering arrival, and the meekness of a towhee skulking around.

On the water, some ducks, such as Mallard and Northern Pintail, tip up (or "dabble") to reach submerged vegetation. Others, including scaup and Redhead, disappear from view as they dive for shellfish and other prey. Among the divers, you'll notice that some species, such as eiders, open their wings just before they dive. These ducks flap their wings for propulsion underwater, and they almost always begin a dive this way.

Flight Pattern

Certain birds have flight patterns that give them away.

Almost nothing flaps as slowly as a Great Blue Heron—you can see this from miles away. Learn the long swooping flight of most woodpeckers and you'll be able to pick them out before they've even landed.

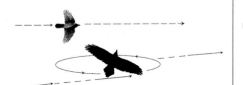

Crows and Ravens
Flight style can be a great way to identify birds at a distance. Although crows and ravens look very similar, they fly quite differently. American Crows flap slowly and methodically, whereas Common Ravens take frequent breaks from flapping to soar or glide.

Many small birds, particularly finches, have bouncy, roller-coaster-like trajectories caused by fluttering their wings and then actually folding them shut for a split second.

Birds of prey have their own distinct styles. Red-tailed Hawks and other buteos fly with deep, regular wingbeats or soar in circles on broad wings. Falcons fly with powerful beats of their sharply pointed wings.

Feeding Style

Much of the time that you watch birds on the move, you'll be watching them feed, so it pays to become familiar with foraging styles.

Some are obvious: the patient stalking of a heron; the continual up-and-back sprints of Sanderlings; the plunge of a kingfisher. But you can develop a surprisingly specific impression of almost any bird just from a few seconds of watching it forage.

For example, swallows, flycatchers, vireos, finches, and thrushes are all roughly the same size, but they feed in totally different manners: swallows eat on the wing; flycatchers dart out from perches and quickly return; vireos creep through leaves; finches sit still and crush seeds; and thrushes hop low to the ground eating insects and fruit.

Flocking

A flock of kingfishers? A single starling all on its own? Some species seem to be born loners, and others are never found solo.

Even among flocking birds, there are those content to travel in threes and fours, and others that gather by the dozens and hundreds. A noisy group of yellow birds in a treetop is much more likely to be a flock of American Goldfinches than a group of Yellow Warblers. A visit to northern coasts in winter might net you several thousand Brant, but you'll probably only see Harlequin Ducks by the handful. Learning the tendencies of birds to flock and their tolerance for crowding is one more aspect of behavior you can use. Just remember that many species get more sociable as summer draws to a close. After nesting is over and young are feeding themselves, adults can relax and stop defending their territories.

Herring Gulls

You'll often see gulls in flocks, whether standing on a beach, or in a parking lot, or wheeling overhead.

4 HABITAT

*A habitat is a bird's home, and many birds are choosy.
Narrow down your list by keeping in mind where you are.*

Identifying birds quickly and correctly is often about probability.
By knowing what's likely to be seen you can get a head start on
recognizing the birds you run into. And when you see a bird you
weren't expecting, you'll know to take an extra look.

Habitat is both the first and last question to ask yourself when
identifying a bird. Ask it first, so you know what you're likely
to see, and last as a double-check. You can fine-tune your
expectations by taking geographic range and time of year into
consideration.

Birding by Probability

We think of habitats as collections of plants—grassland, cypress,
pine woods, deciduous forest. But they're equally collections of
birds. By noting the habitat you're in, you can build a hunch about
the kinds of birds you're most likely to see.

Of course, if you only let yourself identify birds you expect to see,
you'll have a hard time finding unusual birds. The best way to find
rarities is to know your common birds first (the ones left over are
the rare ones). Birding by probability just helps you sort through
them that much more quickly.

Red-breasted Nuthatch

Use Range Maps

You don't have to give yourself headaches trying to keep straight every last bird in your field guide. They may all be lined up next to each other on the pages, but that doesn't mean they're all in your backyard or local park.

Breeding
Migration
Winter
Winter (scarce)
Year-round

Make it a habit to check the range maps before you make an identification. For example, you can strike off at least half of the

Range map of the Yellow-rumped Warbler.

devilishly similar *Empidonax* flycatchers at once, just by taking into account where you are when you see one. Similarly, North America has two kinds of small nuthatches with brown heads, but they don't occur within about 800 miles of each other.

Of course, birds do stray from their home ranges, sometimes fantastically—that's part of the fun. But remember that you're birding by probability, so first compare your bird against what's likely to be present. If nothing matches, then start taking notes.

Check the Time of Year

Range maps hold another clue to identification—they tell you when a bird is likely to be around.

Many of summer's birds, including most of the warblers, flycatchers, thrushes, hummingbirds, and shorebirds, are gone by late fall. Other birds move in to replace them. This mass exodus and arrival is part of what makes bird watching during migration so exciting.

Yellow-rumped Warbler

Use eBird to Help

eBird's online species maps are a great way to explore both range and season. You can zoom in to see bird records from your immediate surroundings, and you can filter the map to show you just sightings from a particular month or season.

Another way to focus on the most likely birds near you is to use our free Merlin® Bird ID app for iOS and Android. Merlin takes your location and date, asks you a few simple questions, and gives you a short list of matching possibilities. See page 30 for more on Merlin.

USING FIELD MARKS TO IDENTIFY BIRDS

Once you've looked at Size and Shape, Color Pattern, Behavior, and Habitat to decide what general type of bird you're looking at, you may still have a few similar birds to choose between. To be certain of your identification, you'll need to look at field marks.

Birds display a huge variety of patterns and colors, which they have evolved in part to recognize other members of their own species. Birders can use these features (called "field marks") to help distinguish species. Pay particular attention to the field marks of the head and the field marks of the wing.

Ornithologists divide a bird's body into topographical regions: beak (or bill), head, back, wings, tail, breast, belly, and legs. To help with identification, many of these regions are divided still further. This diagram shows some of the commonly used descriptive terms.

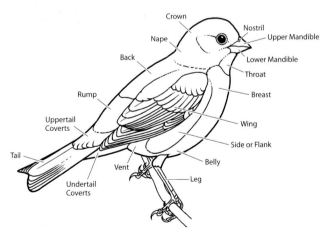

Field Marks of the Head

When identifying an unknown bird, markings on the head are particularly important, as are beak shape and size. Here are head markings visually displayed to help you along.

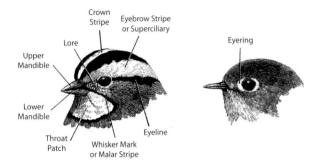

Field Marks of the Wing

A bird's wings are another great place to pick up clues about its identity. In a few groups, notably warblers and vireos, the presence of wingbars and patches of color on the wing can give positive identification even when the bird is in nonbreeding plumage. In other groups, such as flycatchers and sparrows, the absence of wing markings may be important. It also pays to learn the main feather groups, such as primaries, secondaries, tertials, and coverts, and to look for "feather edging"—a different color running along the edges of feathers.

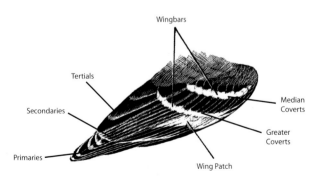

USE MERLIN APP TO SEE THE POSSIBILITIES

Merlin®, an instant bird identification app from the Cornell Lab of Ornithology, can make many identifications simple. It works by narrowing down your choices, prompting you to enter the date, location, and the bird's size, colors, and behavior.

Merlin was designed to be a birding coach for beginning and intermediate bird watchers. Merlin asks you the same questions that an expert birder would ask to help solve a mystery bird sighting. Notice that date and location are Merlin's first and most important questions.

It takes years of experience in the field to know what species are expected at a given location and date. Merlin shares this knowledge with you based on more than 100 million sightings submitted to eBird from birders across the United States and Canada.

Merlin also asks you to describe the color, size, and behavior of the bird you saw. Because no two people describe birds exactly the same way, Merlin presents a shortlist of matching species based on descriptions from Cornell Lab experts as well as thousands of bird enthusiasts who helped "teach" Merlin by participating in online activities.

Much like a modern field guide app, Merlin also provides world-class photos, ID text, sounds, and range maps. You can browse more than 2,000 stunning images taken by top photographers and listen to a selection of songs and calls for each species.

Download Merlin FREE (see page 14 for details).

THE RIGHT STUFF

10 TIPS FOR BEGINNING BIRD WATCHERS

Birding mainly involves patience, careful observation, and a willingness to let the wonder and beauty of the natural world overtake you. But having the right equipment can help too:

1 Binoculars.
Your enjoyment of birds depends hugely on how great they look through your binoculars, so make sure you're getting a big, bright, crisp picture through yours. In recent years excellent binoculars have become available at surprisingly low prices. So while binoculars under $100 may seem tempting, it's truly worth it to spend $250 to $300 for vastly superior images as well as lifetime warranties, waterproof housing, and lighter weight. We suggest getting 7-power or 8-power binoculars—they're a nice mix of magnification while still allowing you a wide enough view that your bird won't be constantly hopping out of your image.

2 Field Guide.
Field guides like this one focus on the most common species in your area and are meant to be portable. Unlike their digital counterparts, they often earn a special place on windowsills, providing a ready resource at home for hours of study and daydreaming.

3 Bird Feeders.
With binoculars for viewing and a guide to help you figure out what's what, the next step is to attract birds to your backyard, where you can get a good look at them. Bird feeders come in all types, but we recommend starting with a black oil sunflower feeder, adding a suet feeder in winter and a hummingbird feeder in summer (or all year in parts of the continent). From there you can diversify to feeders that house millet, thistle seeds, mealworms, and fruit to attract other types of species. In sections that follow, we describe the main types of bird feeders along with images of what they look like, to help

you choose the right feeders for your yard and to attract the birds you want to see.

4 Spotting Scope.

By this point in our list, you've got pretty much all the gear you need to be a birder—that is, until you start looking at those ducks on the far side of the pond, or shorebirds in mudflats, or that Golden Eagle perched on a tree limb a quarter-mile away. Though they're not cheap, spotting scopes are indispensable for seeing details at long range—or simply reveling in intricate plumage details that can be brought to life only with a 20x to 60x zoom. And scopes, like binoculars, are coming down in price while going up in quality.

5 Camera.

With the proliferation of digital gadgetry, you can take photos anywhere, anytime. Snapping even a blurry photo of a bird can help you or others clinch its ID. And birds are innately artistic creatures—more and more amateur photographers are connecting with birds through taking gorgeous pictures. There's also the growing practice of digiscoping—pointing your smartphone's camera through a spotting scope or binoculars.

6 Keeping a List.

"Listing" doesn't have to be for hardcore birders only; it's fun to record special moments from your days of birding. Many people save their records online using eBird. A Cornell Lab project, eBird allows you to keep track of every place and day you go bird watching, enter notes, share sightings with friends, and explore the data other eBirders have entered. Learn more about eBird and how to use it for free on pages 57–58.

7 Birding by Ear.

Many people love bird sounds—calls, songs, and other avian utterances that fill the air. You can use these sounds as clues to identify species. Based on the success of our *Backyard Birdsong Guide* series by world-renowned audiologist Donald Kroodsma, we've added audio capabilities to this book with the Bird QR app. See the next section, "Listening to Birds," for more.

8 **Visual Bird Identification Skills.**
Now that we've covered the physical tools that equip you for bird watching, let's loop back to your mental tools. Once you're outside and surrounded by birds, practice the four-step approach to identification that we shared earlier in Birding 101: Size and Shape; Color Pattern; Behavior; and Habitat.

9 **Birding Apps and Digital Field Guides.**
If you have a smartphone, you can carry a bookshelf in your pocket. You've already learned about Merlin® Bird ID app, but there are many other resources at your disposal. Download the eBird app to keep track of your bird observations in the field. There are also digital field guides—most of the major printed field guides have an app or eBook version. Some specialized apps cover specific groups of species, such as the Warbler Guide and Raptor ID apps. Others, like LarkWire, focus on helping you learn bird song. Search for them in Apple and Android stores.

And our All About Birds species guide works on mobile devices, giving you access to free ID information and sound recordings straight from your smartphone's Internet browser. With the free Bird QR book companion app, you can scan the QR symbols in this guide to display specific web pages related to what you're reading about right inside the app, so you can learn even more.

10 **Connect with Other Birders.**
Bird watching can be a relaxing solo pursuit, like a walk in the woods decorated with bird sightings. But birding can also be a social endeavor, and the best way to learn is from other people. A great way to connect with people is to look on *birding.aba.org* and sign up for a listserv for your area. You'll get emails that will tell you what people have been seeing, announce local bird outings, and connect you with members of your local birding club. Many regions also have Facebook groups where people share what they've been seeing and welcome newcomers. There's a decent chance that someone's leading a bird walk near you this weekend—and they'd love to have you come along.

LISTENING TO BIRDS

When a bird sings, it's telling you what it is, where it is, and often what is happening.

You can only see straight ahead, but you can hear in all directions at once. Learning bird songs is a great way to identify birds hidden by dense foliage, birds far away, birds at night, and birds that look identical to each other.

Song Sparrow

And then there's the "dawn chorus," that time as the sun begins to light up the world, when birds join together in a symphony of sound. When you first listen to a dawn chorus in full swing, the sheer onslaught of bird song can be overwhelming. How does anyone begin to pick apart the chirps, whistles, and trills that are echoing out of the woods? The answer, of course, is to concentrate on one bird at a time—and that approach holds true when you're trying to learn individual songs, too. Don't try to memorize each entire song you hear; instead, focus on one quality of the sound at a time. Many birds have a characteristic rhythm, pitch, or tone to their song. Here's how to use them:

Rhythm

Get used to a bird's characteristic tempo as well as the number of distinct sections to its song. Marsh Wrens sing in a hurry, while White-throated Sparrows are much more leisurely.

Repetition

Some birds characteristically repeat syllables or phrases before moving on to a new sound. Northern Mockingbirds do this many times in a row. Though Brown Thrashers sound similar, they typically repeat only twice before changing to a new syllable.

Pitch

Most birds sing in a characteristic range, with smaller birds (such as the Cedar Waxwing) typically having higher voices and larger birds (such as the Common Raven) usually having deeper voices. Many bird songs change pitch, so it helps to pay attention to the overall pitch trend in a song. Some birds are distinctive for having steady voices, such as the Chipping Sparrow's trill.

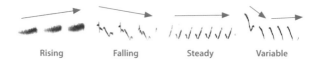

| Rising | Falling | Steady | Variable |

Tone

The tone of a bird's song is sometimes hard to describe, but it can be very distinctive. As a start, pay attention to whether a bird's voice is a clear whistle, harsh or scratchy, liquid and flutelike, or a clear trill. If you can remember the quality of a bird's voice, it can give you a clue to the bird's identity even if the bird doesn't sing the same notes every time.

- **Buzzy**: Like a bee–a good example would be Townsend's Warbler song.
- **Clear**: Something you could whistle. Northern Cardinals have a clear song, as do Yellow Warblers.
- **Trilled**: A lot of sounds in a row that are too fast to count (technically, more than 11 sounds per second). Chipping Sparrows and Dark-eyed Juncos sing trills.

Buzzy

Clear

Trilled

Use Bird QR

Scan the sound QR symbol on each species page to see and listen to different bird sounds. With Bird QR, this book instantly becomes an audio field guide and will also keep track of all your history for future quick access in the app.

PHOTOGRAPHING BIRDS

5 BASICS OF GOOD BIRD PHOTOGRAPHY

With the explosion in availability and design of digital cameras, it's now possible for hobbyists to take amazingly good photos. Though your photos may not show up on the cover of *National Geographic*, you can up the "wow" factor by paying attention to a few basics.

Beyond the mechanical aspects of shutter speed, aperture, and ISO (which digital cameras increasingly handle automatically), there is an indefinable something that transforms an image into a work of art. Often thought of as talent, just as often it's the result of hours of practice and attention to detail. Here are five basics of good bird photography to bear in mind:

1 **Lighting.** The best times to shoot are morning and late afternoon when the light is angled, warmer, and more subdued. It's harder to take a good picture in the middle of a bright, clear day because images end up with too much contrast, where light areas get washed out and shadows turn inky black. Having the source of light behind and slightly to one side of you creates a more three-dimensional subject. Having your subject backlit rarely works well unless you're deliberately going after a silhouette.

2 **Framing.** Professionals usually avoid placing any subject in the exact center of a photograph. It tends to be more visually stimulating to see the bird off to one side, facing inward. Our own eyes naturally follow the same trajectory. Likewise, avoid placing the horizon line in the middle of a picture, which cuts it in half and divides the image. It's better to frame the horizon in the top or bottom third of your photograph.

3 **Composition.** Non-bird elements in your picture can add or detract from a pleasing composition. Branches, shrubbery, rocks, and flowers can be a distraction—or they can be used artfully to frame the bird within the picture.

Although you want to avoid having a branch right behind the bird, looking like it's growing out of its head, incorporating some part of the bird's habitat often makes a shot better. If the background is too busy, try opening the aperture to blur the background and make your subject stand out.

4 Angle. You can shoot from a position that is higher than your subject, lower, at eye level, or somewhere in between. Each situation can be different—but adjusting your height to shoot the bird at eye level is often a

Great Egret

good choice, as it puts the viewer on the same plane as the bird.

To get closer to wary birds, you can wear muted clothing, hide behind vegetation, and move slowly and calmly in a zigzag pattern. It is never a good idea to bait a bird or to approach so closely that you flush it or alter its behavior.

5 Knowledge of Your Subject. To be the best bird photographer you can be, you really have to know birds. For example, knowing the habitat and behavior of a species allows you to predict where you're likely to find them and anticipate what they might do next. For example, berry bushes attract Cedar Waxwings; herons haunt the edges of marshes and ponds; waterfowl often rest and preen in the same spot every day. Study your subject and you'll know when and where to get the shot.

What Kind of Camera?

We're in a golden age of camera design and there are great options at every level of interest. Serious enthusiasts tend toward DSLRs (digital single-lens reflex cameras) with interchangeable lenses, but these can be expensive. At the entry level, so-called "superzoom" cameras can produce surprisingly good results while remaining compact and fairly inexpensive.

DIGISCOPING

Placing the lens of a digital camera to the eyepiece of a spotting scope is called "digiscoping." It's an inexpensive way to take decent pictures without a heavy, expensive telephoto lens.

Digiscoped Yellow-bellied Sapsucker.

Both scopes and digital cameras have improved tremendously since the dawn of digiscoping, in 1999. One of the most significant advances has been the advent of smartphones, which are now arguably the best tool for digiscoping and certainly the most convenient. Scopes, too have begun to come down in price.

There can be different goals in digiscoping. It can be practiced slowly and patiently to capture frame-worthy photos, whether detail-rich or artistically blurred. More often, it's a handy way to capture shots to remind yourself of a special moment or to back up a rare bird report. It's even becoming common for people to record video while digiscoping.

Granted, digiscoping does require a spotting scope, which can cost as much as a camera and telephoto lens—but some birders are happy to put their money toward a scope that can do double duty in both bird watching and photography.

Getting a good image when digiscoping comes down to gathering plenty of light, getting the camera lens the correct distance from the scope's eyepiece, and holding everything steady.

Getting Connected

There are a variety of ways to bring the camera lens and scope eyepiece together. For smartphones, the earliest method involved placing a finger between phone and eyepiece both to steady the lens and keep it at the correct distance. Today you can find phone adapters custom-sized to hold a phone in the proper position—greatly cutting down on fiddliness and frustration.

If you don't line up camera and eyepiece perfectly, you may get uneven focus, part of the image cut off, or shadows creeping in as light leaks in between scope and camera lenses.

Remember that the many commercial adapters are not universal, so make sure you get what fits your gear.

Standing Steady

The magnification produced by digiscoping is just what you need to pull your subject in close, but it also magnifies small movements from wind or a shaky trigger finger. Keeping extraneous motion to a minimum is of paramount importance. A quality tripod for your scope will provide stable support and prevent your photos from turning into a blurry mess. You'll find that a rock-steady tripod will be well worth it anyway—even in routine bird watching without attaching a camera.

5 TIPS FOR SUCCESSFUL DIGISCOPING

Digiscoped Northern Cardinal.

1 Let There Be Light.
One cause of blurry photos is low light coming through the scope, which forces a slower shutter speed and increases the effect of motion. Using larger, brighter scopes, such as 85-mm models rather than 65-mm models, results in noticeably better digiscoped photos. If you can change your camera's ISO (a feature becoming more common on smartphones), set it as high as you can and you'll get a faster shutter speed.

2 Resist the Zoom.
For scopes with a zoom, bear in mind that you quickly lose light as you zoom in. The human eye is good at compensating for this; cameras less so. Take advantage of your camera's many megapixels by shooting at a lower, brighter zoom setting and then cropping later.

3 Capture the Motion.
Many cameras and phones have a continuous shooting feature that takes photos one after another. This setting can help you catch birds in just the right pose. As an alternative, consider shooting video of a fast-moving subject—this can be more helpful than still photos when trying to identify a bird later.

4 **Try with Your Binoculars.**
Sometimes called "digibinning," this advanced technique can sometimes produce decent photos. If you don't already have a spotting scope, it's a less expensive way to get into digiscoping. But be warned: it's hard to hold the binocular-phone combination steady. It's a good idea to start with large, stationary birds such as herons.

5 **Practice, Practice, Practice.**
Fortunately, once you've got the equipment, taking digital photos is virtually free. It may seem impossible at first, but you'll quickly improve as you become comfortable with setting up the scope and handling your camera's controls. Don't be afraid to experiment—you never know what you'll come away with.

ATTRACTING BIRDS TO YOUR BACKYARD

Song Sparrow
Photo by Bob Vuxinic

BIRDSCAPING

You can watch birds anywhere.
Parks, nature preserves, and wildlife refuges provide some of the most diverse species, but the easiest place to watch birds is your own backyard. Enhancing your yard to attract and support birds is called "birdscaping."

Putting up a feeder is an easy way to attract birds. But if you'd prefer a more natural approach or you want to satisfy more than birds' nutritional needs, consider landscaping your yard—even just a part of it—to be more bird friendly. Even a small yard can provide vital habitat.

You'll find a trove of tips, techniques, and local landscaping resources at our Habitat Network project. The core concept is simple—all birds need three basic things from their habitats:

1 Food.
Your birds can get food from feeders that you put up. Landscaping your yard to provide the fruit, seeds, beneficial insects, and other small animals that birds feed on adds natural food sources for birds, too.

2 Water.
All living things need water to survive. Providing this habitat necessity is one of the quickest ways to attract birds to your property. If there is a water source in your yard, such as a pond, creek, birdbath, or even a puddle, you've probably noticed birds using it. If you don't have a water feature yet, a birdbath is an easy way to provide this habitat need.

3 Shelter.
Whether it's protection from the elements, safe places to hide from predators, or secure locations to hide nests, providing shelter is one of the best ways to make your property bird-friendly.

Take a "bird's-eye" look at your backyard. Does it provide those things? If not, there are plants you can grow and many other ways you can enhance your yard to make it safe and inviting for birds.

Here are some tips to help you:

Evaluate Your Yard

First, take stock of what you already have. Draw a map of your property including buildings, sidewalks, fences, trees, shrubs, feeders, and nest boxes. Note sunny or shady sites, low or wet areas, sandy sites, and plants you want to keep. You can do this online with a free tool from the Cornell Lab and The Nature Conservancy, called Habitat Network (learn more in *Getting Involved* starting on page 65).

Purple coneflowers

Start With a Plan

Before you start digging holes and rearranging your yard, develop a planting plan. Draw each new plant onto a piece of tracing paper, then place that over the map of your yard—or use the point-and-click tools on the Habitat Network site. Once your plants are in, use your map as a reminder about which ones need to be watered and weeded, especially in the first year after planting. Mulch is great for keeping moisture in and weeds out.

Think "Variety"

Try to include variety and year-round value in your planting plan. Look for places to include grasses, legumes, hummingbird flowers, plants that fruit in summer and fall, winter-persistent plants, and conifers for shelter. Plant native species instead of exotics, and look for places to create shelter with a brush pile or standing dead tree. Habitat Network can give you specific planting recommendations and resources for your zip code.

To learn more about how to improve your backyard habitat, visit *www.Habitat.Network* or scan this symbol with Bird QR.

BIRD FEEDERS

Fifty million people in North America feed birds and it's a great way to attract birds to your backyard. But feeders are not one size fits all—different species are attracted to different designs. Here are the main types of feeders and the types of birds they attract.

Ground

Many species of birds, including sparrows and doves, prefer to feed on large, flat surfaces and may not visit any type of elevated feeder. Song Sparrows and many towhee species, for instance, will rarely land on a feeder, but they will readily eat fallen seed from the ground beneath your feeders. To attract these species, try spreading seed on the ground or on a large surface such as the top of a picnic table. Ground feeders that sit low to the ground with mesh screens for good drainage can also be used. Make sure that there are no predators around, including outdoor cats.

Large and Small Hopper

A hopper feeder is a platform on which walls and a roof are built, forming a "hopper" that protects seed against the weather.

Large hoppers attract most species of feeder birds and will allow larger species, such as doves and grackles, to feed. Small hoppers will attract smaller birds while preventing those larger species from comfortably perching and monopolizing the feeder.

Large and Small Tube

A tube feeder is a hollow cylinder, often made of plastic, with multiple feeding ports and perches. Tube feeders keep seed fairly dry. Feeders with short perches accommodate small birds such as finches but exclude larger birds such as grackles and jays. The size of the feeding ports varies as well, depending on the type of seed to be offered. Note that special smaller feeding ports are required for nyjer (thistle) seed to prevent spillage.

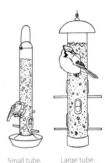

Small tube.   Large tube.

Sugar Water

Sugar-water feeders are specially made to dispense sugar water through small holes. Choose a feeder that is easy to take apart and clean, because the feeder should be washed or run through the dishwasher frequently.

Platform

A platform feeder is any flat, raised surface onto which bird food is spread. The platform should have plenty of drainage holes to prevent water accumulation. A platform with a roof will help keep seeds dry. Trays attract most species of feeder birds. Placed near the ground, they are likely to attract juncos, doves, and sparrows.

Suet Cage

Suet or suet mixes can be placed in a specially made cage, tied to trees, or smeared into knotholes. Cages that are only open at the bottom tend to be starling-resistant but allow woodpeckers, nuthatches, and chickadees to feed by clinging upside down.

Thistle Sock

Thistle "socks" are fine-mesh bags to which birds cling to extract nyjer or thistle seeds. Seed within thistle socks can become quite wet with rain, so only use large ones during periods when you have enough finches to consume the contents in a few days.

Window Feeder

Small plastic feeders affixed to window glass with suction cups, and platform feeders hooked into window frames, attract finches, chickadees, titmice, and some sparrows. They afford wonderful, close-up views of birds, and their placement makes them the safest of all feeder types for preventing window collisions.

FEEDER PLACEMENT & SAFETY

Place feeders in a quiet area where they are easy to see and convenient to refill. Place them close to natural cover, such as trees or shrubs. Evergreens are ideal, as they provide thick foliage that hides birds from predators and buffers winter winds.

Be careful not to place feeders too close to trees with strong branches that can provide jump-off points for squirrels and cats. A distance of about 10 feet is a good compromise.

American Goldfinches and Pine Siskins

Place hummingbird feeders in the shade if possible, as sugar solution spoils quickly in the sun. Don't use honey, artificial sweeteners, or food coloring. If bees or wasps become a problem, try moving the feeder.

Ornithologists estimate that more than 600 million birds are killed by hitting windows in the United States and Canada each year. Placing feeders close to your windows (ideally within 3 feet) can help reduce this problem. When feeders are close, a bird leaving the feeder cannot gain enough momentum to do harm if it strikes the window.

You can prevent more window strikes by breaking up reflections of trees and open space, which birds perceive as a flight path through your home. Techniques include attaching streamers, suction- cup feeders, or decals to windows, crisscrossing branches within the window frames, or installing awnings or screens. Another method is to attach netting to the outside of the window to buffer the impact. Deer netting (the kind used to keep deer from eating plants in your yard) works well.

To learn more about window crashes and how to prevent them, scan this symbol with Bird QR.

BIRD FOOD

Sunflower seeds attract the widest variety of birds and are the mainstay food used in most bird feeders. Other varieties of seed can help attract different types of birds to your feeders and yard and this section highlights many of them. When buying mixtures, note that those that contain red millet, oats, and other fillers are not attractive to most birds and can lead to a lot of waste.

Sunflower

There are two kinds of sunflower—black oil and striped. The black oil seeds ("oilers") have very thin shells, easy for virtually all seed-eating birds to crack open, and the kernels within have a high fat content, which is extremely valuable for most winter birds. Striped sunflower seeds have a thicker shell, much harder for House Sparrows and blackbirds to crack open. So if you're inundated with species you'd rather not subsidize at your feeder, before you do anything else, try switching to striped sunflower. Sunflower in the shell can be offered in a wide variety of feeders, including trays, tube feeders, hoppers, and acrylic window feeders. Sunflower hearts and chips shouldn't be offered in tube feeders where moisture can collect. Since squirrels love sunflower seeds, be prepared to take steps to squirrel-proof your feeder if needed.

Safflower

Safflower has a thick shell, hard for some birds to crack open, but is a favorite among cardinals. Some grosbeaks, chickadees, doves, and native sparrows also eat it. According to some sources, House Sparrows, European Starlings, and squirrels don't like safflower, but in some areas seem to have developed a taste for it. Cardinals and grosbeaks tend to prefer tray and hopper feeders, which makes these feeders a good choice for offering safflower.

Nyjer or Thistle

Small finches including American Goldfinches, Lesser Goldfinches, Indigo Buntings, Pine Siskins, and Common Redpolls often devour these tiny, black, needlelike seeds. As invasive thistle plants became a recognized problem in North America, suppliers shifted to a daisylike plant, known as *Guizotia abyssinica*, that produces a similar type of small, oily, rich seed. The plant is now known as niger or nyjer, and is imported from overseas. The seeds are heat-sterilized during importation to limit their chance of spreading invasively, while retaining their food value.

White Proso Millet

White millet is a favorite with ground-feeding birds including quails, native sparrows, doves, towhees, juncos, and cardinals. Unfortunately it's also a favorite with cowbirds, other blackbirds, and House Sparrows, which are already subsidized by human activities and supported at unnaturally high population levels by current agricultural practices and habitat changes. When these species are present, it's wisest to not use millet; virtually all the birds that like it are equally attracted to black oil sunflower. Because white millet is so preferred by ground-feeding birds, scatter it on the ground or set low platform feeders with excellent drainage.

Shelled and Cracked Corn

Corn is eaten by grouse, pheasants, turkeys, quail, cardinals, grosbeaks, crows, ravens, jays, doves, ducks, cranes, and other species. Unfortunately, corn has two serious problems. First, it's a favorite of House Sparrows, cowbirds, starlings, geese, bears, raccoons, and deer. Second, corn is the bird food most likely to be contaminated with aflatoxins, which are extremely toxic even at low levels. Never buy corn in plastic bags, never allow it to get wet, never offer it in amounts that can't be consumed in a day during rainy or very humid weather, and be conscientious about raking up old corn. Never offer corn covered in a red dye. Corn should be offered in fairly small amounts at a time on tray feeders. Don't offer it in tube feeders that could harbor moisture.

Peanuts

Peanuts are very popular with jays, crows, chickadees, titmice, woodpeckers, and many other species, but are also favored by squirrels, bears, raccoons, and other animals. Like corn, peanuts have a high likelihood of harboring aflatoxins, so must be kept dry and used up fairly quickly.

Peanuts in the shell can be set out on platform feeders or right on a deck railing or window feeder as a special treat for jays. If peanuts or mixtures of peanuts and other seeds are offered in tube feeders, make sure to change the seed frequently, especially during rainy or humid weather, completely emptying out and cleaning the tube every time.

Milo or Sorghum

Milo is a favorite with many western ground-feeding birds. On Cornell Lab of Ornithology seed preference tests, Steller's Jays, Curve-billed Thrashers, and Gambel's Quails preferred milo to sunflower. In another study, House Sparrows did not eat milo, but cowbirds did. Milo should be scattered on the ground or on low tray feeders.

Golden Millet, Red Millet, Flax, and Others

These seeds are often used as fillers in packaged birdseed mixes, but most birds shun them. Waste seed becomes a breeding ground for bacteria and fungus, contaminating fresh seed more quickly. Make sure to read the ingredients list on birdseed mixtures, avoiding those with these seeds. If a seed mix has a lot of small, red seeds, make sure they're milo or sorghum, not red millet.

Mealworms

Mealworms are the larvae of the mealworm beetle, *Tenebrio molitor*, and they provide a high-protein treat for many birds. Some people provide live mealworms, while others prefer offering dried larvae. Birds such as chickadees, titmice, wrens, and nuthatches relish this food, and mealworms are one of the few food items that reliably attracts bluebirds. Offer mealworms on a flat tray or in a specialized mealworm feeder.

Fruit

Various fruits can prove quite attractive to many species of birds. Oranges cut in half will often attract orioles which will sip the juice and eat the flesh of the orange. Grapes and raisins are a favorite of many fruit-eating birds. Mockingbirds, catbirds, bluebirds, robins, and waxwings are also likely to feed on fruit. Many species are also attracted to the dried seeds of fruits such as pumpkins or apples. Be sure to dispose of any fruit that becomes moldy because some molds create toxins that are harmful to birds.

Sugar Water or Nectar

To make nectar for hummingbirds, add one part table sugar to four parts boiling water and stir. A slightly more diluted mixture can be used for orioles (one part sugar to six parts water). Allow the mixture to cool before filling the feeder.

Store extra sugar water in the refrigerator for up to one week (after that it may become moldy, which is dangerous for birds). Adding red food coloring is unnecessary and possibly harmful to birds. Red portals on the feeder, or even a red ribbon tied on top, will attract the birds just as well.

Grit

Birds "chew" their food in the muscular part of their stomach, called the gizzard. To aid in the grinding, birds swallow small, hard materials such as sand, small pebbles, ground eggshells, and ground oyster shells. Grit, therefore, attracts many birds as a food supplement or even by itself. Oyster shells and eggshells have the added benefit of being a good source of calcium, something birds need during egg laying. If you decide to provide eggshells, be sure to sterilize them first. You can boil them for 10 minutes or heat them in an oven (20 minutes at 250°F). Let the eggshells cool, then crush them into pieces about the size of sunflower seeds. Offer the eggshell in a dish or low platform feeder.

To learn more about bird food, scan this symbol with Bird QR.

WATER SOURCES

Like all animals, birds need water to survive. Though they can extract some moisture from their food, most birds drink water every day. Birds also use water for bathing, to clean their feathers and remove parasites. After splashing around in a bath for a few minutes, a bird usually perches in a sunny spot and fluffs its feathers out to dry. Then it carefully preens each feather, adding a protective coating of oil secreted by a gland at the base of its tail.

Because birds need water for drinking and bathing, they are attracted to water just as they are to feeders. A dependable supply of fresh, clean water is highly attractive. In fact, a birdbath will even bring in birds that don't eat seeds and won't visit your feeders. Providing water for birds can improve the quality of your backyard bird habitat and should provide you with a fantastic opportunity to observe bird behavior.

Birds seem to prefer baths that are at ground level, but these can make birds more vulnerable to predators. Raised baths will attract birds as well, so we recommend them over ground-level baths. Change the water daily to keep it fresh and clean. You can also arrange a few branches or stones in the water so that birds can stand on them and drink without getting wet (this is particularly important in winter).

Birdbaths should be only an inch or two deep with a shallow slope. One of the best ways to make your birdbath more attractive is to provide dripping water. You can buy a dripper or sprayer, or you can recycle an old bucket or plastic container by punching a tiny hole in the bottom, filling it with water, and hanging it above the birdbath so the water drips out. Don't add antifreeze; it is poisonous to all animals including birds.

To learn more about birdbaths, scan this symbol with Bird QR.

NEST BOXES

FEATURES OF A GOOD BIRDHOUSE

BUILD A SAFE AND SUCCESSFUL HOME

IT'S WELL CONSTRUCTED

Untreated Wood. Use untreated, unpainted wood, preferably cedar, pine, cypress, or for larger boxes (owls) non-pressure-treated CDX exterior grade plywood.

Galvanized Screws. Use galvanized screws for the best seal. Nails can loosen over time, allowing rain into the nest box. Screws are also easier to remove for repairs or maintenance. Do not use staples.

IT KEEPS BIRDS DRY

Sloped Roof. A sloped roof that overhangs the front by 2–4" and the sides by 2" will help keep out driving rain, while also thwarting predators. Add 1/4"-deep cuts under the roof on all three edges to serve as gutters that channel rain away from the box.

side view (cutaway)

Recessed Floor. A recessed floor keeps the nest from getting wet and helps the box last longer. Recess the floor at least 1/4" up from the bottom.

bottom view

Drainage Holes. Add at least four drainage holes (3/8" to 1/2" diameter) to the floor to allow any water that enters the box to drain away. Alternatively, you can cut away the corners of the floorboard to create drainage holes.

IT HELPS REGULATE TEMPERATURE

Thick Walls. Walls should be at least 3/4" thick to insulate the nest properly. (Note that boards sold as 1" are actually 3/4" thick.)

Ventilation Holes. For adequate ventilation, there should be two 5/8"-diameter holes on each of the side walls, near the top (four total).

IT KEEPS OUT PREDATORS

No Perches. A perch is unnecessary for the birds and can actually help predators gain access to the box.

Types of Predator Guards. Although predators are a natural part of the environment, birdhouses are typically not as well concealed as natural nests and some predators can make a habit of raiding your boxes. Adding a baffle or guard helps keep nestlings and adults safe from climbing predators. Below are some time-tested options.

 Collar Baffle. A metal collar of about 3 feet in diameter surrounding the pole underneath the nest box.

 Stovepipe Baffle. The most complex, and perhaps the most effective. These baffles are generally 8" in diameter and 24"–36" long.

 Noel Guard. A wire tube attached to the front of the nest box. Use this guard in combination with another, or attach it to boxes installed on trees.

COMMON NEST BOX PREDATORS

 Snakes. Many snakes are excellent climbers and can easily surmount an unguarded pole. Snakes most likely to climb into birdhouses are generally nonvenomous (such as racers and rat snakes) and helpful at controlling rodents. Avoid installing nest boxes next to brush piles.

Raccoons. Raccoons are intelligent and can remember nest box locations from year to year. They can be abundant in populated areas. Mount nest boxes on a metal pole equipped with a baffle; avoid mounting them on trees or fence posts.

 Chipmunks. Chipmunks are both a nest predator and a competitor for nest boxes. To keep chipmunks out, mount boxes away from trees on a metal pole equipped with a baffle.

Cats. Cats are excellent jumpers and can leap to the top of a nest box from a nearby tree or from the ground. Mount your box high enough and far enough from trees so cats cannot spring to the top of the box in a single leap. Keep pet cats indoors for their own safety and for the safety of birds.

IT HAS THE RIGHT ENTRANCE SIZE FOR THE RIGHT BIRD

By providing a properly sized entrance hole, you can attract desirable species to your birdhouses while excluding predators and unwanted occupants. Below are the requirements for entrance-hole size for some common species that nest in boxes.

3"	Screech-owls and American Kestrel
2 ½"	Northern Flicker
1 ⁹⁄₁₆"	Ash-throated Flycatcher, Great Crested Flycatcher, Mountain Bluebird
1 ½"	Eastern Bluebird, Western Bluebird, Bewick's Wren, Carolina Wren
1 ⅜"	White-breasted Nuthatch, Tree Swallow, Violet-green Swallow
1 ¼"	Prothonotary Warbler, Red-breasted Nuthatch, Tufted Titmouse
1 ⅛"	House Wren and chickadees

IT HELPS FLEDGLINGS LEAVE THE NEST

Rough Interior Walls. The interior wall below the entrance hole should be rough to help nestlings climb out of the box. For small boxes (wrens and chickadees), plain wood is usually rough enough, but you can roughen smooth boards with coarse sandpaper.

Interior Grooves. A series of shallow horizontal cuts, like a small ladder, works well in medium-sized boxes meant for swallows and bluebirds. Swallows, in particular, need a little help climbing out of boxes.

Duck Boxes. For duck boxes, staple a strip of 1/4"-mesh hardware cloth from floor to hole to help ducklings escape deep boxes.

IT MAKES PLACEMENT AND MAINTENANCE EASY

Extended Back. A few extra inches at the top and bottom of your birdhouse can make it easier to mount on a metal pole. Alternatively, you can predrill mounting holes in the back panel before assembly and use a short-handled screwdriver to install the box.

Hinged Door with a Sturdy Closing Mechanism. A hinged side gives you access for cleaning and monitoring your nest box, both of which are important for a successful nesting season. A latch or nail keeps the box securely closed until you are ready to open it.

Into DIY? Scan this symbol with Bird QR app or visit *nestwatch.org/birdhouses* to get FREE downloadable nest-box plans.

GETTING INVOLVED

Great Blue Heron
Photo by Gerrit Vyn

CITIZEN SCIENCE

Each month, bird watchers report millions of bird observations to citizen-science projects at the Cornell Lab of Ornithology, contributing to the world's most dynamic and powerful source of information on birds.

The Cornell Lab has been at the forefront of citizen science since 1966. Today, the birding community can use our innovative online tools to tap into millions of records and see how their own sightings fit into the continental picture. Scientists can analyze the same data to reveal striking changes in the movements, distributions, and numbers of birds across time, and to determine how birds are affected by habitat loss, pollution, and disease.

If you enjoy watching birds, you can help and contribute to science, whether you are a beginner or a seasoned birder. Participating can take as little or as much time as you want—you decide!

There's a Project for Every Bird Watcher

Our fun and meaningful citizen-science projects enable people to watch birds at their favorite locations and share their sightings:

- **eBird** is a powerful tool for keeping track of your sightings and for exploring what others have seen—with global coverage and millions of sightings recorded per month.
- **Great Backyard Bird Count** is possibly the easiest project of all and the best one to start with—a global effort to count birds over one long weekend each February.
- **Project FeederWatch** is a winter project where you count birds at your feeders to help track bird populations and distributions.
- **NestWatch** challenges you to monitor the nest success of birds breeding around you—training and best practices are provided.
- **Celebrate Urban Birds** combines art and science to help communities connect to nature in urban and suburban settings.
- **Habitat Network** is a growing community of people documenting their landscaping to track the impact of wildlife gardening and green infrastructure around the world.

eBird

Since its inception in 2002, eBird has grown into one of the world's largest data sources about living things—thanks to bird watchers contributing more than 370 million sightings of birds.

eBird works in two ways: It gives bird watchers a convenient, free way to enter, store, and organize their sightings. And it makes those sightings available to others, turning it into a useful resource for studying or finding birds anywhere in the world.

Use eBird to start or maintain your birding lists—or use it to find out where and when to go bird watching. It works all over the world and provides endless ideas about what to do and where to go next. And it's free.

eBird provides easy-to-use online tools for birders and critical data for science. With eBird, you can:

- Record the birds you see
- Keep track of your bird lists
- Learn where to find birds near you
- Share your sightings and join the eBird community
- Contribute to science and conservation

How to Record and Store Sightings in eBird

eBird uses a simple and intuitive interface to allow you to record your bird sightings easily. You simply enter when, where, and how you went birding, then fill out a checklist of all the birds you saw and heard. A free mobile app allows you to track sightings faster than ever. Data-quality filters review all submissions automatically, and local experts review any unusual records before they enter the database.

eBird automatically organizes your checklists into local and national lists, state lists, year lists, and more. eBird also keeps your recordings current with new information that affects nomenclature. For example, when official bird names change, or species are split apart or lumped together, eBird automatically adjusts your lists accordingly. You can also add all of your bird photos to your checklist, letting you share with friends while helping build automatic photo-identification tools that can help you learn more. All these features work in any country in the world and are available in many languages.

How to Explore Data and Learn with eBird

One of eBird's greatest strengths is its ability to show you where and when birds occur, using innovative visualization tools. These free tools are used annually by millions of bird watchers, scientists, and conservationists worldwide. Here are a few:

Range Maps: Choose a species, then explore a map of everywhere it has been reported. Filter the map by date or zoom in to anywhere in the world with pinpoint precision.

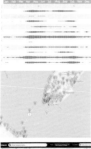

Photo and Sound Archive: Each month, eBirders upload thousands of images and sounds. All of them are searchable in the Macaulay Library archive, so you can explore birds both familiar and new.

Bar Charts: Create a customized checklist for any region and season. The list tells you which species to expect when; bars tell you how rare or common each bird is during the year.

Hotspot Explorer: Using an interactive map, explore birding spots in any part of the world and discover which have the most sightings—a great tool for travelers looking for local tips on where to go birding.

Explore a Region: See the full species list, plus recent sightings, best hotspots, and top birders for any county, state, province, or country.

To learn more about eBird and the birds recently seen in your area, visit *ebird.org* or scan this symbol with the Bird QR app.

GREAT BACKYARD BIRD COUNT

The Great Backyard **Bird Count**

Art by Charley Harper

Begun in 1998, the four-day Great Backyard Bird Count (GBBC) was the first citizen-science program to collect and display bird observation data online on a large scale. Today, the GBBC is one of the most popular annual events among bird watchers and has expanded to cover the whole world. More than 160,000 people of all ages and walks of life take part. In 2016, more than 162,000 counts flooded in from 130 countries, recording a total of 5,689 species of birds—more than half of all bird species in the world!

Why Count Birds?

Scientists and bird enthusiasts can learn a lot by knowing where the birds are. No single scientist or team of scientists could hope to document and understand the complex distribution and movements of so many species in such a short time. Scientists use information from the GBBC, along with observations from other citizen-science projects, to see the big picture about what is happening to bird populations. You can help scientists investigate far-reaching questions, such as these:

- How do weather and climate change influence bird populations?

- Some birds appear in large numbers during some years but not others. Where are these species from year to year, and what can we learn from these patterns?

- How does the timing of bird migrations compare across years?

- What kinds of differences in bird diversity are apparent in cities versus suburban, rural, and natural areas?

Why Is the GBBC in February?

Originally the GBBC was held in the U.S. and Canada each February to create a snapshot of the distribution of birds just before spring migrations ramped up in March. Scientists at the Cornell Lab of Ornithology, National Audubon Society, Bird Studies Canada, and elsewhere can combine this information with data from surveys conducted at different times of the year. In 2013, the count went global, creating snapshots of birds wherever they are in February, regardless of seasons across the hemispheres.

How to Participate

We invite you to participate! Visit *birdcount.org* to find out when the next GBBC is happening (it falls in February during the U.S. Presidents' Day weekend). If you're new to citizen science, you'll need to register for a free online eBird account to enter your checklist counts. If you have already participated in another Cornell Lab citizen-science project, you can use that login information for GBBC.

Once registered, simply tally the numbers and kinds of birds you see for at least 15 minutes on one or more days of the count every February. You can count from any location, anywhere in the world, for as long as you wish. During the count, you can explore what others are seeing in your area or around the world. You can also participate in an annual photo contest (with great bird-themed prizes), and contribute to a cascade of great images to enjoy as they pour in from across the globe.

To learn more and participate in the GBBC, visit *birdcount.org* or scan this symbol with Bird QR.

The Great Backyard Bird Count is led by the Cornell Lab of Ornithology and National Audubon Society, with Bird Studies Canada and many international partners. The Great Backyard Bird Count is powered by eBird.

PROJECT FEEDERWATCH

Project FeederWatch is a winter-long survey of birds that visit feeders in backyards and at nature centers, community areas, and other locales in North America. Each year, almost 20,000 people participate in Project FeederWatch and count birds at their feeders from November through early April. With more than 1.5 million checklists submitted since 1987, FeederWatchers have contributed valuable data enabling scientists to monitor changes in the distribution and abundance of birds.

Using FeederWatch data, scientists have studied the influence of nonnative species on native bird communities, examined the association between birds and habitats, and tracked unpredictable movements in winter bird populations. Participants gain from the rewarding experience of watching birds at their feeders and contributing their own observations to reveal larger patterns in bird populations across the continent.

Downy Woodpecker

Why Are FeederWatch Data Important?

With each season, FeederWatch increases in importance as a unique monitoring tool for more than 100 bird species that winter in North America.

What sets FeederWatch apart from other monitoring programs is the detailed picture that FeederWatch data provide about weekly changes in bird distribution and abundance across North America. FeederWatch data tell us where birds are as well as where they are not. This crucial information enables scientists to piece together accurate population maps.

Because FeederWatchers count the number of individuals of each species they see several times throughout the winter, FeederWatch data are extremely powerful for detecting and explaining gradual changes in the wintering ranges of many species. In short, FeederWatch data are important because they provide information about bird population biology that cannot be detected by any other available method.

How Are FeederWatch Data Used?

The massive amounts of data collected by FeederWatchers across the continent help scientists understand:

- Long-term trends in bird distribution and abundance
- The timing and extent of winter irruptions of winter finches and other species
- Expansions or contractions in winter ranges of feeder birds
- Kinds of foods and environmental factors that attract birds
- How disease is spread among birds that visit feeders

How to Participate

Anyone interested in birds can participate, including people of all skill levels and backgrounds. FeederWatch is a great project for children, families, individuals, classrooms, retirees, youth groups, nature centers, and bird clubs. You can count birds as often as every week, or as infrequently as you like—the schedule is very flexible. All you need is a bird feeder, birdbath, or plantings that attract birds.

New participants receive a research kit with complete instructions for participating, as well as a bird identification poster and access to the digital version of *Living Bird*, the Cornell Lab's award-winning magazine, plus the year-end report, *Winter Bird Highlights*. As of 2017, there is an $18 annual participation fee for U.S. residents ($15 for Cornell Lab members). Canadians can participate by joining Bird Studies Canada for CAN$35. The participation fee covers materials, staff support, web design, data analysis, and the year-end report. Project FeederWatch is supported almost entirely by participation fees. Without the support of our participants, this project wouldn't be possible.

 To learn more about Project FeederWatch, visit *feederwatch.org* or use your Bird QR app and scan this symbol.

Project FeederWatch is operated by the Cornell Lab of Ornithology and Bird Studies Canada.

NESTWATCH

NestWatch is a nationwide monitoring program designed to track status and trends in the reproductive biology of birds, including when nesting occurs, how many eggs are laid, how many hatch, and how many hatchlings survive. The database is used to study the current condition of breeding bird populations and how they may be changing over time.

By finding and monitoring bird nests, NestWatch participants help scientists track the breeding success of birds across North America. Participants witness fascinating behaviors of birds at the nest, and collect information on the location,

American Robin nest.

habitat, species, number of eggs, and number of young. Launched in 2007 with funding from the National Science Foundation, NestWatch has collected more than 300,000 nesting records. Combined with historic data, this information will help scientists address how birds are affected by large-scale changes such as global climate change, urbanization, and land conversion.

How to Participate

Participating in NestWatch is free and just about anyone can do it (children should always be accompanied by an adult when observing bird nests). Simply follow the directions on the website to become a certified NestWatcher, find a bird nest using the helpful tips, visit the nest every 3–4 days to record what you see, and then report this information on the website. Your observations will be added to those of thousands of other NestWatchers in a continually growing database used by researchers to understand and study birds. While you contribute extremely valuable information to science, you will also learn firsthand about the breeding behaviors of birds.

To learn more about NestWatch, visit *nestwatch.org* or use your Bird QR app and scan this symbol.

CELEBRATE URBAN BIRDS

Celebrate Urban Birds is a year-round project developed by the Cornell Lab for people in cities, suburbs, and rural areas. It is an easy, fun project for the entire family; no prior knowledge of birds is required, and your data will help scientists understand how birds use green spaces in

cities. Since 2007, Celebrate Urban Birds has partnered with 11,000 community organizations and distributed 400,000 educational kits. Educational materials and online trainings are offered in both English and Spanish.

How to Participate

1. Register for free at *CelebrateUrbanBirds.org* and get your educational kit with instructions, ID guides, and sunflower seeds for planting.

2. Learn to identify 16 focal species. You can get additional species lists online at *CelebrateUrbanBirds.org/regional*.

3. Pick a place to watch birds in an area that is 50 feet by 50 feet (the size of half a basketball court).

4. Spend 10 minutes watching birds in the selected area.

5. Repeat observations three times in the same area in one month.

6. Enter data online or send to the Cornell Lab by mail.

Every year Celebrate Urban Birds awards dozens of mini-grants to community organizations, including Alzheimer's support groups, youth clubs, oncology centers, businesses, and rehabilitation centers throughout the Americas to lead community activities focused on birds, greening, and the arts. Anybody can apply for a grant—the application is simple! Visit *CelebrateUrbanBirds.org* to order educational materials, apply for a community grant, or find hundreds of fun, creative activities that involve the arts, greening, and birds for people of all ages.

To learn more, visit *CelebrateUrbanBirds.org* or use your Bird QR app and scan this symbol.

HABITAT NETWORK

Habitat Network is creating a citizen-science movement to explore how our collective efforts to transform yards and urban landscapes into more diverse habitat can support wildlife and connect people to nature in communities around the world.

IT'S A MAP
Habitat Network is a citizen-science mapping tool used to capture, identify, and share the state of private and public lands and other data about ecologically relevant practices in those places.

IT'S A RESOURCE
Habitat Network provides a search tool and local information you need to make informed decisions to plan for and improve a yard, park, school, or other green space.

IT'S EDUCATIONAL
Habitat Network provides informative articles and videos on a wide variety of topics, including native plants, healthy ecosystems, D.I.Y., cover, water, food, birds, pollinators, design advice, and more.

IT'S A COMMUNITY
Habitat Network gives like-minded people the ability to communicate and share their maps by either joining or forming specialized groups.

IT'S ECOLOGICAL
Habitat Network helps you revolutionize and transform your property by expanding native habitat and engaging you as part of the conservation solution to our shared environmental concerns.

How to Participate

Habitat Network is year-round. You can participate from anywhere in the world, although some of its resource tools are specific to North America. To begin mapping habitat, sign up for a free account at *www.Habitat.Network*. You can also browse the project's many gardening and landscaping resources and find tips and tutorials on how to use the mapping tools.

ANATOMY OF A HABITAT MAP

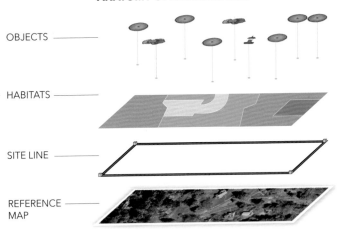

OBJECTS

HABITATS

SITE LINE

REFERENCE
MAP

To learn more about Habitat Network and to create your own habitat map, visit *www.Habitat.Network* or use your Bird QR app and scan this symbol.

Habitat Network is a partnership between The Nature Conservancy and the Cornell Lab of Ornithology.

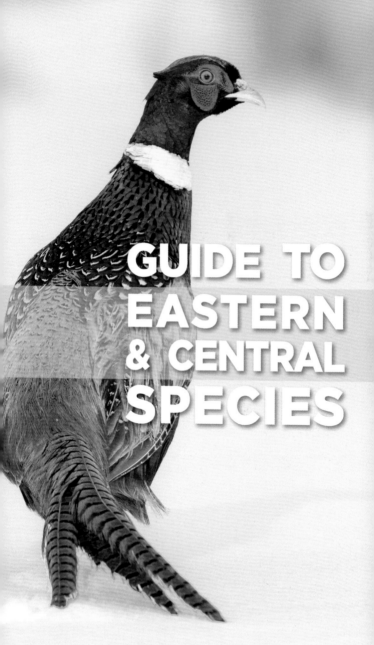

GUIDE TO EASTERN & CENTRAL SPECIES

Ring-necked Pheasant
Photo by B. N. Singh

CANADA GOOSE *(Branta canadensis)*

The big, black-necked Canada Goose, with its signature white chinstrap mark, is a familiar bird of fields and parks. Thousands of these "honkers" migrate north and south each year, filling the sky with long V formations. As lawns have proliferated, more and more of these grassland-adapted birds are staying put in urban and suburban areas year-round, where some people enjoy them while others regard them as pests.

AT A GLANCE

Food In spring and summer, Canada Geese concentrate their feeding on grasses and herbs, including skunk cabbage and eelgrass. During fall and winter they rely more on berries and seeds, including agricultural grains. They're also very efficient at removing kernels from dry corncobs. Two subspecies have adapted to urban environments and graze on domesticated grasses year-round.

Nesting The nest of the Canada Goose is a large, open cup on the ground, made of dry grasses, lichens, mosses, and other plant materials. It's lined with down and some body feathers. The nests are usually located near water, on muskrat mounds or other slightly elevated sites.

Habitat Canada Geese can be found just about anywhere near lakes, rivers, ponds, or other small or large bodies of water, and also in yards, parks, lawns, and farm fields.

RANGE MAP

- Breeding
- Nonbreeding
- Year-round

KEYS TO IDENTIFICATION

MEASUREMENTS (Both sexes)

Length	Wingspan	Weight
30–43 in	50–67 in	105.8–318 oz
76–110 cm	127–170 cm	3000–9000 g

SIZE & SHAPE. The Canada Goose is a big waterbird with a long neck, large body, large webbed feet, and a wide, flat bill. Adult Canada Geese can vary widely in size.

COLOR PATTERN. The Canada Goose has a black head with white cheeks and a chinstrap, black neck, tan breast, and brown back. Its bill, legs, and feet are all black.

BEHAVIOR. Canada Geese feed by dabbling in the water or grazing in fields and large lawns. They are known for their honking call and are often very vocal in flight. They often fly together in pairs or in V formation in flocks, which reduces wind resistance and conserves energy.

Cool Facts

At least 11 subspecies of Canada Goose have been recognized. In general, the farther north they breed, the smaller they are, and the farther west, the darker.

Backyard Tips

Mowing and maintaining large lawns anywhere near water is an open invitation to Canada Geese. If you want to keep them from walking on your lawn, plastic mesh on the grass may do the trick.

WOOD DUCK *(Aix sponsa)*

The Wood Duck is one of the most stunningly beautiful of all ducks. The male is iridescent chestnut and green, whereas the elegant female has a distinctive profile and delicate white pattern around the eye. They live in wooded swamps, where they nest in holes in trees, or in nest boxes put up near lakes and ponds. They are one of the few duck species equipped with strong claws that can grip bark and perch on branches.

AT A GLANCE

Food
Wood Ducks eat seeds, fruits, acorns, insects, and other arthropods. Some feed heavily on corn and other grains in agricultural fields. Studies indicate that their diets can vary greatly, but plants make up 80% or more of their diet.

Nesting
Wood Ducks nest in tree holes with openings that range from 4 inches to a couple of feet across. The cavity depth is variable, averaging about 2 feet deep, but in rotten trees can be as much as 15 feet deep. The young use their clawed feet to climb out. The female lines the nest with down feathers taken from her breast.

Habitat
Look for Wood Ducks in wooded swamps, marshes, streams, beaver ponds, and small lakes. They prefer to stick to wet areas with trees or cattails. As cavity nesters, Wood Ducks take readily to nest boxes.

RANGE MAP

- ■ Breeding
- ■ Nonbreeding
- ■ Nonbreeding (scarce)
- ■ Year-round

KEYS TO IDENTIFICATION

MALE

FEMALE

MEASUREMENTS (Both sexes)

Length	Wingspan	Weight
18.5–21.3 in 47–54 cm	26–28.7 in 66–73 cm	16–30.4 oz 454–862 g

SIZE & SHAPE. The Wood Duck has a unique shape among ducks—boxy, crested head, thin neck, and long, broad tail. In flight, they hold their heads up high, sometimes bobbing them. Overall, their silhouettes show skinny necks, long bodies, thick tails, and short wings.

COLOR PATTERN. In good light, males have a glossy green head with white stripes, a chestnut breast, and buffy sides. In low light, they look dark overall with paler sides. The female is gray-brown with a white-speckled breast. In late summer, males lose their pale sides and bold stripes, but retain their bright eyes and bills.

BEHAVIOR. Unlike most waterfowl species, the Wood Duck perches and nests in trees and often flies through woods. When swimming, its head jerks back and forth, similar to the head movement of a walking pigeon. Wood Ducks often gather in small groups, separate from other waterfowl. Listen for the female's call when these wary birds flush.

Cool Facts

Wood Ducks nest in trees near water. Soon after hatching, ducklings jump down from the nest and go to the water. Ducklings can jump from heights of over 50 feet without injury.

Backyard Tips

Consider putting up a nest box to attract a breeding pair of Wood Ducks. You can find instructions for building one at *nestwatch.org/birdhouses*. Attach a predator guard to protect eggs and young.

MALLARD *(Anas platyrhynchos)*

The Mallard is perhaps the most familiar of all ducks, occuring throughout North America and Eurasia in ponds and parks, as well as wilder wetlands and estuaries. The male's gleaming green head, black tail-curl, and gray flanks arguably make it the most easily identified duck.

Almost all domestic ducks come from this species, and odd-looking hybrid Mallards can be commonly found in parks and towns.

AT A GLANCE

Food

Mallards eat a wide variety of food. They don't dive but instead dabble to feed, tipping forward in the water to eat seeds and aquatic vegetation. On the shore, they pick at prey and vegetation on the ground. In city parks, they readily accept handouts from parkgoers.

Nesting

Mallards nest on the ground on dry land near water. Nests are generally concealed under overhanging grass or other vegetation, occasionally in agricultural fields. Females construct their nests, which are usually about a foot across, with a bowl for the eggs that is usually 1–6 inches deep and 6–9 inches across.

Habitat

Mallards can live in almost any wetland habitat. Look for them on lakes, ponds, marshes, rivers, and coastal habitats, as well as city and suburban parks and residential backyards.

RANGE MAP

- Breeding
- Nonbreeding
- Year-round

KEYS TO IDENTIFICATION

MALE

FEMALE

MEASUREMENTS (Both sexes)

Length	Wingspan	Weight
19.7–25.6 in	32.3–37.4 in	35.3–45.9 oz
50–65 cm	82–95 cm	1000–1300 g

SIZE & SHAPE. Mallards are large ducks with hefty bodies, rounded heads, and wide, flat bills. Like many "dabbling ducks," their bodies are long and their tails ride high out of the water, giving them a blunt shape. In flight, their wings are broad and set back toward the rear.

COLOR PATTERN. Male Mallards have dark, iridescent-green heads and bright yellow bills. Their gray bodies are sandwiched between a brown breast and black rear. Females and juveniles are mottled brown with orange-and-brown bills. Both sexes have a white-bordered, blue "speculum" or bright patch in their wing.

BEHAVIOR. Mallards are "dabbling ducks"—they feed in the water by tipping forward and grazing on underwater plants. They almost never dive. They can be very tame, especially in city ponds, and often group together with other Mallards, other species of dabbling ducks, or even farm ducks.

Cool Facts

The classic quack of a duck comes from the female Mallard. Males don't quack; they make a quieter, rasping sound. Male Mallards don't incubate or care for ducklings after they hatch.

Backyard Tips

If you have a pond or marshy area on your property, Mallards might be attracted to your yard. Mallards sometimes feed on corn and other seeds beneath feeders.

NORTHERN BOBWHITE *(Colinus virginianus)*

An emphatic, whistled *bob-white* ringing from a grassy field or piney woods has long been a characteristic sound of summers in the eastern countryside. These small, round birds are not easy to spot, as their dappled plumage offers excellent camouflage. They forage in groups, scurrying between cover or bursting into flight if alarmed. Bobwhites have been in sharp decline over the past half-century and are a priority for conservation.

AT A GLANCE

Food
Northern Bobwhites eat mostly seeds and leaves, supplemented with varying amounts of insects during the breeding season. They forage as a group, scratching and pecking through leaf litter or foraging on low plants. During fall and winter, they eat many seeds and acorns. In the spring, they eat more leafy green parts of plants. In the summer, their diet includes grass seeds, some fruits, and arthropods.

Nesting
Both sexes work together to dig a scrape in the ground, about 6 inches across and 2 inches deep, and line it with grass and other dead vegetation. They often weave weeds and grasses into an arch to completely hide the nest from view. Nest building takes about 5 days.

Habitat
Northern Bobwhites live in open pine forests, overgrown fields, shrubby areas, and grasslands. They respond well to areas managed with prescribed fire, which helps to maintain an open, grassy ground layer.

RANGE MAP

Year-round

KEYS TO IDENTIFICATION

MALE

MEASUREMENTS (Both sexes)

Length	Wingspan	Weight
10 in	13.5 in	4.6–5.6 oz
25 cm	34 cm	129–159 g

SIZE & SHAPE. Bobwhites are small quail with rounded bodies, small heads, rounded wings, and short tails. Males have a small crest that becomes erect when they are alert and their heads are raised.

COLOR PATTERN. Northern Bobwhites are intricately patterned in brown, rufous, buff, and black. Males have bold black-and-white head patterns. Females have buffy throats and eyebrows.

BEHAVIOR. Northern Bobwhites travel in coveys and run across the ground from the shelter of one shrubby patch to another. When they are flushed, they explode into flight with quick wingbeats and then duck into the nearest cover.

Cool Facts

The Northern Bobwhite is one of the most intensively studied bird species in the world. Scientists have focused on them to learn how pesticides and prescribed fires affect habitats.

Backyard Tips

In places where bobwhites are common, they may eat birdseed from ground feeders in open backyards with shrub cover. Keep an ear out for their beautiful calls that signify their presence.

RING-NECKED PHEASANT *(Phasianus colchicus)*

The Ring-necked Pheasant can be found striding across open fields and weedy roadsides in the U.S and southern Canada. The male sports iridescent copper-and-gold plumage, a red face, and a crisp white collar. Its crowing can be heard as far as a mile away. Introduced to the U.S. from Asia in the 1880s, pheasants quickly became one of North America's most popular upland game birds. Watch for them along roads or bursting into flight from brushy cover.

AT A GLANCE

Food In fall and winter, Ring-necked Pheasants eat seeds, grasses, leaves, roots, wild fruits, nuts, and insects. Their spring and summer diet is similar but with a greater emphasis on animal prey and fresh greenery. They forage in grasslands, hayfields, and brushy areas.

Nesting The Ring-necked Pheasant's nest, built on the ground, is a rudimentary affair—unlined or sparsely lined with vegetation taken from beside the nest depression. The average nest bowl is about 7 inches across and 3 inches deep. Nests are usually surrounded by tall vegetation.

Habitat Ring-necked Pheasants are birds of agricultural areas intermixed with areas of taller vegetation, which they use for cover. Look for them along rural roadsides, in overgrown or recently harvested fields, and in brushy areas and hedgerows.

RANGE MAP

■ Year-round

KEYS TO IDENTIFICATION

MALE

FEMALE

MEASUREMENTS (Both sexes)

Length	Wingspan	Weight
19.7–27.6 in	22–33.9 in	17.6–105.8 oz
50–70 cm	56–86 cm	500–3000 g

SIZE & SHAPE. The Ring-necked Pheasant is a large, chickenlike bird with a long, pointed tail. It has fairly long legs, a small head, long neck, and plump body.

COLOR PATTERN. The male Ring-necked Pheasant is a gaudy bird with a red face and an iridescent green neck with a bold white ring. The male's very long tail is coppery with thin, black bars. The female is brown with paler scaling on its upperparts, buff or cinnamon on its underparts, black spotting on its sides, and thin, black bars on its tail.

BEHAVIOR. Ring-necked Pheasants forage on the ground in fields, where they eat waste grain, other seeds, and insects when available. They usually walk or run, only occasionally resorting to flying (usually when disturbed at close range by humans or predators). Males give a loud, cackling display that can be heard over long distances.

Cool Facts

Along with most of the grouse family, pheasants have strong breast muscles which create extreme power, allowing them to escape trouble in a hurry when needed.

Find This Bird

Keep an eye out for Ring-necked Pheasants running between patches of cover as you travel through agricultural areas—particularly along dirt roads where they often forage in weedy areas.

The Wild Turkey is a big, spectacular bird and a common sight throughout the year as flocks stride around woods and clearings. The courting male puffs itself into a feathery ball and fills the air with exuberant gobbling. Many North American kids learn turkey identification by tracing outlines of their hands to make Thanksgiving cards. Reintroductions have made them even more widespread today than historically. They now occur in every state except Alaska.

AT A GLANCE

Food Wild Turkeys forage in flocks, mostly on the ground. Sometimes they climb into shrubs or low trees for fruits. Throughout the year they eat seeds, nuts, berries, buds, and other plant matter, occasionally supplementing their diet with insects and small vertebrates.

Nesting Wild Turkeys nest on the ground in dead leaves at the base of a tree, under a brush pile or shrubbery, or occasionally in an open hayfield. The female scratches a shallow depression in the soil and lines it with only the dead leaves or other plant materials already present at the site.

Habitat Wild Turkeys live in mature forests, particularly with nut trees such as oak, hickory, or beech, interspersed among edges and fields. You may also see them along roads and in woodsy backyards.

RANGE MAP

Year-round

KEYS TO IDENTIFICATION

MALE

MEASUREMENTS (Both sexes)

Length	Wingspan	Weight
43.3–45.3 in	49.2–56.7 in	88–381 oz
110–115 cm	125–144 cm	2500–10800 g

SIZE & SHAPE. The Wild Turkey is a very large, plump bird with long legs, a wide rounded tail, and a small head on a long, slim neck.

COLOR PATTERN. The Wild Turkey is dark overall, with a bronze-green iridescence on most of its plumage. Its wings are dark and boldly barred with white, and its rump and tail feathers are broadly tipped rusty or white. The bare skin of its head and neck varies from red to blue to gray.

BEHAVIOR. Wild Turkeys travel in flocks and search on the ground for nuts, berries, insects, and snails. They use their strong feet to scratch leaf litter out of the way. In early spring, males gather in clearings to perform courtship displays. They puff up their body feathers, flare their tails into a vertical fan, and strut slowly while giving a characteristic gobbling call. At night, Wild Turkeys fly up into trees to roost in groups.

Cool Facts

Newly hatched chicks follow the female, which feeds them for a few days until they learn to find food on their own. As the chicks grow, they band into groups. Male Wild Turkeys don't help out at all.

Backyard Tips

If you have a large yard near woods, you can attract Wild Turkeys by planting nut-bearing or berry trees. Some people attract turkeys by scattering birdseed or corn on their lawns.

PIED-BILLED GREBE *(Podilymbus podiceps)*

Part bird, part submarine, the Pied-billed Grebe is commonly found across much of North America. These expert divers inhabit sluggish rivers, freshwater marshes, lakes, and estuaries. They use their chunky bills to kill and eat large crustaceans along with a great variety of fish, amphibians, insects, and other invertebrates. Rarely seen in flight and often hidden amid vegetation, the Pied-billed Grebe announces its presence with a loud call.

AT A GLANCE

Food Pied-billed Grebes eat mostly crustaceans (particularly crayfish) and small fish, which they capture and crush with their stout bills and strong jaws. Collecting most of their food underwater during foraging dives, they also eat mussels, snails, beetles, dragonfly nymphs, and other aquatic insects and their larvae.

Nesting Pied-billed Grebes create an open bowl nest on a platform of floating vegetation, usually situated among tall emergent plants. Its nest bowl is 4–5 inches in diameter and about an inch deep, and may be expanded during the egg-laying period.

Habitat Look for Pied-billed Grebes on small, quiet ponds and marshes where thick vegetation grows out of the water. In winter, they occur on larger water bodies, occasionally in large groups.

RANGE MAP

- Breeding
- Nonbreeding
- Year-round

KEYS TO IDENTIFICATION

MEASUREMENTS (Both sexes)

Length	Wingspan	Weight
11.8–15 in	17.7–24.4 in	8.9–20 oz
30–38 cm	45–62 cm	253–568 g

SIZE & SHAPE. The Pied-billed Grebe is a small, chunky swimming bird. It has a compact body and a slender neck, with a relatively large, blocky head and short, thick bill. It has virtually no tail.

COLOR PATTERN. These brown birds are slightly darker on their upperparts and more tawny-brown on the underparts. During spring and summer, the crown and nape are dark and the throat is black. While breeding, the bill is whitish with a black band ("pied"), but it's yellow-brown at other times of year. The juvenile has a striped face.

BEHAVIOR. Pied-billed Grebes can adjust their buoyancy and often float with just the upper half of the head above the water. They catch small fish and invertebrates by diving or slowly submerging. After a dive, they may reappear quite a distance from where they went down.

Cool Facts

Pied-billed Grebes create their varying buoyancy by trapping water in their feathers, giving them great control. They can sink deeply or stay just at or below the surface with this ability.

Find This Bird

Look for small-bodied, large-headed Pied-billed Grebes in summer on large ponds and small lakes with emergent vegetation. In winter, look for them in small flocks on larger water bodies.

The gangly Double-crested Cormorant is a prehistoric-looking, matte-black fishing bird with yellow-orange facial skin. Cormorants are a common sight around fresh and salt water across North America—perhaps attracting the most attention when standing in a large group on docks, rocky islands, and channel markers, wings spread out to dry. These solid, heavy-boned birds chase and catch small fish underwater.

AT A GLANCE

Food Double-crested Cormorants eat mostly fish, but may also consume insects, crustaceans, or amphibians. They dive and chase fish underwater with powerful propulsion from webbed feet. The tip of a cormorant's bill is shaped like a hook, helpful for seizing its prey.

Nesting Cormorants often nest in colonies. Nests may be on the ground, on rocks or reefs with no vegetation, or atop trees. They're constructed of small sticks, with some seaweed and flotsam, and lined with grass. The male delivers the material and the female does the building. Nests are 1.5–3 feet in diameter and 4–17 inches high.

Habitat Double-crested Cormorants are the most widespread cormorants in North America, and the ones most often seen in fresh water. They breed on coastlines and along large inland lakes. A colony's stick nests, built high in trees on an island or patch of flooded timber, can be conspicuous.

RANGE MAP

- ■ Breeding
- ■ Migration
- ■ Nonbreeding
- ■ Year-round

KEYS TO IDENTIFICATION

MEASUREMENTS (Both sexes)

Length	Wingspan	Weight
27.6–35.4 in	44.9–48.4 in	42.3–88.2 oz
70–90 cm	114–123 cm	1200–2500 g

SIZE & SHAPE. The Double-crested Cormorant is a large waterbird with a small head on a long, kinked neck. It has a thin, strongly hooked bill, roughly the length of its head. Its heavy body sits low in the water; from a distance or in poor light, it may sometimes be mistaken for a loon.

COLOR PATTERN. Adults are brown-black with a small patch of yellow-orange skin on the face. Immatures are browner overall, palest on the neck and breast. In the breeding season, adults develop a small double crest of stringy black or white feathers.

BEHAVIOR. Double-crested Cormorants float low on the surface of water and dive to catch small fish. After fishing, they stand on docks, rocks, and tree limbs with wings spread open to dry. In flight, they often travel in V-formation flocks that shift and reform as the birds alternate between bursts of choppy flapping and short glides.

Cool Facts

Up close, the all-black Double-crested Cormorant puts lots of bright colors on show, with an orange-yellow throat, sparkling aquamarine eyes, and a mouth that is bright blue on the inside.

Find This Bird

Look near lakes and coastlines for these perched black waterbirds. On the water they sit low, head usually tilted slightly upward. You may also see them holding their wings out to sun themselves.

GREAT BLUE HERON *(Ardea herodias)*

Whether poised at a river bend or cruising along the coastline with slow, deep wingbeats, the Great Blue Heron is a majestic sight. This widespread heron with subtle blue-gray plumage often stands motionless as it scans for prey, or it may wade belly deep with deliberate steps. It may move slowly, but the Great Blue Heron can strike like lightning to grab a fish or snap up a gopher. In flight, look for its tucked-in neck and long legs trailing out behind.

AT A GLANCE

Food

Great Blue Herons eat nearly any prey within striking distance, including fish, amphibians, reptiles, small mammals, insects, and other birds. They grab small prey in their strong mandibles or use the closed bill to impale larger fish.

Nesting

The male Great Blue Heron gathers the sticks that serve as the bulk of the nest material, presenting them to the female. She builds a platform to support the saucer-shaped nest cup, lining it with smaller materials. The finished nest may be from 20 inches to 4 feet across and nearly 3.5 feet deep.

Habitat

Look for Great Blue Herons in saltwater and freshwater habitats, from open coasts, marshes, sloughs, riverbanks, and lakes to backyard goldfish ponds. They also forage in grasslands and agricultural fields. Breeding birds gather in colonies called "heronries," where they build stick nests high off the ground.

RANGE MAP

Breeding
Nonbreeding
Year-round

KEYS TO IDENTIFICATION

MEASUREMENTS (Both sexes)

Length	Wingspan	Weight
38–54 in	65–79 in	74–88 oz
97–137 cm	167–201 cm	2100–2500 g

SIZE & SHAPE. This largest of North American herons has long legs, a sinuous neck, and a thick, daggerlike bill. Head, chest, and wing plumes give a shaggy appearance. In flight, the Great Blue Heron curls its neck into a tight "S" shape. Its wings are broad and rounded, and the legs trail well beyond the tail.

COLOR PATTERN. The Great Blue Heron appears blue-gray from a distance, with a wide black stripe over the eye. In flight, the upper side of the wings are two-toned, pale on the forewings and darker on the flight feathers.

BEHAVIOR. Hunting Great Blue Herons wade slowly or stand statuelike, stalking fish and other prey in shallow water or open fields. Watch for the lightning-fast thrust of the neck and head as they stab with their strong bills. Their very slow wingbeats, tucked-in neck, and trailing legs create an unmistakable image in flight.

Cool Facts

These birds can hunt day and night thanks to a high percentage of rod-type photoreceptors in their eyes for night vision. Specially shaped vertebrae help them strike prey at a distance.

Backyard Tips

Great Blue Herons sometimes visit yards that feature fish ponds. A length of drain pipe placed in the pond can provide fish with a place to hide from feeding herons.

GREAT EGRET *(Ardea alba)*

Great Egrets are a dazzling sight in many North American wetlands. Slightly smaller and more svelte than Great Blue Herons, Great Egrets are still large with an impressive wingspan. They hunt in classic heron fashion, standing immobile or wading through wetlands to capture fish. Great Egrets were hunted nearly to extinction for their plumes in the late nineteenth century, sparking conservation movements and some of the first laws to protect birds.

AT A GLANCE

Food

The Great Egret eats mainly small fish but also takes amphibians, reptiles, birds, small mammals, and invertebrates. It hunts in belly-deep or shallower water, alone or in groups. It wades in search of prey or simply stands still waiting for prey to approach.

Nesting

The male builds the nest platform from long sticks and twigs before pairing up with a female; both members of the pair may collaborate to complete the nest, though the male sometimes finishes it himself. The nest is up to 3 feet across and 1 foot deep.

Habitat

Great Egrets live in freshwater, brackish, and marine wetlands. During the breeding season, they are found in colonies in trees or shrubs with other waterbirds. The colonies are located on lakes, ponds, marshes, estuaries, impoundments, and islands. Great Egrets use similar habitats for migration stopover sites and wintering grounds.

KEYS TO IDENTIFICATION

MEASUREMENTS (Both sexes)

Length	Wingspan	Weight
37–41 in	51–57 in	35 oz
94–104 cm	131–145 cm	1000 g

SIZE & SHAPE. Great Egrets are tall, long-legged wading birds with long, daggerlike bills and long necks that may be stretched to full length or folded in an S curve. In flight, the long neck is tucked in and the legs extend far beyond the tip of the short tail.

COLOR PATTERN. Every feather on a Great Egret is white. The bill is solid yellowish-orange and the legs and feet are entirely black.

BEHAVIOR. Great Egrets wade in shallow water (both fresh and salt) to hunt fish, frogs, and other small aquatic animals. They typically stand still and watch for unsuspecting prey to pass by, and then, with startling speed, strike with a jab of the long neck and bill.

RANGE MAP

- Breeding
- Migration
- Nonbreeding
- Year-round

Cool Facts

During the breeding season, Great Egrets grow long, beautiful plumes on their backs called *aigrettes*. These feathers, once prized for ladies' hats, almost led to the bird's extinction in the late 1800s.

Find This Bird

At any pond, wetland, or coastal marsh within their range, you may see a few kinds of all-white herons. Look for the Great Egret's large size, black legs, and yellow bill.

GREEN HERON (Butorides virescens)

From a distance, the Green Heron is a dark, stocky bird hunched on slender yellow legs at the water's edge, often hidden behind a tangle of leaves. From close range, it is a striking bird with a velvet-green back, rich chestnut body, and a dark cap often raised into a short crest. This small heron crouches patiently to surprise fish with quick snatches of its daggerlike bill.

AT A GLANCE

Food Green Herons eat mainly small fish. They also feed on insects, spiders, crustaceans, snails, amphibians, reptiles, and rodents. When a fish is close, the heron lunges and darts its head, grasping (or sometimes spearing) the fish with its sharp, heavy bill.

Nesting The male begins building the nest before pairing up, but his mate finishes its construction as he gathers more materials. She shapes the long, thin sticks he gives her into a nest 8–12 inches across, with a shallow central depression averaging less than 2 inches deep. The nest is usually set in a large fork of a tree or bush, usually concealed by overhanging branches.

Habitat Green Herons live near wooded ponds, marshes, rivers, reservoirs, and estuaries. They may nest in dry woods and orchards as long as there is water nearby for foraging.

RANGE MAP

- Breeding
- Migration
- Nonbreeding
- Year-round

KEYS TO IDENTIFICATION

MEASUREMENTS (Both sexes)

Length	Wingspan	Weight
16.1–18.1 in	25.2–26.8 in	8.5 oz
41–46 cm	64–68 cm	240 g

SIZE & SHAPE. Compared with most herons, Green Herons are short and stocky, with fairly short legs and thick necks often drawn up against their bodies. They have broad, rounded wings and a long, daggerlike bill; in flight they can resemble crows. They often raise their crown feathers into a short crest.

COLOR PATTERN. From a distance, Green Herons look all dark. In better light they are deep green on the back with a rich chestnut breast and neck. The wings are dark gray. Juveniles are browner, with pale streaking on the neck and spots on the wings.

BEHAVIOR. Green Herons stand motionless at the water's edge as they hunt for fish and amphibians. They typically stand on vegetation or solid ground, seldom wading as do larger herons. In flight, these compact herons can look ungainly, often partially uncrooking their necks to give a front-heavy appearance.

Cool Facts

The Green Heron is one of the world's few tool-using bird species, creating fishing lures with bread crusts, insects, and other objects, then dropping them on water surfaces to entice small fish.

Find This Bird

Green Herons sometimes pay visits to ornamental fish ponds. A length of drain pipe placed in the pond can provide fish with a place to hide from feeding herons.

BLACK VULTURE *(Coragyps atratus)*

With sooty black plumage, a bare black head, and neat white patches under the wingtips, Black Vultures are almost dapper. Whereas Turkey Vultures are lanky birds with teetering flight, Black Vultures are compact birds with broad wings, short tails, and powerful wingbeats. Highly social birds with fierce family loyalty, Black Vultures share food with relatives, feeding young for months after they've fledged.

AT A GLANCE

Food

Black Vultures feed almost exclusively on carrion, locating it by sight as they soar high in the skies on thermals. From this vantage they can spot carcasses and pay attention to Turkey Vultures, which have a more developed sense of smell. The Black Vultures can follow them to find food. They also occasionally kill skunks, opossums, turtle hatchlings, and other animals. They often investigate dumpsters and landfills.

Nesting

Black Vultures usually nest in dark cavities such as caves, hollow trees, abandoned buildings, brush piles, thickets, and stumps. They lay their eggs directly on the ground.

Habitat

Look for Black Vultures in open areas within forested landscapes. They typically nest and roost in wooded areas and soar above open areas to find food. Black Vultures have substantially increased their range northward in recent decades.

RANGE MAP

■ Year-round
■ Year-round (scarce)

KEYS TO IDENTIFICATION

MEASUREMENTS (Both sexes)

Length	Wingspan	Weight
23.6–26.8 in	53.9–59.1 in	56.4–77.6 oz
60–68 cm	137–150 cm	1600–2200 g

SIZE & SHAPE. Black Vultures are large and raptorlike. In flight they hold their broad, rounded wings flat and angled slightly forward. The tail is very short and rounded. They have small, bare heads and narrow but strongly hooked bills.

COLOR PATTERN. These birds are uniform black except for white patches or "stars" on the undersides of their wingtips. These can be hard to see in strong light or from far away. The bare skin of the head is gray.

BEHAVIOR. During the day, Black Vultures soar in flocks, often with Turkey Vultures and hawks. Their flight style is distinctive: strong wingbeats followed by short glides, giving them a batlike appearance. Look for them along highway margins eating roadkill, as well as picking through dumpsters. They roost in groups in trees and on transmission towers, typically waiting through early morning until the air warms up and they can soar on thermals.

Cool Facts

Black Vultures lack a voice box, so their vocal abilities are limited to raspy hisses and grunts. They are the most numerous vulture in the Western Hemisphere.

Find This Bird

On warm or sunny days, look for Black Vultures soaring high on thermals. Their broad, forward-angled wings, small head, and short tail give them a distinctive silhouette.

TURKEY VULTURE *(Cathartes aura)*

If you've gone looking for raptors on a clear day, your heart has probably leaped at the sight of a large, soaring bird in the distance. If it's soaring with its wings raised in a V and making wobbly circles, it's probably a Turkey Vulture. These birds ride thermals in the sky and use their keen sense of smell to detect fresh carcasses.

They are consummate scavengers, cleaning up the countryside one bite of their sharply hooked bills at a time.

AT A GLANCE

Food
Turkey Vultures eat carrion, which they find largely by their excellent sense of smell. Mostly they eat mammals but also feed on dead reptiles, other birds, amphibians, fish, and even invertebrates. Unlike their Black Vulture relatives, Turkey Vultures almost never attack living prey.

Nesting
Turkey Vultures don't build much of a nest. They may scrape out a spot in the soil or leaf litter, pull aside obstacles, or arrange scraps of vegetation or rotting wood. Some use rotting logs or even old barns. Many nest sites are used repeatedly for a decade or more.

Habitat
Turkey Vultures are common in open areas, along roadsides, and near food sources such as landfills, trash heaps, and construction sites. On sunny days, look for them in the air; in colder weather and at night they roost on poles, towers, and dead trees.

RANGE MAP

- Breeding
- Year-round

KEYS TO IDENTIFICATION

MEASUREMENTS (Both sexes)

Length	Wingspan	Weight
25.2–31.9 in	66.9–70.1 in	70.5 oz
64–81 cm	170–178 cm	2000 g

SIZE & SHAPE. Turkey Vultures are large dark birds with long, broad wings. Bigger than most raptors except eagles and condors, they have long "fingers" at their wingtips and long tails that extend past their toe tips in flight. When soaring, Turkey Vultures hold their wings slightly raised, making a V when seen head-on.

COLOR PATTERN. Turkey Vultures appear black from a distance but up close are dark brown with a featherless red head and pale bill. While most of their body and forewing are dark, the undersides of the flight feathers (along the trailing edge and wingtips) are paler, giving a two-toned appearance.

BEHAVIOR. Turkey Vultures are majestic but unsteady soarers. Their teetering flight with very few wingbeats is characteristic. Look for them gliding relatively low to the ground, sniffing for carrion, or riding thermals to higher vantage points. They may soar in small groups and roost in larger numbers. You may see them on the ground in small groups, huddled around roadkill.

Cool Facts

Turkey Vultures have excellent immune systems and can feast on carcasses without contracting botulism, anthrax, cholera, or salmonella.

Find This Bird

Turkey Vultures are accustomed to living near humans and cleaning up messes. Look for them at farm fields or on road edges, as well as in the sky on hot days.

Unique among North American raptors for their diet of live fish and ability to dive into water to catch them, Ospreys are common sights soaring over shorelines, patrolling waterways, and standing on their huge stick nests, white heads gleaming. These large, rangy hawks do well around humans and have rebounded in numbers following the ban on the pesticide DDT.

AT A GLANCE

Food
The Osprey is the only hawk on the continent that eats almost exclusively live fish. In North America, more than 80 species of freshwater and saltwater fish account for 99% of the Osprey's diet.

Nesting
Osprey nests are built of sticks and lined with bark, sod, grasses, vines, algae, or flotsam and jetsam. Nests on artificial platforms, especially in a pair's first season, are less than 2.5 feet in diameter and 3–6 inches deep. After generations of adding to the nest, Ospreys can end up with nests 10–13 feet deep and 3–6 feet in diameter.

Habitat
Look for Ospreys around nearly any body of water: saltmarshes, rivers, ponds, reservoirs, estuaries, and even coral reefs. Their conspicuous stick nests are placed in the open atop poles, channel markers, and dead trees, often over or near water.

RANGE MAP

- ◼ Breeding
- ◼ Migration
- ◼ Winter
- ◼ Year-round

KEYS TO IDENTIFICATION

MEASUREMENTS (Both sexes)

Length	Wingspan	Weight
21.3–22.8 in	59.1–70.9 in	49.4–70.5 oz
54–58 cm	150–180 cm	1400–2000 g

SIZE & SHAPE. Ospreys are very large, distinctively shaped hawks. Despite their size, their bodies are slender, with long, narrow wings and long legs. Ospreys fly with a marked kink in their wings, making an M shape when seen from below.

COLOR PATTERN. Ospreys are brown above and white below, and overall they are whiter than most raptors. From below, the wings are mostly white with a prominent dark patch at the wrists. The head is white with a broad brown stripe through the eye. Juveniles have white spots on the back and buffy shading on the breast.

BEHAVIOR. Ospreys search for fish by flying on steady wingbeats and bowed wings, or circling high in the sky over relatively shallow water. They often hover briefly before diving, feet first, to grab a fish. You can often clearly see an Osprey's catch in its talons as the bird carries it back to a nest or perch.

Cool Facts

Ospreys have a reversible outer toe that allows them to grasp with two toes in front and two behind. Barbed pads on the soles of the birds' feet help them grip slippery fish.

Find This Bird

Thanks to environmental laws, Ospreys are much more common now than 40 years ago—look for their kinked-wing silhouettes over most large water bodies in summer and during migration.

BALD EAGLE *(Haliaeetus leucocephalus)*

The Bald Eagle has been the national emblem of the United States since 1782 and has served as a spiritual symbol for native people for far longer than that. These regal birds aren't really bald, but their white-feathered heads gleam in contrast to their chocolate-brown body and wings. Look for them soaring in solitude, chasing other birds for their food, or gathering by the hundreds near open water in winter.

AT A GLANCE

Food

Fish of many kinds constitute the centerpiece of the Bald Eagle's diet, but eagles also eat other birds, reptiles, amphibians, invertebrates, and small mammals. They take their prey dead or alive. Bald Eagles sometimes gorge, ingesting a large amount of food and digesting it over several days.

Nesting

Bald Eagles build some of the largest of all bird nests—typically 5–6 feet in diameter and 2–4 feet tall, ranging in shape from cylindrical to conical to flat, depending on the supporting tree. Near shorelines they may nest on the ground using whatever materials are available, such as kelp and driftwood.

Habitat

Look for Bald Eagles near lakes, reservoirs, rivers, marshes, and coasts. For a chance to see large Bald Eagle congregations, check out wildlife refuges or large bodies of water over much of the continent during winter.

RANGE MAP

■ Breeding
■ Nonbreeding
■ Year-round

KEYS TO IDENTIFICATION

ADULT

IMMATURE

MEASUREMENTS (Both sexes)

Length	Wingspan	Weight
28–37.8 in	80.3 in	105.8–222.2 oz
71–96 cm	204 cm	3000–6300 g

SIZE & SHAPE. The Bald Eagle dwarfs most other birds, including the Turkey Vulture and Red-tailed Hawk. It has a heavy body, large head, and long, hooked bill. In flight, a Bald Eagle holds its broad wings flat like a board.

COLOR PATTERN. Adult Bald Eagles have white heads and tails with dark brown bodies and wings. Their legs and bills are bright yellow. Immature birds have mostly dark heads and tails; their brown wings and bodies are mottled with white in varying amounts. Young birds attain adult plumage in about 5 years.

BEHAVIOR. Bald Eagles soar high in the sky, flapping low over treetops with slow wingbeats. They perch in trees or stand on the ground. Bald Eagles scavenge many meals by harassing other birds or by eating carrion or garbage. They mostly eat fish, but also take mammals, gulls, and waterfowl.

Cool Facts

Rather than do its own fishing, the Bald Eagle often goes after other creatures' catches. It often forces Ospreys to drop their prey, and sometimes snatches a fish right out of an Osprey's talons.

Find This Bird

Bald Eagles are widespread across North America in winter. Look for their rock-steady soaring on very broad wings or find them perched on sturdy branches near rivers and lakes.

The tiny Sharp-shinned Hawk often appears in a blur of motion and disappears in a flurry of feathers. This smallest hawk in North America is a daring, acrobatic flier. An "accipiter," it has long legs, short wings, and a very long tail, an ideal shape for navigating its deep-woods home at top speed in pursuit of songbirds and occasionally small rodents. The Sharp-shinned Hawk is easiest to spot in fall on its southward migration.

AT A GLANCE

Food

Songbirds make up about 90% of the Sharp-shinned Hawk's diet. Birds the size of American Robins or smaller are the most frequent prey; bigger birds are at less risk but not completely safe. Sharp-shinned Hawks also eat small rodents and an occasional moth or grasshopper.

Nesting

The nest is a broad, flat mass of dead twigs, sometimes lined with flakes of bark. Both members of the pair bring material to the site, but the female does most or all of the construction. The shallow, platformlike nest is usually 1–2 feet in diameter and 4–6 inches deep.

Habitat

Sharp-shinned Hawks breed in deep forests. During migration, look for them in open habitats or high in the sky, migrating along ridgelines. During the nonbreeding season they hunt small birds and mammals along forest edges, and sometimes at backyard bird feeders.

RANGE MAP

■ Breeding
■ Migration
■ Nonbreeding
■ Year-round

KEYS TO IDENTIFICATION

MEASUREMENTS (Both sexes)

Length	Wingspan	Weight
9.4–13.4 in	16.9–22 in	3.1–7.7 oz
24–34 cm	43–56 cm	87–218 g

SIZE & SHAPE. Sharp-shinned Hawks are small, long-tailed hawks with short, rounded wings. They have small heads that in flight do not usually project beyond the "wrists" of the wings. The tail tends to be square-tipped and may show a notch at the tip. Females are considerably larger than males.

COLOR PATTERN. Adults are slaty blue-gray above, with narrow red-orange bars on the breast. Immature birds are mostly brown with coarse vertical streaks on white underparts. Adults and young have broad dark bands across their long tails.

BEHAVIOR. Sharp-shinned Hawks are agile fliers that speed through dense woods to surprise their prey, typically songbirds. They may also pounce from low perches. When flying across open areas, they have a distinctive flap-and-glide flight style.

Cool Facts

Sharp-shinned Hawks carry their prey to a stump or low branch to pluck before eating. Unlike owls, they seldom swallow feathers.

Backyard Tips

Bird feeders sometimes attract hawks. If you want to give the small birds a break, take down feeders for a few weeks. The hawk will move on and the songbirds will return when you put your feeders back up.

COOPER'S HAWK (Accipiter cooperii)

Among the bird world's most skillful fliers, Cooper's Hawks are common woodland hawks that tear through tree canopies at high speed in pursuit of other birds. You're most likely to see one prowling above a forest edge or field using just a few stiff wingbeats followed by a glide. Their smaller lookalike, the Sharp-shinned Hawk, makes Cooper's Hawks famously tricky to identify.

AT A GLANCE

Food

Cooper's Hawks eat mainly medium-sized birds which they chase. They sometimes rob nests and also eat some rodents and bats.

Nesting

Cooper's Hawks build nests in pines, firs, spruces, oaks, beeches, and other trees, in dense woods or suburban neighborhoods. The male builds the nest over about 2 weeks, with a little help from the female. Nests are piles of sticks roughly 27 inches in diameter and 6–17 inches high. The cup, 8 inches wide and 4 inches deep, is lined with bark flakes and sometimes green twigs.

Habitat

Cooper's Hawks are forest and woodland birds, but they do well in leafy suburbs, too. These lanky hawks are a regular sight in parks, quiet neighborhoods, fields, backyard feeders, and even along busy streets if there are trees around.

RANGE MAP

Breeding
Nonbreeding
Year-round

KEYS TO IDENTIFICATION

MEASUREMENTS

	Length	Wingspan	Weight
Male	14.6–15.4 in 37–39 cm	24.4–35.4 in 62–90 cm	7.8–14.5 oz 220–410 g
Female	16.5–17.7 in 42–45 cm	29.5–35.4 in 75–90 cm	11.6–24 oz 330–680 g

SIZE & SHAPE. This medium-sized hawk has the classic accipiter shape: broad, rounded wings and a long tail. It has a more bull-headed look than the Sharp-shinned, its head often jutting past the bend of the wings, and its tail tip is usually more rounded.

COLOR PATTERN. Adults are steely blue-gray above with warm reddish bars on the underparts and thick dark bands on the tail. Juveniles are brown above and crisply streaked on the upper breast, giving them a cleaner look than the more blurry streaking of young Sharp-shinned Hawks.

BEHAVIOR. Cooper's Hawks fly with the flap-flap-glide pattern typical of accipiters, seldom flapping continuously. One hunting strategy is to fly fast and low to the ground, then up and over an obstruction to surprise prey on the other side.

Cool Facts

A Cooper's Hawk captures a bird with its feet and kills it by squeezing. Falcons tend to kill their prey by biting it, but Cooper's Hawks hold their catch away from the body until it dies.

Find This Bird

During migration, organized hawk watches on ridgetops in both East and West are great places to see lots of Cooper's Hawks.

Whether wheeling over a swamp forest or whistling plaintively from a riverine park, a Red-shouldered Hawk is typically a sign of wet deciduous woodlands. It's one of our most distinctively marked common hawks, with barred reddish-peachy underparts and a strongly banded tail. In flight, translucent crescents near the wingtips help to identify the species at a distance.

AT A GLANCE

Food

Red-shouldered Hawks hunt from perches below the forest canopy or at the edge of a pond, sitting silently until they detect prey below. Then they descend swiftly, gliding and snatching a vole, chipmunk, or toad. They also eat frogs, snakes, and crayfish.

Nesting

Each year both male and female build a new nest or refurbish a prior year's nest. The stick nest is about 2 feet in diameter, typically placed in a broad-leaved tree (occasionally in a conifer), below the forest canopy but toward the treetop, usually in a crotch of the main trunk.

Habitat

Look for Red-shouldered Hawks in deciduous woodlands, often near rivers and swamps. During migration they often move high overhead along ridges or coastlines. They may be abundant at some hawk-watching overlooks.

RANGE MAP

- Breeding
- Nonbreeding
- Year-round

KEYS TO IDENTIFICATION

MEASUREMENTS (Both sexes)

Length	Wingspan	Weight
16.9–24 in	37–43.7 in	17.1–27.3 oz
43–61 cm	94–111 cm	486–774 g

SIZE & SHAPE. Red-shouldered Hawks are medium sized, with broad, rounded wings and medium-length tails that they fan out when soaring. In flight, they often glide or soar with their wingtips pushed slightly forward, giving them a distinctive "reaching" posture.

COLOR PATTERN. Adults are colorful hawks with dark-and-white checkered wings and warm reddish barring on the breast. The tail is black with narrow white bands. Immatures are brown above and white below streaked with brown. All ages show narrow, pale crescents near the wingtips in flight.

BEHAVIOR. Red-shouldered Hawks soar over forests or perch on tree branches or utility wires. Their rising, whistled *kee-rah* is a distinctive sound of the forest. They hunt small mammals, amphibians, and reptiles either from perches or while flying.

Cool Facts

American Crows often mob Red-shouldered Hawks, and both species may chase each other to steal food. The two species may also join forces to attack a Great Horned Owl and chase it away.

Find This Bird

A good way to find Red-shouldered Hawks is to learn their distinctive whistle and listen for it in and around wet forests, where you may find them hunting from a perch along a stream or pond.

RED-TAILED HAWK *(Buteo jamaicensis)*

The Red-tailed Hawk is probably the most common hawk in North America. If you've got sharp eyes, you may see several on almost any long car ride. Red-tailed Hawks soar above open fields, slowly turning circles on their broad, rounded wings. They also perch atop telephone poles, eyes fixed on the ground to catch the movements of a vole or a rabbit, or simply waiting out cold weather before climbing a thermal air current into the sky.

AT A GLANCE

Food
Mammals make up the bulk of most Red-tailed Hawk meals. Frequent prey items include voles, mice, wood rats, rabbits, snowshoe hares, jackrabbits, and ground squirrels. They also take birds, including pheasants, bobwhite, starlings, and blackbirds, as well as snakes and carrion.

Nesting
Both adults build the nest or refurbish one from a previous year. The nest is a tall pile of dry sticks up to 3 feet high, lined with bark strips and fresh green twigs. It's usually placed near the crown of a tall tree where the adults and young have a commanding view of the landscape.

Habitat
Red-tailed Hawks occupy just about every type of open habitat on the continent, including desert, grasslands, roadsides, fields and pastures, parks, broken woodland, and (in Mexico) tropical rainforest. They're also found in many large cities.

RANGE MAP

Breeding
Year-round

KEYS TO IDENTIFICATION

ADULT

IMMATURE

MEASUREMENTS

Male	Length 17.7–22 in 45–56 cm	Wingspan 44.9–52.4 in 114–133 cm	Weight 24.3–45.9 oz 690–1300 g
Female	Length 19.7–25.6 in 50–65 cm	Wingspan 44.9–52.4 in 114–133 cm	Weight 31.7–51.5 oz 900–1460 g

SIZE & SHAPE. Red-tailed Hawks are large hawks with typical buteo proportions: very broad, rounded wings and a short, wide tail. Large females seen from a distance may deceptively appear as large as an eagle.

COLOR PATTERN. Most Red-tailed Hawks are rich brown above and pale below, with a streaked belly and, on the wing underside, a dark bar between shoulder and wrist. The tail is usually pale below and cinnamon-red above, though in young birds it's brown and banded.

BEHAVIOR. Red-tailed Hawks are most conspicuous when soaring in wide circles high above a field. When flapping, their wingbeats are heavy. They often face into a high wind to hover without flapping, eyes fixed on the ground. They attack in a slow, controlled dive with legs outstretched.

Cool Facts

Whenever a hawk or eagle appears in a TV show or movie, no matter what species, the shrill cry on the soundtrack is almost always that of a Red-tailed Hawk.

Backyard Tips

Red-tailed Hawks eat mostly mammals; they may soar over your house while hunting, but are less likely to be a problem at bird feeders than Cooper's Hawks and Sharp-shinned Hawks.

AMERICAN COOT *(Fulica americana)*

The waterborne American Coot is a good reminder that not everything that swims is a duck. A close look at the small head, scrawny legs, and funny lobed toes reveals a different kind of bird entirely. The coot's dark body and white bill is a common sight in nearly any open water across the continent. Coots often mix with ducks, but they're actually related to cranes and rails.

AT A GLANCE

Food

American Coots eat mainly aquatic plants including duckweed, sedges, water lilies, and cattails. When on land, they pick at terrestrial plants and sometimes grains or leaves. You may also see them eating insects, crustaceans, snails, and small vertebrates.

Nesting

Nests are usually built over water on floating platforms and are often associated with dense stands of vegetation such as reeds, sedges, and grasses. The nest material is woven into a shallow basket and lined with finer smooth material to hold the eggs. The average diameter is 12 inches, with an egg cup about 1 inch deep and 6 inches in diameter.

Habitat

The American Coot inhabits a wide variety of mainly freshwater wetlands, including prairie potholes, swamps and marshes, suburban parks, sewage ponds, and the edges of large lakes.

RANGE MAP

- ■ Breeding
- ■ Breeding (scarce)
- ■ Migration
- ■ Nonbreeding
- ■ Year-round

KEYS TO IDENTIFICATION

MEASUREMENTS (Both sexes)

Length	Wingspan	Weight
15.5–16.9 in	23–25 in	21.2–24.7 oz
39.4–42.9 cm	58.4–63.5 cm	600–700 g

SIZE & SHAPE. The American Coot is a plump, chickenlike bird with a rounded head and a sloping bill. Its tiny tail, short wings, and large feet are visible on the rare occasions when it takes flight.

COLOR PATTERN. American Coots are dark-gray to black, with a bright-white bill and forehead. The legs are yellow-green. At close range, you may see a small patch of red on the forehead. American Coots have small, bright-red eyes.

BEHAVIOR. You'll find American Coots eating aquatic plants on almost any body of water. When swimming and diving they look like small ducks, but on land they look more chickenlike, walking rather than waddling. An awkward flier, the American Coot requires a long, noisy running takeoff to get airborne.

Cool Facts

American Coots in the winter can be found in rafts of mixed waterfowl and in groups numbering up to several thousand individuals.

Find This Bird

To find American Coots, scan lakes and ponds for small black birds with bright white bills. You may also see them walking around on land on their long, yellow-green legs.

SANDHILL CRANE *(Antigone canadensis)*

Whether stepping singly across a wet meadow or filling the sky by the hundreds or thousands, Sandhill Cranes have an elegance that draws attention. These tall, gray-bodied, crimson-capped birds breed in open wetlands, fields, and prairies across North America. They group together in great numbers, filling the air with distinctive rolling cries. Mates display to each other with exuberant dances characterized by a gangly grace.

AT A GLANCE

Food

The omnivorous Sandhill Crane feeds on land or in shallow marshes, picking from the surface and probing with its bill. Its diet is heavy in seeds and cultivated grains. It may also include berries and tubers, as well as small vertebrates and invertebrates.

Nesting

Pairs of Sandhill Cranes build their nests using dried plant material early in the season, adding green matter as it becomes available. They toss nesting material over their shoulders to form a mound, which the female stands atop arranging. The mound may be 30-40 inches across and 4-6 inches high; those built over water must be larger and higher than those built on dry land.

Habitat

Sandhill Cranes breed and forage in open prairies, grasslands, farmlands, and wetlands. Outside of the breeding season, they often roost in deeper water of ponds or lakes, where they are safer from predators.

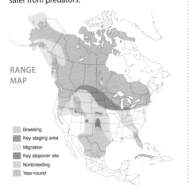

RANGE MAP

- Breeding
- Key staging area
- Migration
- Key stopover site
- Nonbreeding
- Year-round

KEYS TO IDENTIFICATION

MEASUREMENTS (Both sexes)

Length	Wingspan	Weight
47.2 in	78.7 in	119.9–172.8 oz
120 cm	200 cm	3400–4900 g

SIZE & SHAPE. Sandhill Cranes are very large birds with long necks, long legs, and very broad wings. The bulky body tapers into a slender neck; the short tail is covered by drooping feathers that form a "bustle." The head is small. The bill is straight and longer than the head.

COLOR PATTERN. Fresh adult feathers are slate gray, but preening birds often "paint" themselves with soil; any iron stains the plumage rusty. Adults have pale cheeks and red, bumpy, bare skin on the crown. Their legs are black. Juveniles are gray and rusty brown, without the adult's pale cheek or red crown.

BEHAVIOR. Sandhill Cranes forage for grains and invertebrates in prairies, grasslands, farms, and marshes. They do not hunt in open water or hunch their necks the way herons do. Sandhill Cranes form extremely large flocks—into the tens of thousands—on their wintering grounds and during migration. They often migrate very high in the sky.

Cool Facts

Sandhill Cranes are known for their dancing skills. Courting cranes stretch their wings, pump their heads, bow, and leap into the air in a graceful and energetic dance.

Find This Bird

In summer, cranes are found in small bogs and prairies across northern North America and the southeastern United States. In winter, they form huge flocks in places like Bosque del Apache, New Mexico.

KILLDEER *(Charadrius vociferus)*

A shorebird you can see without going to the beach, the Killdeer is a graceful plover common on large lawns, golf courses, athletic fields, and parking lots. This tawny bird runs across the ground in spurts, stopping with a jolt every so often. Its voice, a far-carrying, excited *kill-deer*, is a common sound even after dark, often given in flight as the bird circles overhead on slender wings.

AT A GLANCE

Food

Killdeer feed primarily on invertebrates such as earthworms, snails, crayfish, grasshoppers, beetles, and aquatic insect larvae. They follow farmers' plows and take advantage of any unearthed prey; they also eat seeds left on agricultural fields.

Nesting

Killdeer nests are simple scrapes, often made on slight rises in open habitats. The nest is a shallow depression scratched into the bare ground, typically 3–3.5 inches across. After egg-laying begins, Killdeer often add rocks, bits of shell, sticks, and trash to the nest.

Habitat

Look for Killdeer on open ground with low vegetation (or no vegetation at all), such as on lawns, golf courses, driveways, parking lots, and gravel-covered roofs, as well as pastures, fields, sandbars, and mudflats. It's one of the least water-associated of all shorebirds.

RANGE MAP

- Breeding
- Nonbreeding
- Year-round

KEYS TO IDENTIFICATION

MEASUREMENTS (Both sexes)

Length	Wingspan	Weight
7.9–11 in	18.1–18.9 in	2.6–4.5 oz
20–28 cm	46–48 cm	75–128 g

SIZE & SHAPE. Killdeer have the large, round head, large eyes, and short bill characteristic of other plovers, but are more slender and lanky, with a long, pointed tail and long wings.

COLOR PATTERN. Killdeer are brownish-tan on top and white below. The white chest is barred with two black bands, and the brown face is marked with black and white patches. The bright orange-buff rump is conspicuous in flight.

BEHAVIOR. Killdeer walk along the ground or run ahead a few steps, stopping to look around before running again. When disturbed, they break into flight and circle overhead, calling repeatedly. Their flight is rapid, with stiff, intermittent wingbeats.

Cool Facts

A well-known denizen of dry habitats, the Killdeer is actually a proficient swimmer. Adults swim well in swift-flowing water, and chicks can swim across small streams.

Backyard Tips

Killdeer don't visit feeders, but they do nest in open habitat including driveways and short lawns. Keep an eye out for them in spring and you may find a little Killdeer family at your home.

RING-BILLED GULL *(Larus delawarensis)*

Adapted to life around humans, Ring-billed Gulls frequent parking lots, garbage dumps, beaches, and fields. They are the gulls you're most likely to see far away from coastal areas—in fact, most Ring-billed Gulls nest in the interior of the continent, near fresh water. A black band encircling the yellow bill helps distinguish adults from other gulls, but some other species have black or red spots on the bill that may look from a distance like this ring.

AT A GLANCE

Food
Able to thrive on almost any source of nutrition, Ring-billed Gulls eat mostly fish, insects, earthworms, rodents, grain, and garbage. In addition to their more common fare, Ring-billed Gulls have been known to eat some fruits as well as French fries and other food discarded—or left unguarded—by people.

Nesting
Ring-billed Gulls nest in colonies numbering from 20 to tens of thousands of pairs. They build their nests on the ground near fresh water, usually on low, sparsely vegetated terrain. The male and female cooperate in constructing the nest—a scrape in the ground lined with plant materials.

Habitat
Ring-billed Gulls are often found in urban, suburban, and agricultural areas. Near coasts, they frequent estuaries, beaches, mudflats, and coastal waters. In winter, they're common around docks, wharves, and harbors.

RANGE MAP

Breeding
Migration
Nonbreeding
Year-round

KEYS TO IDENTIFICATION

MEASUREMENTS (Both sexes)

Length	Wingspan	Weight
16.9–21.3 in	41.3–46.1 in	10.6–24.7 oz
43–54 cm	105–117 cm	300–700 g

SIZE & SHAPE. The Ring-billed is a medium-sized gull with a fairly short, slim bill. When perched, its long, slender wings extend well past its square-tipped tail. In flight, the birds move lightly on easy flaps of their fairly slender wings.

COLOR PATTERN. Adults are clean gray above with a white head, body, and tail; their black wingtips are spotted with white. They have yellow legs and a yellow bill with a black band around it. Nonbreeding adults have brown-streaked heads. During their first two years, Ring-billed Gulls are mottled brown and gray with a pinkish bill and legs.

BEHAVIOR. These sociable gulls often fly overhead by the hundreds or feed together on golf courses, beaches, and fields. Strong, nimble flyers and opportunistic feeders, Ring-billed Gulls circle and hover acrobatically looking for food; they also forage afloat and on foot.

Cool Facts

Ring-billed Gulls are dedicated parents—maybe too dedicated. They sometimes pull egg-shaped pebbles into their nests and incubate them along with the rest of their clutch.

Find This Bird

Look for these gulls near parking lots, fast food joints, sporting events, sewage ponds, and garbage dumps. They also frequent reservoirs, lakes, marshes, mudflats, and beaches.

HERRING GULL (*Larus argentatus*)

Spiraling above a fishing boat or gathered near shore, Herring Gulls are the quintessential "seagulls," the most familiar gulls of the North Atlantic. They are also found across much of coastal North America, including on the Great Lakes, in winter. The variety of plumages they wear during their first four years makes identification tricky—so begin by learning to recognize their beefy size and shape.

AT A GLANCE

Food Herring Gulls prey on marine and freshwater invertebrates, fish, insects, smaller seabirds, and even on adults, young, and eggs of other gulls. Some specialize on a single food type such as crabs, sea urchins, or clams.

Nesting Herring Gull pairs pick nesting sites together in soft soil, sand, or short vegetation. Several days before egg-laying, they hollow out up to four scrapes 10–15 inches across with a central depression 4–8 inches wide and about the depth of an egg. They line them with vegetation, feathers, plastic, rope, or other materials. They'll choose the actual nest from these options.

Habitat Look for Herring Gulls in winter along coasts and near large reservoirs, lakes, and major rivers. They feed in habitats as diverse as open water, mudflats, plowed fields, and garbage dumps. Flocks gather in almost any open space near food.

RANGE MAP

- ■ Breeding
- ■ Migration
- ■ Nonbreeding
- ■ Year-round

KEYS TO IDENTIFICATION

MEASUREMENTS (Both sexes)

Length	Wingspan	Weight
22–26 in	53.9–57.5 in	28.2–44.1 oz
56–66 cm	137–146 cm	800–1250 g

SIZE & SHAPE. Herring Gulls are large gulls with hefty bills and robust bodies. In flight, they look barrel chested and broad winged compared to smaller species such as Ring-billed Gulls.

COLOR PATTERN. Adults have light-gray backs, black wingtips, and white heads and underparts. In winter, dusky streaks mark their heads. Juveniles are mottled brown; second-year birds are brown but show gray on the back. Third-years have more gray on the back and more white on the head and underparts. The legs are dull pink at all ages.

BEHAVIOR. Herring Gulls patrol shorelines and open ocean, picking scraps off the surface. Rallying around fishing boats or refuse dumps, they are loud and competitive scavengers that snatch other birds' meals. They spend much of their time perched near food sources, often in large congregations of gulls.

Cool Facts

For many people there's only one type of gull, the "seagull." But in fact, nearly two dozen species of gulls live in North America alone. The Herring Gull is one of the most common.

Find This Bird

Look for Herring Gulls in winter soaring along coastal shorelines, feeding on beaches, or squabbling at refuse dumps. Within their range, almost any large open space near water can become a hangout.

ROCK PIGEON *(Columba livia)*

A common sight in cities around the world, Rock Pigeons crowd streets and public squares, living on discarded food and offerings of birdseed. You'll often see flocks with plain, spotted, pale, or rusty-red varieties in them. Introduced to North America from Europe in the early 1600s, city pigeons nest on buildings and window ledges. In the countryside they also nest on barns and grain towers, under bridges, and on natural cliffs.

AT A GLANCE

Food

Rock Pigeons feed on seeds, fruits, and, more rarely, invertebrates. Pigeons also readily eat food left out by people, including breadcrumbs and litter.

Nesting

Males usually choose the nest site, then sit in place and coo to attract a mate. The site is a nook or ledge on a cliff or structure, often beneath an overhang. The female makes a flimsy platform of straw, stems, and sticks brought to her one at a time by the male. Pigeons reuse their nests and don't carry away the feces of their nestlings. Over time, the nest grows into a sturdy mound, sometimes incorporating unhatched eggs and mummified remains of dead nestlings.

Habitat

Rock Pigeons live in urban areas, on farmlands, and near rocky cliffs. They may gather in large flocks in urban parks where people feed them.

RANGE MAP

Year-round
Year-round (scarce)

KEYS TO IDENTIFICATION

MEASUREMENTS (Both sexes)

Length	Wingspan	Weight
11.8–14.2 in	19.7–26.4 in	9.3–13.4 oz
30–36 cm	50–67 cm	265–380 g

SIZE & SHAPE. Larger and plumper than a Mourning Dove, Rock Pigeons are tubby birds with small heads and short legs. Their wings are broad but pointed and the tail is wide and rounded. In flight they may resemble falcons.

COLOR PATTERN. Rock Pigeons are extremely variable in color, but most are bluish gray with two black bands on each wing and a black tip to the tail. They usually have iridescent throat and neck feathers. Wings may be patterned with two bars or dark spots, or may be plain. The tail is usually dark tipped.

BEHAVIOR. Pigeons often gather in flocks, walking or running on the ground and pecking for food. When alarmed, the flock may suddenly fly into the air and circle several times before coming down again.

Cool Facts

Rock Pigeons carried messages for the U.S. Army Signal Corps during World War I and II, saving lives and providing vital strategic information.

Backyard Tips

Pigeons come to open areas with food on the ground. However, seed on the ground can attract rodents, so provide only as much food as the pigeons will eat during a visit.

EURASIAN COLLARED-DOVE (Streptopelia decaocto)

With a flash of white tail feathers and a flurry of dark-tipped wings, the Eurasian Collared-Dove settles onto a phone wire or fence post to give its rhythmic three-parted coo. This chunky relative of the Mourning Dove gets its name from the black half-collar at the nape of the neck. A few Eurasian Collared-Doves were introduced to the Bahamas in the 1970s. They made their way to Florida by the 1980s and then rapidly colonized most of the continent.

AT A GLANCE

Food Eurasian Collared-Doves eat mainly seed and cereal grain such as millet, sunflower, milo, wheat, and corn. They also eat some berries and green parts of plants, as well as some invertebrates.

Nesting The male brings the female twigs, grasses, roots, and other nesting materials, which he sometimes pushes directly under her. Over 1–3 days, she builds a simple platform nest that may include feathers, wool, string, and wire. A pair often uses the same nest for multiple broods during the year, and may renovate old nests. Nests are usually built 10 or more feet above the ground.

Habitat Eurasian Collared-Doves live in urban and suburban areas throughout much of the U.S. except the Northeast. In rural settings, look for them on farms and in livestock yards where grain is available. In cooler months, flocks may roost together in large trees.

RANGE MAP

Year-round

Year-round (scarce)

KEYS TO IDENTIFICATION

MEASUREMENTS (Both sexes)

Length	Wingspan	Weight
11.4–11.8 in	13.8 in	4.9–6.3 oz
29–30 cm	35 cm	140–180 g

SIZE & SHAPE. Eurasian Collared-Doves have plump bodies, small heads, and long tails. They're larger than Mourning Doves but slimmer and longer-tailed than Rock Pigeons. The wings are broad and slightly rounded. The broad tail is squared off at the tip rather than pointed like a Mourning Dove's.

COLOR PATTERN. Eurasian Collared-Doves are chalky light brown to gray-buff birds with broad white patches in the tail. The "collar" is a narrow black crescent around the nape of the neck. In flight and when perched, the wingtips are darker than the rest of the wing.

BEHAVIOR. Eurasian Collared-Doves perch on telephone poles, wires, and in large trees while giving incessant three-syllable coos. Their flight pattern features bursts of clipped wingbeats and looping glides. When walking, they bob their heads and flick their tails.

Cool Facts

Bird feeders and trees planted in urban and suburban areas are cited as two of the main factors in the species' colonization of the continent.

Backyard Tips

Eurasian Collared-Doves readily come to backyards for seed and grain, particularly millet. They often nest near houses and other developed areas where food is easily available.

INCA DOVE *(Columbina inca)*

The tiny Inca Dove is a delicate bird with fine black scalloping on its back and rich rusty wings that flash when it bursts into flight. This 1.5-ounce dove of Mexico and Central America has become a common resident of settled areas in Texas and the Southwest. Its call, a plaintive "no-hope," can be heard all day.

AT A GLANCE

Food
The Inca Dove eats mainly grains, weeds, and grass seeds. Inca Doves usually forage on the ground amid low vegetation, but they often come to feeders with elevated platforms.

Nesting
The male Inca Dove gathers plant materials and brings them to the female, which builds an insubstantial twig nest. When he carries materials to her, he climbs on her back and gives them directly to her or sets them next to her in an apparently important ritual. The nest is a compact platform, usually unlined. Inca Doves do not clean their nests and use them repeatedly. Over time, excrement collects, binding the materials and, as it builds up on the sides, deepening the cup.

Habitat
Inca Doves usually live around people, in towns, cities, and farms, where they feed on open ground and at feeders. They nest in shrubs and small trees.

RANGE MAP

■ Year-round

KEYS TO IDENTIFICATION

MEASUREMENTS (Both sexes)

Length	Wingspan	Weight
7.1–9.1 in	11 in	1.1–2 oz
18–23 cm	28 cm	30–58 g

SIZE & SHAPE. The Inca Dove is a small dove with a long, square-tipped tail. It's smaller than all other North American doves except for the ground-doves.

COLOR PATTERN. The Inca Dove is brownish-gray with a delicate scaly pattern of black feather edges on its back and wings. The tail has white corners and edges. In flight, the wings flash a rich rufous-brown color and the center of the tail shows black.

BEHAVIOR. This sociable dove of aridlands and urban areas flocks and roosts communally except during the nesting season. It spends its days feeding, resting, bathing, and sunning.

Cool Facts

The Inca Dove engages in an odd behavior known as "pyramid roosting." Pairs or groups of Inca Doves huddle together in the sunshine, with some sitting on the backs of the others.

Backyard Tips

This species takes millet, sunflower, and other seeds at feeders and on the ground beneath them. It also uses birdbaths.

A dove the size of a sparrow, the Common Ground-Dove forages in dusty open areas, sometimes shaded by the grass clumps it feeds beneath. Its dusty plumage camouflages it until the bird springs into flight with a soft rattling of feathers and a flash of reddish-brown in the wings. These small, attractive doves are common across the southernmost parts of the U.S. from California to Florida.

AT A GLANCE

Food Common Ground-Doves glean small seeds from wild grasses and weeds. They are common visitors to bird feeders and also eat small erries and insects. In spring and summer they ometimes eat snail shells, possibly to replenish e calcium they expend producing eggs and op milk during nesting.

Nesting Ground-doves invest minimal time building nests, but both sexes share the labor. When nesting on the ground, they dig a slight depression the earth and line it with a few plant aterials. For above-ground nests, they build structure of twigs or pine needles lined with otlets and grasses. Each nest is up to 3 inches cross.

Habitat Common Ground-Doves live in open or shrubby areas with tall grasses or groves of trees, including riparian corridors and open savannas. They so live in towns and suburbs, where they equent yards and hedges.

ANGE
MAP

■ Year-round

KEYS TO IDENTIFICATION

MEASUREMENTS (Both sexes)

Length	Wingspan	Weight
5.9–7.1 in	10.6 in	1–1.4 oz
15–18 cm	27 cm	28–40 g

SIZE & SHAPE. Common Ground-Doves are tiny doves with short, round wings, short tails, and short, thin bills. They are stocky, with short legs, and they shuffle as they walk.

COLOR PATTERN. Common Ground-Doves are sandy brown overall, with large, dark spots on the wing coverts. In flight the wings show rich rufous patches. Males have a pinkish wash on the head, neck, and chest, and bluish crowns; females are duller. Both sexes have fine, dark scaling on the neck and chest, and pinkish-red bills with a dark tip.

BEHAVIOR. Common Ground-Doves are relatively shy, usually staying hidden in grasslands and small groves of trees. Males sing a series of quiet, moaning coos. Mostly seen on the ground at backyard bird feeders, Common Ground-Doves eat seeds and grains, along with some insects.

Cool Facts

ike other doves and pigeons, Common Ground-Doves feed their young a milky-colored, nutritious secretion called crop milk.

Backyard Tips

Common Ground-Doves come to ground feeders for commercial birdseed mixes, millet, buckwheat, and other seeds.

WHITE-WINGED DOVE (Zenaida asiatica)

Originally a bird of desert thickets, the White-winged Dove has become a common sight in cities and towns across the southern U.S. When perched, this bird's unspotted brown upperparts and large, neat white crescent along the wing edge distinguish it from the Mourning Dove. In flight, those subdued crescents become flashing white stripes worthy of the bird's name. Look closely to see a remarkably colorful face, bright orange eyes, and blue "eye shadow."

AT A GLANCE

Food The White-winged Dove eats mostly grains and other agricultural crops, and also takes fruits and large seeds. It seems adapted to large food items because of its large bill and slow eating style (it never pecks quickly, the way Mourning Doves do). White-winged Doves often feed from perches above the ground.

Nesting The male gathers twigs and brings them to the female; she constructs the nest over a couple of days, arranging twigs and some weeds or grasses into a flimsy bowl about 4 inches across. The nest is usually on a tree branch or crotch under heavy shade.

Habitat White-winged Doves live in dense, thorny forests, streamside woodlands, deserts full of cactus and palo verde, and, more recently, urban and suburban areas of the southwestern U.S.

RANGE MAP

- Breeding
- Nonbreeding
- Nonbreeding (scarce)
- Year-round

KEYS TO IDENTIFICATION

MEASUREMENTS (Both sexes)

Length	Wingspan	Weight
19 in	11.5 in	4.4–6.6 oz
48 cm	29 cm	125–187 g

SIZE & SHAPE. White-winged Doves are plump, square-tailed doves with relatively long, thin bills and small heads.

COLOR PATTERN. White-winged Doves are brown overall, with a dark line on the cheek. A white stripe at the edge of the folded wing becomes, as the bird takes flight, a bright flash in the middle of a dark wing. The tail is tipped in white. Their faces are ornately marked with blue skin around the red eyes.

BEHAVIOR. Look for White-winged Doves in deserts of the Southwest and in cities and suburbs of Texas and the coastal Southeast. Individuals travel widely and irregularly across the continent after the breeding season ends.

Cool Facts

In the early 1980s, the singer Stevie Nicks introduced millions of Americans to the White-winged Dove with her song "Edge of Seventeen," which hit #11 on the Billboard charts.

Backyard Tips

White-winged Doves often eat at elevated bird feeders, taking sunflower, milo, corn, and safflower. They may also eat berries from shrubs.

MOURNING DOVE *(Zenaida macroura)*

These graceful, slender-tailed, small-headed doves are common across the continent. Mourning Doves perch on telephone wires and forage for seeds on the ground; their flight is fast and bullet straight. Their soft, drawn-out calls sound like laments. When taking off, their wings make a sharp whistling or whinnying sound. Mourning Doves are the most hunted species in North America, but their numbers remain strong throughout their range.

AT A GLANCE

Food
Seeds make up 99% of a Mourning Dove's diet, which includes cultivated grains and peanuts, wild grasses, weeds, herbs, and occasionally berries. Mourning Doves eat roughly 12% to 20% of their body weight per day, averaging about 71 calories.

Nesting
The nest is a flimsy, unlined assembly of pine needles, twigs, and grass stems. The male carries twigs to the female, passing them to her while standing on her back; the female weaves them into a nest 8 inches across. The nest is typically set amid dense foliage on the branch of an evergreen, orchard tree, mesquite, or cottonwood, or on the ground.

Habitat
Mourning Doves are primarily birds of open fields, areas with scattered trees, and woodland edges, but large numbers roost in woodlots during winter. They feed on the ground in grasslands, agricultural fields, backyards, and roadsides.

RANGE MAP

- Breeding
- Year-round
- Nonbreeding

KEYS TO IDENTIFICATION

MEASUREMENTS (Both sexes)

Length	Wingspan	Weight
9.1-13 in	17.7 in	3.0-6.0 oz
23-34 cm	45 cm	86-170 g

SIZE & SHAPE. Mourning Doves are plump-bodied and long-tailed, with short legs, a small bill, and a head that looks tiny in comparison to the body. The long, pointed tail is unique among North American doves.

COLOR PATTERN. Mourning Doves often match their open-country surroundings in color. They're delicate brown to buffy-tan overall, with black spots on the wings and black-bordered white tips to the tail feathers.

BEHAVIOR. Mourning Doves fly fast on powerful wingbeats, sometimes making sudden ascents, descents, and dodges, their pointed tails stretching behind them.

Cool Facts

In spring you might see three Mourning Doves flying in formation. It's a display: the first two are males in a chase. The third is a female paired with the first, and apparently just along for the ride.

Backyard Tips

Scatter seeds, particularly millet, on the ground or on platform feeders. Plant dense shrubs or evergreen trees in your yard to provide nesting sites.

EASTERN SCREECH-OWL *(Megascops asio)*

If you hear a mysterious trill in the night, the spooky sound may come from an owl no bigger than a pint glass. Common east of the Rockies in woods, suburbs, and parks, Eastern Screech-Owls are found wherever trees are, sometimes even nesting in backyard woodpecker holes or nest boxes. These supremely camouflaged birds hide out in nooks and tree crannies through the day, so your best chance of finding one is to listen at night.

AT A GLANCE

Food

Eastern Screech-Owls eat many small animals, including birds and mammals as well as invertebrates, including earthworms, insects, and crayfish. They are agile enough to occasionally prey on bats, and can rarely even be cannibalistic. When prey is plentiful, Eastern Screech-Owls cache extra food in tree holes for as long as 4 days.

Nesting

Eastern Screech-Owls nest in woodpecker holes and natural tree cavities, but never dig holes themselves. They depend on woodpeckers, fungus, rot, and squirrels to make them. Screech-owls also often use nest boxes. The female lays her eggs on whatever debris is on the bottom of the nest cavity.

Habitat

This owl is fairly common in most types of woods (evergreen and deciduous; urban and rural), especially near water. It shuns treeless expanses of mountains and plains.

RANGE MAP

Year-round

KEYS TO IDENTIFICATION

MEASUREMENTS (Both sexes)

Length	Wingspan	Weight
6.3–9.8 in	18.9–24 in	4.3–8.6 oz
16–25 cm	48–61 cm	121–244 g

SIZE & SHAPE. The Eastern Screech-Owl is a short, stocky bird with a large head and almost no neck. Its wings are rounded; its tail is short and square. Pointed ear tufts are often raised, lending its head a distinctive silhouette.

COLOR PATTERN. Eastern Screech-Owls can be either mostly gray or mostly reddish-brown (rufous). Whatever the overall color, they are patterned with complex bands and spots that give the bird excellent camouflage against tree bark. The catlike eyes are yellow.

BEHAVIOR. Eastern Screech-Owls are active at night and are far more often heard than seen—most bird watchers know this species only from its trilling or whinnying calls. However, this cavity-roosting owl can be attracted to nest boxes and may be spotted in daylight at the entrance to its box or tree cavity.

Cool Facts

Eastern Screech-Owls of the suburbs may fledge more young than their rural counterparts, probably because their predators are scarcer in the suburbs.

Backyard Tips

Eastern Screech-Owls readily use nest boxes, so consider putting one up to attract a breeding pair. Instructions and plans are available at *nestwatch. org/birdhouses*.

The Great Horned Owl is the quintessential owl of storybooks. This powerful predator can grab birds and mammals even larger than itself, but it also dines on daintier fare such as tiny scorpions, mice, and frogs. It's one of the most common owls in North America, equally at home in deserts, wetlands, forests, grasslands, backyards, cities, and almost any other semiopen habitat between the Arctic and the tropics.

AT A GLANCE

Food

Great Horned Owls have the most diverse diet of all North American raptors. Their prey range in size from rodents and scorpions to skunks, geese, and raptors. They eat mostly mammals and birds. Although they are usually nocturnal hunters, Great Horned Owls sometimes hunt in broad daylight.

Nesting

Great Horned Owls typically nest in trees such as cottonwood, juniper, beech, and pine. They usually use a nest built by another species, such as a Red-tailed Hawk, but also use tree cavities, deserted buildings, cliff ledges, and human-made platforms.

Habitat

Look for this widespread owl in young woods interspersed with fields or other open areas. The broad range of habitats they use includes deciduous and evergreen forests, swamps, desert, tundra edges, and tropical rainforest, as well as cities, orchards, suburbs, and parks.

RANGE MAP

- Year-round
- Year-round (scarce)

KEYS TO IDENTIFICATION

MEASUREMENTS (Both sexes)

Length	Wingspan	Weight
18.1–24.8 in	39.8–57.1 in	32.1–88.2 oz
46–63 cm	101–145 cm	910–2500 g

SIZE & SHAPE. These large, thick-bodied owls have a catlike silhouette thanks to two prominent feathered tufts on the head. The wings are broad and rounded. In flight, the rounded face and short bill combine to create a blunt-headed appearance.

COLOR PATTERN. Great Horned Owls are mottled gray-brown, with reddish-brown faces and a neat white patch on the throat. Their overall color tone varies regionally from sooty to pale.

BEHAVIOR. Great Horned Owls are usually nocturnal. You may see them at dusk sitting on fence posts or tree limbs at the edges of open areas, or flying across roads or fields with stiff, deep beats of their rounded wings. Their call is a deep, stuttering series of four or five mellow hoots.

Cool Facts

When clenched, a Great Horned Owl's strong talons require a force of 28 pounds to open. The owls use this deadly grip to sever the spine of large prey.

Find This Bird

It's a thrill to stay up late around wooded areas and listen for owls. The Great Horned is one of the most widespread: listen for its deep, four- or five-noted, stuttering series of hoots.

BARRED OWL *(Strix varia)*

The Barred Owl's strident *Who cooks for you? Who cooks for you-all?* is a classic sound of old forests and swamps. But this attractive owl, with soulful brown eyes and brown-and-white-striped plumage, can also pass completely unnoticed as it flies noiselessly through the dense canopy or roosts on a tree limb. Originally a bird of the East, during the twentieth century it spread through the Pacific Northwest and southward into California.

AT A GLANCE

Food Barred Owls eat many small animals, including mammals, birds (up to the size of grouse), amphibians, reptiles, and invertebrates. They hunt by sitting and waiting on an elevated perch, scanning for prey with their sharp eyes and ears. They do most of their hunting in the evening and night, but sometimes feed during the day.

Nesting Barred Owls usually nest in a natural cavity, 20–40 feet high in a large tree. They may also use stick nests built by other animals, or human-made nest boxes. Barred Owls do little or nothing to change an existing cavity or platform nest.

Habitat Barred Owls live in large, mature forests made up of both deciduous trees and evergreens, often near water.

RANGE MAP

■ Year-round

KEYS TO IDENTIFICATION

MEASUREMENTS (Both sexes)

Length	Wingspan	Weight
17–20 in	39–43 in	17–37 oz
43–50 cm	99–110 cm	470–1050 g

SIZE & SHAPE. Barred Owls are large, stocky owls with rounded heads, no ear tufts, and medium-length, rounded tails.

COLOR PATTERN. Barred Owls are mottled brown and white, with dark brown eyes. The underparts are marked with vertical brown bars on a white background; the upper breast is crossed with brown horizontal bars. The wings and tail are barred brown and white.

BEHAVIOR. Barred Owls roost quietly in trees during the day, though they occasionally call or hunt. By night they hunt small animals, including fish and frogs, and occasionally belt out their distinctive hoots and screeching calls.

Cool Facts

Young Barred Owls can climb trees by grasping the bark with their bill and talons, flapping their wings, and working their way up the trunk.

Backyard Tips

Barred Owls may nest in large nest boxes in mature forests. You can download plans for building the right-size box at nestwatch.org/birdhouses.

On warm summer evenings, Common Nighthawks roam the skies over treetops, grasslands, and cities. Their sharp, electric *peent* call is often the first clue they're overhead. In the dim half-light, these long-winged birds fly in graceful loops, flashing a white crescent patch just past the bend of each wing as they chase insects. These fairly common but declining birds build no nest.

AT A GLANCE

Food

Common Nighthawks eat flying insects almost exclusively. They hunt on the wing at dawn and dusk, opening their tiny beaks to reveal a cavernous mouth well suited for devouring flying insects. They often take advantage of clouds of insects attracted to streetlamps, stadium lights, and other bright lights.

Nesting

Common Nighthawks typically lay eggs right on the bare ground, usually on material such as gravel, sand, bare rock, wood chips, leaves, needles, tar paper (on flat roofs), cinders, or occasionally living vegetation.

Habitat

Common Nighthawks are most visible when they forage on the wing over cities and open areas near woods or wetlands. They migrate over fields, river valleys, marshes, woodlands, towns, and suburbs.

RANGE MAP

- Breeding
- Migration

KEYS TO IDENTIFICATION

MALE

MEASUREMENTS (Both sexes)

Length	Wingspan	Weight
8.7–9.4 in	20.9–22.4 in	2.3–3.5 oz
22–24 cm	53–57 cm	65–98 g

SIZE & SHAPE. Common Nighthawks are medium-sized, slender birds with very long, pointed wings and medium-long tails. The tiny bill, large eyes, and short neck give the bird a big-headed, somewhat owl-like appearance.

COLOR PATTERN. Common Nighthawks are well camouflaged in gray, white, buff, and black. The long, dark wings have a striking white blaze about two-thirds of the way out to the tip. In flight, the male's V-shaped white throat patch contrasts with the rest of his mottled plumage.

BEHAVIOR. Look for Common Nighthawks flying about in early morning and evening. During the day, they roost motionless on tree branches, fence posts, or the ground, and can be very difficult to see. When migrating or feeding over insect-rich areas such as lakes or well-lit billboards, nighthawks may gather in large flocks. Their buzzy, American Woodcock–like *peent* call is distinctive.

Cool Facts

The Common Nighthawk's impressive booming sounds during courtship dives, in combination with its erratic, batlike flight, have earned it the colloquial name "bullbat."

Find This Bird

Common Nighthawks are easiest to see in flight at dawn and dusk as they forage for aerial insects. In towns, look for nighthawks over brightly lit areas.

CHIMNEY SWIFT (Chaetura pelagica)

A bird best identified by silhouette, the cigar-shaped Chimney Swift nimbly maneuvers over rooftops, fields, and rivers to catch insects. Its tiny body, curved wings, and stiff, shallow wingbeats give it a flight style as distinctive as its fluid, chattering call. This enigmatic little bird spends almost its entire life airborne. Its tiny feet can't grasp normal perches—instead it clings to vertical walls inside chimneys, hollow trees, and caves.

AT A GLANCE

Food Chimney Swifts eat airborne insects, grabbing large ones with their bills; small ones go right down the throat. They feed over urban and residential neighborhoods, fields, grasslands, shrublands, orchards, forests, and marshes, often some distance away from nest sites.

Nesting Although they originally nested in natural sites such as caves and hollow trees of old-growth forests, Chimney Swifts now nest primarily in chimneys and other artificial sites with vertical surfaces. The nest is a half-saucer of loosely woven twigs, stuck together and cemented to the chimney wall with the bird's gluelike saliva.

Habitat Chimney Swifts forage widely, wherever flying insects are found. They gather to roost in chimneys and other dim, enclosed areas with a vertical surface on which to cling, such as air vents, wells, hollow trees, and caves.

RANGE MAP

■ Breeding
□ Migration

KEYS TO IDENTIFICATION

MEASUREMENTS (Both sexes)

Length	Wingspan	Weight
4.7–5.9 in	10.6–11.8 in	0.6–1.1 oz
12–15 cm	27–30 cm	17–30 g

SIZE & SHAPE. Chimney Swifts are small birds with slender bodies and long, narrow, curved wings. Their round head, thick but short neck, and short, tapered tail give them the appearance of a flying cigar. The tiny bill is hard to see.

COLOR PATTERN. Chimney Swifts are dark gray-brown all over, slightly paler on the throat. They can appear to be all black from a distance and when backlit against the sky.

BEHAVIOR. Chimney Swifts fly rapidly with nearly constant wingbeats, often twisting from side to side and banking erratically. Their wingbeats are stiff, with very little flex at the wrists. They often give a high, chattering call while they fly.

Cool Facts

Swifts are so aerial that they even bathe in flight: they glide down to the water, smack the surface with their bodies, and then bounce up and shake themselves dry as they fly away.

Backyard Tips

Chimney Swifts may take up residence in a brick chimney without a cap. To accommodate them, keep the damper closed during summer and schedule chimney cleanings before or after the breeding season.

This brilliant, tiny, precision-flying creature glitters like a jewel in full sun, then vanishes with a zip toward the next nectar source. Feeders and flower gardens are great ways to attract Ruby-throated Hummingbirds, and some gardeners turn their yards into buzzing clouds of hummers each summer. This is the only breeding hummingbird in the East outside of Texas. Enjoy them while they're around; by early fall, they're bound for Central America.

AT A GLANCE

Food Ruby-throated Hummingbirds feed on the nectar of red or orange tubular flowers such as trumpet creeper, cardinal flower, honeysuckle, jewelweed, bee-balm, red buckeye, and red morning glory, as well as sugar water at feeders and sap at Yellow-bellied Sapsucker drill holes. They also catch tiny insects in midair or pull them out of spiderwebs.

Nesting The female builds the nest on a slender, often descending branch. The nest, the size of a large thimble, is made of thistle or dandelion down and bits of lichen and moss, held together with strands of spider silk and sometimes pine resin.

Habitat Ruby-throated Hummingbirds live in open woodlands, forest edges, meadows, grasslands, parks, gardens, and backyards.

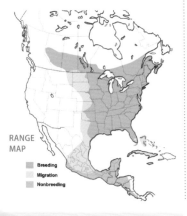

RANGE MAP

- Breeding
- Migration
- Nonbreeding

KEYS TO IDENTIFICATION

MALE

FEMALE

MEASUREMENTS (Both sexes)

Length	Wingspan	Weight
2.8–3.5 in	3.1–4.3 in	0.1–0.2 oz
7–9 cm	8–11 cm	2–6 g

SIZE & SHAPE. The Ruby-throated Hummingbird is a small hummingbird with a slender, slightly curved bill. The fairly short wings don't reach all the way to the tail when the bird is sitting.

COLOR PATTERN. Ruby-throated Hummingbirds are bright emerald or golden-green on the back and crown, with gray-white underparts. Males have a brilliant iridescent red throat that looks dark when it's not in good light.

BEHAVIOR. Ruby-throated Hummingbirds fly straight and fast but can stop instantly, hover, and adjust their position up, down, or backwards with exquisite control. They often visit hummingbird feeders and tube-shaped flowers and defend these food sources against others. You may also see them plucking tiny insects from the air or from spiderwebs.

Cool Facts

The extremely short legs of the Ruby-throated Hummingbird prevent it from walking or hopping. The best it can do with its tiny legs is to shuffle along a perch.

Backyard Tips

Plant tubular flowers or set up hummingbird feeders to attract these birds. Make sugar-water mixtures with about one-quarter cup of sugar per cup of water—there's no need to use food coloring.

BLACK-CHINNED HUMMINGBIRD (Archilochus alexandri)

Black-chinned Hummingbirds are small green-backed hummingbirds of the West, with no brilliant colors on their throat except a thin strip of iridescent purple bordering the black chin, visible when light hits it just right. Black-chinned Hummingbirds are exceptionally widespread, found from deserts to mountain forests. Many winter along the Gulf Coast. Their wings produce a low-pitched humming sound.

AT A GLANCE

Food

Black-chinned Hummingbirds feed on flower nectar, tiny insects, spiders, and sugar water at feeders.

Nesting

When newly built, the nest is a compact, deep cup constructed of soft plant matter, spider silk, and cocoon fibers. The female builds it on an exposed, horizontal dead branch well below the canopy. As the nestlings grow, the nest stretches into a wider, shallower cup. Nests in cool areas have thicker walls than nests in warmer areas.

Habitat

This bird is most often seen at feeders or perched on dead branches in tall trees. It may be found anywhere, from lowland deserts to mountainous forests, natural habitats to very urbanized areas. Its only requirements are a few tall trees, and shrubs and vines with nectar-bearing flowers.

RANGE MAP

- Breeding
- Migration
- Nonbreeding
- Year-round

KEYS TO IDENTIFICATION

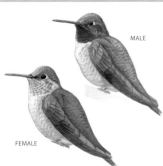

MALE

FEMALE

MEASUREMENTS (Both sexes)

Length	Wingspan	Weight
3.5 in	4.3 in	0.1–0.2 oz
9 cm	11 cm	2–5 g

SIZE & SHAPE. The Black-chinned Hummingbird is a dainty hummingbird with a fairly straight bill, quite similar in shape to a Ruby-throated Hummingbird.

COLOR PATTERN. The Black-chinned Hummingbird is dull metallic green above and dull grayish-white below. Males have a velvety black throat with a thin, iridescent purple base. Females have a pale throat. In both sexes, the flanks are glossed with dull metallic green. The female's three outer tail feathers on each side have broad white tips. The bill is black.

BEHAVIOR. Black-chinned Hummingbirds hover at flowers and feeders, dart erratically to take tiny swarming insects, and perch atop snags to survey their territory, watching for competitors to chase off and for flying insects to eat. During courtship and territorial defense, males do high-speed display dives from as high as 100 feet.

Cool Facts

A Black-chinned Hummingbird egg is about the size of a coffee bean. The nest, made of plant down and spider silk, expands as the babies grow.

Backyard Tips

It's fairly easy to attract hummingbirds to feeding stations. Mix about one-quarter cup of table sugar to one cup of water. Food coloring is unnecessary.

RUFOUS HUMMINGBIRD (Selasphorus rufus)

The brilliant orange Rufous Hummingbird is the feistiest hummingbird in North America. Relentless attackers at flowers and feeders, they chase (if not always defeat) even the large hummingbirds of the Southwest, which may be double their weight. Rufous Hummingbirds are wide ranging and breed farther north than any other hummingbird. Though they breed in the West, they frequently show up in the East in fall and winter.

AT A GLANCE

Food Rufous Hummingbirds feed primarily on nectar from colorful, tubular flowers including columbine, scarlet gilia, penstemon, Indian paintbrush, mints, lilies, fireweeds, larkspurs, currants, and heaths. They get protein and fat from eating insects, particularly gnats, midges, flies, and aphids.

Nesting The female builds the nest alone, using soft plant down held together with spiderweb. She builds it anywhere from eye level up to about 30 feet high in a tree. The finished nest is about 2 inches across on the outside.

Habitat Rufous Hummingbirds breed in open areas, yards, parks, and forests up to the treeline. On migration, they pass through mountain meadows as high as 12,600 feet where nectar-rich, tubular flowers bloom. Winter habitat in Mexico includes shrubby openings and oak-pine forests.

RANGE MAP

- Breeding
- Migration
- Nonbreeding

KEYS TO IDENTIFICATION

MALE

FEMALE

MEASUREMENTS (Both sexes)

Length	Wingspan	Weight
2.8–3.5 in	4.3 in	0.1–0.2 oz
7–9 cm	11 cm	2–5 g

SIZE & SHAPE. The Rufous Hummingbird is a fairly small hummingbird with a slender, nearly straight bill, a tail that tapers to a point when folded, and fairly short wings that don't reach the end of the tail when the bird is perched.

COLOR PATTERN. In good light, male Rufous Hummingbirds glow like coals: bright orange on the back and belly, with a vivid iridescent-red throat. Females are green above with rufous-washed flanks, rufous patches in the green tail, and often a spot of orange on the throat.

BEHAVIOR. Rufous Hummingbirds have the characteristic hummingbird flight: fast and darting with pinpoint maneuverability. They are pugnacious, tirelessly chasing away other hummingbirds, even in places they're only visiting on migration. Like other hummers, they eat insects as well as nectar, taking them from spiderwebs or catching them in midair.

Cool Facts

Rufous Hummingbirds, like most other hummingbirds, beat their wings extremely fast to hover in place. The wingbeat frequency has been recorded at 52–62 wingbeats per second.

Backyard Tips

Rufous hummers may claim your yard if you have hummingbird flowers or feeders. They'll probably try to chase off any other hummingbirds that visit.

BELTED KINGFISHER *(Megaceryle alcyon)*

With its top-heavy physique, energetic flight, and piercing rattle, the Belted Kingfisher seems to have an air of self-importance as it patrols up and down rivers and shorelines. It nests in burrows along earthen banks and feeds almost entirely on aquatic prey, diving to catch fish and crayfish with its heavy, straight bill. These ragged-crested birds are a powdery blue-gray. Males have one blue band across the white breast; females have a blue and a chestnut band.

AT A GLANCE

Food

Belted Kingfishers eat mostly fish, as well as crustaceans, mollusks, insects, amphibians, reptiles, young birds, small mammals, and berries. They watch for prey from a perch overhanging water, such as a bare branch, telephone wire, or pier piling, or while hovering.

Nesting

Belted Kingfishers excavate a nest burrow in an earthen bank, usually one without vegetation. They generally choose a bank near water, but may use a ditch, road cut, or gravel pit. The male and the female take turns digging the burrow 3–6 feet into the bank.

Habitat

Kingfishers live near streams, rivers, ponds, lakes, and estuaries. They spend winter in areas where the water doesn't freeze so that they have continual access to their aquatic foods.

RANGE MAP

■ Breeding
■ Nonbreeding
■ Year-round

KEYS TO IDENTIFICATION

FEMALE

MEASUREMENTS (Both sexes)

Length	Wingspan	Weight
11–13.8 in	18.9–22.8 in	4.9–6 oz
28–35 cm	48–58 cm	140–170 g

SIZE & SHAPE. Belted Kingfishers are stocky, large-headed birds with a shaggy crest on the top and back of the head and a straight, thick, pointed bill. Their legs and feet are surprisingly small, and their tails are medium length and square tipped.

COLOR PATTERN. Belted Kingfishers are steel blue above with fine white spotting on the wings and tail. The underparts are white with a broad blue breast band. Females also have a broad rusty band on their belly and sides. Juveniles show irregular rusty spotting in the breast band.

BEHAVIOR. Belted Kingfishers spend much of their time perched alone along the edges of streams, lakes, and estuaries, searching for small fish. They also fly quickly up and down rivers and shorelines giving loud rattling calls. They hunt either by plunging directly from a perch, or by hovering over the water, bill downward, before diving after a fish they've spotted.

Cool Facts

The Belted Kingfisher is one of comparatively few bird species in which the female is more brightly colored than the male.

Find This Bird

Listen for this bird's loud rattle, given on the wing. Look up and you may see this stocky bird flashing white in its wings as it flies along a stream.

The gorgeous Red-headed Woodpecker is so boldly patterned it's been called a "flying checkerboard," with an entirely crimson head, a snow-white body, and half-white, half-black wings. It doesn't act like most other woodpeckers: it's adept at catching insects in the air, and eats many acorns and beech nuts, often hiding away extra food in tree crevices for later.

AT A GLANCE

Food
Red-headed Woodpeckers eat insects, fruits, and seeds. They typically catch aerial insects by spotting them from a tree limb or fence post and then flying out to grab them. They sometimes raid bird nests to eat eggs and nestlings; they also eat mice and occasionally adult birds.

Nesting
Red-headed Woodpeckers nest in dead trees or dead parts of live trees. The male does most of the nest excavation but the female helps; they dig out a gourd-shaped cavity 3–6 inches across and 8–16 inches deep; the entrance hole is near the top.

Habitat
Red-headed Woodpeckers live in pine and oak savannas and other open forests with clear understories. Open pine plantations, tree rows in agricultural areas, and standing timber in beaver swamps and other wetlands all attract them.

RANGE MAP

- Breeding
- Nonbreeding
- Year-round

KEYS TO IDENTIFICATION

MALE

MEASUREMENTS (Both sexes)

Length	Wingspan	Weight
7.5–9.1 in	16.5 in	2–3.2 oz
19–23 cm	42 cm	56–91 g

SIZE & SHAPE. Red-headed Woodpeckers are medium-sized woodpeckers with fairly large, rounded heads, short, stiff tails, and powerful, straight bills.

COLOR PATTERN. Adults have bright-red heads, white underparts, and black backs with large white patches in the wings, making the lower back appear all white when perched. Immatures have gray-brown heads, and the white wing patches show rows of black spots near the trailing edge.

BEHAVIOR. In addition to catching insects by hammering into wood, Red-headed Woodpeckers also catch insects in flight and hunt for them on the ground. They also eat considerable amounts of fruit and seeds. Their raspy calls are shriller and scratchier than those of Red-bellied Woodpeckers.

Cool Facts

Red-headed Woodpeckers are fierce defenders of their territories. They may remove the eggs of other species from nests and nest boxes or destroy other birds' nests.

Backyard Tips

Red-headed Woodpeckers occasionally visit feeders in winter, especially for suet. They eat seeds, corn, acorns, pecans, and many kinds of fruits (including apples, cherries, strawberries, and grapes).

RED-BELLIED WOODPECKER *(Melanerpes carolinus)*

Red-bellied Woodpeckers are pale, medium-sized woodpeckers common in forests of the East. Their strikingly barred backs and gleaming red caps make them an unforgettable sight—just resist the temptation to call them Red-headed Woodpeckers, a rarer species that's mostly black on the back with big white wing patches. Learn the Red-bellied Woodpecker's rolling call and you'll notice these birds in many places.

AT A GLANCE

Food

Though this bird mainly eats insects, spiders, and other arthropods, it also eats acorns, nuts, and pine seeds, as well as some other seeds and a variety of fruit. It also occasionally grabs small lizards, nestling birds, and even minnows.

Nesting

The Red-bellied Woodpecker nests in dead trees (hardwoods or pines), dead limbs of live trees, and fence posts. The same pair may nest in the same tree year after year, but typically excavate a new cavity. They lay their eggs on the bed of wood chips left over after excavating the cavity.

Habitat

Red-bellied Woodpeckers are common in many Eastern woodlands and forests, from old stands of oak and hickory to young hardwoods and pines. They also often venture to backyard feeders, especially in neighborhoods with large shade trees.

RANGE MAP

■ Year-round

KEYS TO IDENTIFICATION

MALE

MEASUREMENTS (Both sexes)

Length	Wingspan	Weight
9.4 in	13–16.5 in	2–3.2 oz
24 cm	33–42 cm	56–91 g

SIZE & SHAPE. The Red-bellied Woodpecker is sleek and round-headed, about the same size as a Hairy Woodpecker but without the blocky outlines.

COLOR PATTERN. The Red-bellied Woodpecker often appears pale overall, even with the boldly black-and-white striped back. It has a flashy red cap and nape, fuller in the male than the female. Look for white patches near the wingtips as this bird flies. The red belly is subtle and hard to see.

BEHAVIOR. Look for Red-bellied Woodpeckers hitching along branches and trunks of medium to large trees, picking at the bark surface more often than drilling into it. Like most woodpeckers, they have a characteristic undulating flight pattern.

Cool Facts

You may sometimes see Red-bellied Woodpeckers wedge large nuts into bark crevices, then whack them into manageable pieces using their beaks.

Backyard Tips

If you live near any wooded patches, you may be able to attract these birds with suet (in winter), peanuts, peanut butter, and sunflower seeds.

On a walk through the forest, look for neat rows of tiny holes in tree bark. In the East, this is the work of the Yellow-bellied Sapsucker, an enterprising woodpecker that laps up the leaking sap and any trapped insects with its specialized, brush-tipped tongue. It sits still on a tree trunk for long intervals while feeding. Its loud mewing calls and stuttered drumming make it easy to detect, especially in spring.

AT A GLANCE

Food

As the name indicates, sapsuckers rely on sap as a main food source. They tend to choose sick or wounded trees for drilling their wells, and they choose tree species with high sugar concentrations in their sap. They drill wells throughout the year on both their breeding and wintering grounds. Yellow-bellied Sapsuckers also eat insects and spiders.

Nesting

Yellow-bellied Sapsuckers are cavity nesters. The eggs are laid on wood chips left over from the excavation. The entrance hole is small, only about 1.5 inches in diameter, but the cavity itself may be 10 inches deep.

Habitat

Yellow-bellied Sapsuckers live in both hardwood and conifer forests. They often nest in groves of small trees such as aspens, and spend winters in open woodlands.

RANGE MAP

Breeding
Migration
Nonbreeding

KEYS TO IDENTIFICATION

MALE

MEASUREMENTS (Both sexes)

Length	Wingspan	Weight
7.1–8.7 in	13.4–15.7 in	1.5–1.9 oz
18–22 cm	34–40 cm	43–55 g

SIZE & SHAPE. Yellow-bellied Sapsuckers are fairly small woodpeckers with stout, straight bills. The long wings extend about halfway to the tip of the stiff, pointed tail at rest. Often, sapsuckers hold their crown feathers up to form a peak at the back of the head.

COLOR PATTERN. Yellow-bellied Sapsuckers are mostly black and white with boldly patterned faces. Both sexes have red foreheads, and males have red throats. Look for a long white stripe along the folded wing. Bold black-and-white stripes curve from the face toward a black chest shield and white or yellowish underparts.

BEHAVIOR. Yellow-bellied Sapsuckers perch upright on trees, leaning on their tails like other woodpeckers. They feed at sap wells—neat rows of shallow holes they drill in tree bark. They drum on trees and metal objects in a distinctive stuttering pattern.

Cool Facts

Yellow-bellied Sapsuckers have been found drilling sap wells in more than 1,000 species of trees and woody plants, though they have a strong preference for birches and maples.

Backyard Tips

Yellow-bellied Sapsuckers occasionally eat at suet feeders, but more regularly appear in yards to feed in trees—especially apple, mountain ash, birch, and maple.

DOWNY WOODPECKER *(Picoides pubescens)*

The active little Downy Woodpecker is a familiar sight at backyard feeders and in parks and woodlots, where it joins flocks of chickadees and nuthatches. An often acrobatic forager, this woodpecker is at home on tiny branches or balancing on slender plant galls and suet feeders. The Downy and its larger lookalike, the Hairy Woodpecker, offer one of the first identification challenges that beginning bird watchers must master.

AT A GLANCE

Food Downy Woodpeckers eat insects such as ants, caterpillars, and beetle larvae living within wood and bark. About a quarter of their diet consists of plant material, especially berries, acorns, and grains. They are common at feeders, taking suet, sunflower seeds, and sometimes sugar water.

Nesting Downy Woodpeckers excavate cavities in dead trees or in dead parts of live trees. Entrance holes are round and 1–1.5 inches across. Cavities are 6–12 inches deep and widen toward the bottom. The cavity is lined only with wood chips.

Habitat You'll find Downy Woodpeckers in open woodlands, particularly among deciduous trees, and brushy or weedy edges. They're also at home in orchards, city parks, backyards and vacant lots.

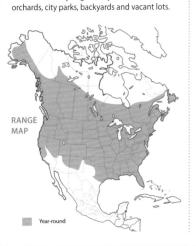

RANGE MAP

◼ Year-round

KEYS TO IDENTIFICATION

MALE

MEASUREMENTS (Both sexes)

Length	Wingspan	Weight
5.5–6.7 in	9.8–11.8 in	0.7–1 oz
14–17 cm	25–30 cm	21–28 g

SIZE & SHAPE. The Downy Woodpecker is a miniaturized version of the classic woodpecker body plan. It has a straight, chisel-like bill, blocky head, wide shoulders, and straight-backed posture as it leans away from tree limbs braced by its tail feathers. The bill seems short for a woodpecker.

COLOR PATTERN. The head is boldly striped black and white, and the gleaming white back stands out between folded black-and-white checkered wings. Males have a small red patch on the back of the head; male fledglings have a reddish crown. The outer tail feathers are white with a few black spots.

BEHAVIOR. Downy Woodpeckers hitch around tree limbs and trunks or drop into tall weeds to feed on galls, moving more acrobatically than larger woodpeckers. In spring and summer, Downy Woodpeckers are noisy, making shrill whinnying calls and drumming on trees.

Cool Facts

Downy Woodpeckers often feed on weed stalks, extracting insects larger woodpeckers can't get. They sometimes follow Pileated Woodpeckers to reach into their deep feeding holes.

Backyard Tips

Downy Woodpeckers are among the most frequent woodpeckers at bird feeders. They eat suet, black oil sunflower seeds, millet, and peanuts. They sometimes drink at hummingbird feeders.

HAIRY WOODPECKER *(Picoides villosus)*

The larger of two lookalikes, the Hairy Woodpecker is small but powerful, using its long, strong bill to forage along trunks and main branches of large trees. Hairy Woodpeckers have a somewhat soldierly bearing due to their erect, straight-backed posture on tree trunks and their neatly striped heads. Look for them at backyard suet or sunflower feeders, and listen for them calling in woodlots, parks, and forests.

AT A GLANCE

Food
More than 75% of the Hairy Woodpecker's diet is insects, particularly beetle larvae, ants, and moth pupae. They also eat bees, wasps, caterpillars, spiders, and millipedes. Hairy Woodpeckers are common visitors at feeders, taking suet and sunflower seeds.

Nesting
Hairy Woodpeckers typically excavate their nests in a dead stub of a living tree. The cavity is often in a branch or stub that isn't perfectly vertical, with the entrance hole on the underside. The entrance to the nest is about 1.5 inches wide, leading to a cavity 8–12 inches deep.

Habitat
Hairy Woodpeckers are birds of mature forests across the continent. They're also found in woodlots, suburbs, parks, and cemeteries, as well as forest edges, open woodlands of oak and pine, recently burned forests, and stands infested by bark beetles.

RANGE MAP

■ Year-round

KEYS TO IDENTIFICATION

MALE

MEASUREMENTS (Both sexes)

Length	Wingspan	Weight
7.1–10.2 in	13–16.1 in	1.4–3.4 oz
18–26 cm	33–41 cm	40–95 g

SIZE & SHAPE. The Hairy Woodpecker is a medium-sized woodpecker with a fairly square head, a long, straight, chisel-like bill, and stiff, long tail feathers it braces against tree trunks. The bill is nearly the same length as the head.

COLOR PATTERN. Hairy Woodpeckers are contrasting bold black and bright white. The black wings are checkered with white; the head has two white stripes and, in males, a bright-red spot above the nape. The back is gleaming white between folded black-and-white wings.

BEHAVIOR. Hairy Woodpeckers hitch up tree trunks and along main branches. They sometimes feed at the bases of trees, along fallen logs, and, rarely, on the ground. They have the slowly undulating flight pattern of most woodpeckers.

Cool Facts

Hairy Woodpeckers sometimes drink sap leaking from wells made by sapsuckers. They've also been seen pecking into sugar cane to drink the sugary juice.

Backyard Tips

To attract Hairy Woodpeckers, offer suet, peanuts, and black oil sunflower seeds from hanging feeders, especially in winter when natural food is scarce.

NORTHERN FLICKER *(Colaptes auratus)*

Northern Flickers are large, brown woodpeckers with a gentle expression and handsome black-scalloped plumage. On walks, don't be surprised if you scare one up from the ground. Flickers eat a great many ants and beetles, digging into the ground with their strong, slightly curved bills. When they fly they show a flash of color in the underwings and undertail—yellow in the East, red in the West—and a bright white rump.

AT A GLANCE

Food Northern Flickers eat mainly insects, especially ants and beetles that they take on the ground. They often hammer at the soil much as other woodpeckers drill into wood, to dig out ant larvae from underground. They also eat fruits and seeds, especially in winter.

Nesting Northern Flickers usually excavate nest holes in dead or diseased tree trunks or large branches. Nests are generally placed 6–15 feet off the ground, but on rare occasions can be over 100 feet high. The entrance hole is about 3 inches in diameter, and the cavity is 13–16 inches deep.

Habitat Look for Northern Flickers in woodlands, forest edges, and open fields with scattered trees, as well as city parks and suburbs. You can also find them in wet areas such as streamside woods, flooded swamps, and marsh edges.

RANGE MAP

- ▇ Breeding
- ▇ Nonbreeding
- ▇ Year-round

KEYS TO IDENTIFICATION

MALE
(YELLOW-SHAFTED FORM)

MEASUREMENTS (Both sexes)

Length	Wingspan	Weight
11–12.2 in	16.5–20.1 in	3.9–5.6 oz
28–31 cm	42–51 cm	110–160 g

SIZE & SHAPE. Flickers are fairly large woodpeckers with a slim, rounded head, long, slightly curved bill, and long, flared tail that tapers to a point.

COLOR PATTERN. Flickers appear brownish overall with a white rump patch that's conspicuous in flight and often visible when perched. The undersides of the wing and tail feathers are bright yellow in eastern birds, or red in western birds. With a closer look you'll see the brown plumage is richly patterned with black spots, bars, and crescents.

BEHAVIOR. Unlike most woodpeckers, Northern Flickers spend lots of time on the ground. When in trees they're often perched upright on horizontal branches instead of leaning against their tails on a trunk. They fly in an up-and-down path using heavy flaps interspersed with glides, like many woodpeckers.

Cool Facts

Woodpeckers drum on trees to seek mates, not to find food. They're interested in making the loudest possible noise, which is why you may see flickers drumming on metal objects such as lampposts.

Backyard Tips

Northern Flickers don't habitually visit bird feeders, but you can find them in your yard if you have a mixture of trees and open ground, especially if there is an anthill or two.

PILEATED WOODPECKER *(Dryocopus pileatus)*

The Pileated Woodpecker is one of the biggest, most striking forest birds on the continent—about the size of a crow. Look and listen for it whacking at dead trees and fallen logs in search of its main prey, carpenter ants and wood-boring beetles, leaving unique rectangular holes in the wood. Its nest and roost holes provide crucial shelter to other species, including swifts, owls, ducks, bats, flying squirrels, and pine martens.

AT A GLANCE

Food

The Pileated Woodpecker's primary food is carpenter ants, supplemented by other ants, beetle larvae, termites, and other insects. It also eats wild fruits and nuts. Occasionally, a Pileated Woodpecker visits backyard bird feeders for seeds, suet, or peanut butter.

Nesting

The male Pileated Woodpecker begins excavating the nest cavity, but the female also contributes. They don't line the nest with anything except fallen wood chips. Cavity depth can range from 10–24 inches. They nest in dead trees within a mature or old stand of coniferous or deciduous trees.

Habitat

Pileated Woodpeckers are forest birds that require large, standing dead trees and downed wood. In the East, they live in young forests as well, and are sometimes seen in partially wooded suburbs and backyards.

RANGE MAP

Year-round

KEYS TO IDENTIFICATION

MALE

MEASUREMENTS (Both sexes)

Length	Wingspan	Weight
15.7–19.3 in	26–29.5 in	8.8–12.3 oz
40–49 cm	66–75 cm	250–350 g

SIZE & SHAPE. The Pileated Woodpecker is a very large woodpecker with a long neck and a triangular crest that sweeps off the back of the head. The bill is long and chisel-like, about the length of the head. In flight, the wings are broad and the bird can seem crowlike.

COLOR PATTERN. Pileated Woodpeckers are mostly black, with white stripes on the face and neck and a flaming-red crest. Males have a red stripe on the cheek; this is black on females. Mostly white underwings and small white crescents on the upper wing at the bases of flight feathers can be seen when they fly.

BEHAVIOR. Pileated Woodpeckers drill distinctive rectangular holes in rotten wood to get at carpenter ants and other insects. They are loud birds with whinnying and yelling calls. They also drum on dead trees in a deep, slow, rolling pattern.

Cool Facts

Pileated Woodpeckers can drill holes so deep and remove so much wood from a tree that they sometimes cause it to break in half.

Backyard Tips

Pileated Woodpeckers sometimes visit backyard bird feeders, especially for suet. If you have dead or dying trees on your property, consider leaving them to attract this species to forage, roost, or even nest.

All About Backyard Birds 113

AMERICAN KESTREL *(Falco sparverius)*

The American Kestrel, North America's smallest falcon, packs a predator's fierce intensity into its tiny body. It's one of the most colorful of all raptors, too: the male has slate-blue wings and a reddish back; the female is warm reddish-brown. Hunting for insects and other small prey in open territory, kestrels perch on wires or poles, or hover facing into the wind, flapping and adjusting their long tails to stay in place.

AT A GLANCE

Food American Kestrels eat mostly insects and other invertebrates, as well as small rodents and birds. Common foods include grasshoppers, dragonflies, spiders, butterflies, mice, bats, and small songbirds. They also sometimes eat small snakes, lizards, and frogs.

Nesting American Kestrels nest in cavities. They cannot excavate their own, so they use old woodpecker holes, natural tree hollows, rock crevices, and nooks in buildings and other structures. Once they've found a suitable hole, American Kestrels do not add any additional nesting materials.

Habitat American Kestrels occupy open habitats ranging from deserts and grasslands to alpine meadows and agricultural fields. They're most often seen perching on telephone wires along roadsides, in open country with short vegetation and few trees.

RANGE MAP

■ Breeding
■ Nonbreeding
■ Year-round

KEYS TO IDENTIFICATION

MALE

MEASUREMENTS (Both sexes)

Length	Wingspan	Weight
8.7–12.2 in	20.1–24 in	2.8–5.8 oz
22–31 cm	51–61 cm	80–165 g

SIZE & SHAPE. The slender American Kestrel is roughly the size and shape of a Mourning Dove, although it has a larger head; longer, narrower wings; and a long, square-tipped tail. In flight, the wings are often bent, the wingtips swept back.

COLOR PATTERN. American Kestrels are pale when seen from below and warm, rusty brown spotted with black above. Males have slate-blue wings; females' wings are reddish brown. Both sexes have two black vertical marks on each side of their pale face, the front one nicknamed a "mustache," the rear one a "sideburn." The tail has a black band near the tip.

BEHAVIOR. American Kestrels usually snatch their prey from the ground, though some catch quarry on the wing. They are gracefully buoyant in flight, and are small enough to get tossed around in the wind. When perched, kestrels often pump their tails as if they are trying to balance.

Cool Facts

Birds can see ultraviolet light. This ability enables kestrels to track their vole prey by following the trails of urine that the mammals leave as they run along the ground.

Backyard Tips

American Kestrels are declining in many parts of their range. One problem is availability of nest sites. You can help by putting up a nest box—find plans and instructions at *nestwatch.org/birdhouses.*

Powerful and fast-flying, the Peregrine Falcon hunts medium-sized birds, dropping down on them from high above in a spectacular stoop. They were virtually eradicated from eastern North America by pesticide poisoning in the middle 20th century. After significant recovery efforts thanks to the Endangered Species Act, Peregrine Falcons have made an incredible comeback and are now regularly seen in many large cities and coastal areas.

AT A GLANCE

Food

Peregrine Falcons eat a wide variety of birds, from species as large as Sandhill Cranes down to hummingbirds, and also take large numbers of bats. They often specialize on ducks and shorebirds, especially during migration. They occasionally pirate prey, including fish and rodents, from other raptors.

Nesting

Peregrine Falcons nest on cliffs, electrical transmission towers, quarries, silos, buildings, bridges, and specially constructed nest boxes. The birds do no nest building beyond a ritualized scraping of the nest ledge to create a depression in the sand or gravel substrate.

Habitat

Historically, Peregrine Falcons were most common during the breeding season along coastlines, where cliffs overlooked rivers and lakes, and in mountainous regions. Reintroduction programs have brought them to cities.

RANGE MAP

■ Breeding
■ Migration
■ Nonbreeding
■ Year-round

KEYS TO IDENTIFICATION

MEASUREMENTS (Both sexes)

Length	Wingspan	Weight
14.2–19.3 in	39.4–43.3 in	18.7–56.4 oz
36–49 cm	100–110 cm	530–1600 g

SIZE & SHAPE. Peregrine Falcons are the largest falcons over most of the continent. They look muscular and robust, with long, pointed wings and a long, tapered tail.

COLOR PATTERN. Although they vary geographically, adults are overall blue-gray above with barred underparts and a dark head with thick sideburns. Juveniles are usually heavily marked, with vertical streaks instead of horizontal bars on the breast.

BEHAVIOR. Peregrine Falcons catch medium-sized birds in the air with high-speed dives called stoops. They often fly high in the sky with powerful but shallow, almost leisurely wingbeats. They occasionally soar on thermals with wings spread. They also sit on high perches such as transmission towers and antennas with a view over open country.

Cool Facts

The Peregrine Falcon averages 25–34 mph in traveling flight, reaching speeds up to 69 mph in direct pursuit of prey, and can reach speeds of 200 mph during dives.

Find This Bird

Watch the skies for a large falcon with strong but shallow wingbeats. If a flock of shorebirds suddenly takes flight, look up—chances are a falcon has spooked them.

EASTERN WOOD-PEWEE *(Contopus virens)*

The olive-brown Eastern Wood-Pewee is inconspicuous until it opens its bill and gives its unmistakable slurred, piercing *pee-a-wee*—a characteristic sound of Eastern summers. This small flycatcher perches on dead branches in the mid-canopy and sallies out after flying insects. Though identifying flycatchers can be confusing, the Eastern Wood-Pewee is overall grayer, with longer wings, than other flycatchers.

AT A GLANCE

Food

The Eastern Wood-Pewee captures small flying insects by sallying out from an exposed branch, often returning to the same branch. The pewee also eats small amounts of plant matter, including dogwood and poison ivy berries.

Nesting

Eastern Wood-Pewees nest in trees down to sapling size, usually 15–70 feet off the ground. The nest is a small cup made of woven grass and other plant materials and camouflaged with lichens. It measures 3 inches across and 1–2 inches deep.

Habitat

Eastern Wood-Pewees are most common in deciduous forest and woodland, but they breed in nearly any forested habitat, even smaller woodlots, as long as it is fairly open. On migration they can occur in nearly any spot with trees.

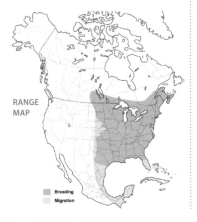

RANGE MAP

Breeding
Migration

KEYS TO IDENTIFICATION

MEASUREMENTS (Both sexes)

Length	Wingspan	Weight
5.9 in	9.1–10.2 in	0.4–0.7 oz
15 cm	23–26 cm	10–19 g

SIZE & SHAPE. Eastern Wood-Pewees are medium-sized flycatchers with long wings and tails. Like other pewees, they have short legs, upright posture, and a peaked crown. Their long wings are an important clue to separate them from *Empidonax* flycatcher species.

COLOR PATTERN. Eastern Wood-Pewees are olive-gray with dark wings and little or no yellow on the underparts. The sides of the breast are dark with an off-white throat and belly, making them appear to wear a vest. They have little or no eyering. The underside of the bill is mostly yellow-orange.

BEHAVIOR. Eastern Wood-Pewees are sit-and-wait predators that sally out from arboreal perches after insects and return to the same or a nearby perch. They often perch high in trees, generally in fairly exposed places providing good viewpoints.

Cool Facts

The Eastern Wood-Pewee's lichen-covered nest is so inconspicuous that it often looks like a knot on a branch.

Backyard Tips

Pewees don't visit feeders but they can be common in woodlots and parks. Listen for their long, lazy *pee-a-wee* call to help track down these nondescript birds.

One of our most familiar eastern flycatchers, the Eastern Phoebe's raspy *fee-bee* call is often heard around yards and farms in spring and summer. This brown-and-white perching bird sits upright and wags its tail from prominent, low perches. It typically constructs its nest in a protected nook on a bridge, barn, or house, which makes it a familiar species for many people.

AT A GLANCE

Food

Flying insects make up the majority of the Eastern Phoebe's diet. Common prey include wasps, beetles, dragonflies, butterflies, moths, flies, midges, and cicadas. Eastern Phoebes also eat spiders, ticks, and millipedes, as well as occasional small fruits or seeds.

Nesting

Eastern Phoebes build nests in sheltered spots where the young can be protected from the elements and be fairly safe from predators. Females construct nests of mud and leaves mixed with grasses and animal hair; an abundance of mosses make them a lovely soft green. The nests are 2.5 inches across and 2 inches deep.

Habitat

These birds favor open woods such as yards, parks, woodlands, and woodland edges. Phoebes usually breed around buildings or bridges, constructing their nests under the protection of an eave or ledge.

RANGE MAP

■ Breeding
■ Migration
■ Nonbreeding
■ Year-round

KEYS TO IDENTIFICATION

MEASUREMENTS (Both sexes)

Length	Wingspan	Weight
5.5–6.7 in	10.2–11 in	0.6–0.7 oz
14–17 cm	26–28 cm	16–21 g

SIZE & SHAPE. The Eastern Phoebe is a plump flycatcher with a medium-length tail. It appears large-headed for its size. The head often appears flat on top, but phoebes sometimes raise the feathers into a peak. Like most small flycatchers, they have short, wide bills useful for snatching insects on the wing.

COLOR PATTERN. The Eastern Phoebe is brownish-gray above and off-white below, with a dusky wash to the sides of the breast. The head is typically the darkest part of the upperparts. Birds in fresh fall plumage show faint yellow on the belly and whitish edging on the folded wing feathers.

BEHAVIOR. Eastern Phoebes generally perch low in trees or on fence lines. They are very active, making short flights to capture insects and often returning to the same perch. They make sharp peeps in addition to their familiar *fee-bee* call. When perched, they wag their tail down and up frequently.

Cool Facts

In 1804, the Eastern Phoebe became the first banded bird in North America. John James Audubon attached silvered thread to an Eastern Phoebe's leg to track its return in successive years.

Backyard Tips

Consider putting up a nest platform under an eave on your house or garage to attract a nesting pair. Make sure you put it up well before they return in spring.

GREAT CRESTED FLYCATCHER *(Myiarchus crinitus)*

The Great Crested Flycatcher is common in Eastern woodlands. Its habit of hunting high in the canopy means it's not particularly conspicuous until you learn its distinctive call, an emphatic rising whistle. It swoops after flying insects and may crash into foliage in pursuit of leaf-crawling prey. This is the only Eastern flycatcher that nests in cavities, and sometimes uses nest boxes or even rural mailboxes. It thrives on the edges of forests.

AT A GLANCE

Food Great Crested Flycatchers eat insects and other invertebrates such as butterflies, moths, beetles, grasshoppers, bees, wasps, flies, and spiders, which they capture on the wing or glean from leaves and crevices. They also take berries and small fruits.

Nesting The female builds the nest. She backfills deep cavities with debris first, then builds the cup, about 3–3.5 inches across and 1.5–2 inches deep, using varied items such as leaves, twigs, hair, snail shells, feathers, bark, cellophane, eggshells, and snakeskin.

Habitat Great Crested Flycatchers nest in open deciduous or mixed woodlands and edges of clearings with dead and dying trees. They tolerate human presence, sometimes choosing cavities in old orchards and woody urban areas such as parks, cemeteries, and golf courses.

RANGE MAP

- Breeding
- Migration
- Nonbreeding
- Year-round

KEYS TO IDENTIFICATION

MEASUREMENTS (Both sexes)

Length	Wingspan	Weight
6.7–8.3 in	13.4 in	1–1.4 oz
17–21 cm	34 cm	27–40 g

SIZE & SHAPE. Great Crested Flycatchers have a powerful build with a large head, broad shoulders, and a fairly long tail. The shaggy crest is not especially prominent. The bill is fairly wide at the base and straight.

COLOR PATTERN. Great Crested Flycatchers are reddish-brown above with a brownish-gray head, gray throat and breast, and bright lemon-yellow belly. The brown upperparts are highlighted by rufous-orange flashes in the primaries and in the tail feathers. The mostly black bill can be pale at the base.

BEHAVIOR. Great Crested Flycatchers are sit-and-wait predators, sallying from high perches (usually near the tops of trees) after large insects, returning to the same or a nearby perch. Their clear, rising *reep!* calls are a very common sound in summer.

Cool Facts

The Great Crested Flycatcher makes the same *reep!* calls on the wintering grounds that it makes in summer.

Backyard Tips

Great Crested Flycatchers need holes or cavities for nesting. To help them, consider putting up a hanging nest box 12–20 feet above the ground. Find details at nestwatch.org/birdhouses.

EASTERN KINGBIRD *(Tyrannus tyrannus)*

With dark gray upperparts and a neat white tip to the tail, the Eastern Kingbird looks like it's wearing a business suit. This big-headed, broad-shouldered bird really means business, harassing other birds that pass over its territory and living up to its scientific name, *Tyrannus tyrannus* (tyrant of all tyrants). Eastern Kingbirds often perch on wires in open areas, sallying out for flying insects and fluttering slowly over the tops of grasses.

AT A GLANCE

Food Eastern Kingbirds eat insects, especially large ones, during spring migration and on the breeding range. During fall migration they consume increasing amounts of fruit, and this becomes their primary diet on their wintering grounds in South America.

Nesting The female builds the sturdy, often exposed nest as the male guards her. The nest is up to 7 inches across and 6 inches deep, made of twigs, roots, bark, and bits of trash. The inside cup, only 2–3 inches across and an inch or two deep, is lined with softer, finer materials.

Habitat The Eastern Kingbird breeds in habitat with tall trees and scattered open spaces, often near water. During migration it stops in more varied habitats. During winter in South America, it forages in flocks in the forest canopy at the edges of rivers and lakes.

RANGE MAP

- ■ Breeding
- ■ Migration

KEYS TO IDENTIFICATION

MEASUREMENTS (Both sexes)

Length	Wingspan	Weight
7.5–9.1 in	13–15 in	1.2–1.9 oz
19–23 cm	33–38 cm	33–55 g

SIZE & SHAPE. The Eastern Kingbird is a sturdy, medium-sized flycatcher with a large head, upright posture, square-tipped tail, and a relatively short, wide, straight bill.

COLOR PATTERN. Eastern Kingbirds are blackish above and white below. The head is a darker black than the wings and back, and the black tail has a conspicuous white tip. If you're lucky, you may see a line of bright-red feathers on the crown of an agitated male, though he usually keeps these hidden.

BEHAVIOR. Eastern Kingbirds often perch in the open atop trees or along utility lines or fences. They fly with very shallow wingbeats and a raised head, making their distinctive metallic, sputtering calls. They are visual hunters, sallying out from perches to snatch flying insects.

Cool Facts

Eastern Kingbirds feed their young for about 7 weeks. Because of this relatively long period of dependence, a pair generally raises only one brood of young per nesting season.

Find This Bird

Look for Eastern Kingbirds on fence lines and in trees bordering wide, grassy expanses. Also watch the sky for kingbirds attacking larger birds such as crows, herons, and hawks that fly through their territory.

RED-EYED VIREO *(Vireo olivaceus)*

A tireless songster, the Red-eyed Vireo is one of the most common summer residents of Eastern forests. It sings its short, robinlike tune almost incessantly throughout the day. When any threat appears on the scene, it makes a distinctive cranky *mew*. In late summer it spends a lot of time in berry-producing shrubs, fattening up before heading for winter digs in the rainforest of the Amazon basin.

AT A GLANCE

Food Red-eyed Vireos eat mostly insects in spring and summer (caterpillars may account for 50% of their summer diet), with increasing amounts of small wild fruits as fall migration approaches. They eat fruit almost exclusively during winter in South America.

Nesting The female constructs the nest, a cup suspended from forked branches, using bark strips and other fibers glued with spider silk and sticky plant fibers. The cup is about 2 inches across and 1.5 inches deep. It rests inside a structure with half-inch walls and an inch-thick floor.

Habitat Red-eyed Vireos breed in deciduous and mixed forests with shrubby understories. They are also found in neighborhoods with large trees. During migration, look for them in more varied habitats.

RANGE MAP

- Breeding
- Breeding (scarce)
- Migration

KEYS TO IDENTIFICATION

MEASUREMENTS (Both sexes)

Length	Wingspan	Weight
4.7–5.1 in	9.1–9.8 in	0.4–0.9 oz
12–13 cm	23–25 cm	12–26 g

SIZE & SHAPE. Red-eyed Vireos are chunky songbirds, a bit bigger than most warblers, with a long, angular head, thick neck, and a strong, long bill with a small but noticeable hook at the tip. The body is stocky and the tail fairly short.

COLOR PATTERN. Red-eyed Vireos are olive-green above and clean white below with a gray crown and white eyebrow stripe bordered above and below by blackish lines. The flanks and under the tail have a green-yellow wash. Adults have red eyes that appear dark from a distance. Immatures have dark eyes.

BEHAVIOR. These vireos forage in deciduous canopies, moving slowly and methodically, carefully scanning leaves above and below for caterpillars and other prey. Their incessant singing in summer, even in the heat of midafternoon, helps draw attention to them.

Cool Facts

When we say "tireless songster," we mean it. One naturalist counted a Red-eyed Vireo singing more than 22,000 times during a single summer day.

Find This Bird

Red-eyed Vireos are very common in summer but hard to see in the leafy treetops. They sing late into the day, so listen for their rising-and-falling song to discover how abundant these birds really are.

This common, large songbird is familiar to many people, with its perky crest; blue, white, and black plumage; and noisy calls. Blue Jays are known for their intelligence and complex social systems with tight family bonds. Their fondness for acorns is credited with helping spread oak trees after the last glacial period. Mark Twain wrote one of his funniest short stories, "Baker's Blue Jay Yarn," about one.

AT A GLANCE

Food Blue Jays eat insects, nuts, and seeds from trees, shrubs, and on the ground. They also eat dead and injured small vertebrates, and sometimes raid nests for eggs and nestlings. Stomach contents over the year reveal that the diet is almost 80% acorns and other plant matter.

Nesting Blue Jays build their open cup nests of twigs, grass, and mud, lined with rootlets, in the crotch or thick outer branches of a tree 10–25 feet above the ground. They fly long distances to obtain rootlets from recently dug ditches, overturned earth, and newly fallen trees.

Habitat Blue Jays are found in all kinds of forests but especially near oak trees; they're more abundant near forest edges than in deep forest. They're common in urban and suburban areas, especially where oaks or bird feeders are found.

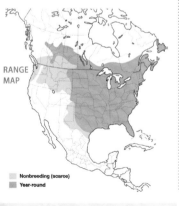

RANGE MAP

■ Nonbreeding (scarce)
■ Year-round

KEYS TO IDENTIFICATION

MEASUREMENTS (Both sexes)

Length	Wingspan	Weight
9.8–11.8 in	13.4–16.9 in	2.5–3.5 oz
25–30 cm	34–43 cm	70–100 g

SIZE & SHAPE. This large songbird has a broad, rounded tail and a crest that it holds up to a sharp peak while calling, but lowers when it's quietly feeding or interacting with family. They are smaller than crows but larger than robins.

COLOR PATTERN. Blue Jays are mostly blue and black above with white or light-gray underparts.

BEHAVIOR. Blue Jays make loud calls including a throaty screech, a squeaky sound like an old pump handle, and imitations of hawk calls. They usually fly across open areas silently. In late summer and fall, flocks of young Blue Jays gather to explore the woods, making a noisy commotion. In autumn they stuff food items such as acorns into a pouch in the throat and carry them away to store for later.

Cool Facts

A Blue Jay can carry five acorns at once: three in a pouch in its throat, one in the mouth, and one grasped in its bill. In this manner they can carry away up to 5,000 acorns to store for winter.

Backyard Tips

Blue Jays prefer tray or hopper feeders rather than hanging feeders. They eat peanuts, sunflower seeds, and suet. Oak trees provide their most important food, acorns. They often drink from birdbaths.

AMERICAN CROW (Corvus brachyrhynchos)

American Crows, familiar over much of the continent, are large, intelligent, all-black birds with hoarse, cawing voices. Common in habitats ranging from open woods and empty beaches to town centers, they usually feed on the ground and eat a huge variety of foods, especially earthworms, insects, small animals, eggs and chicks taken from other birds' nests, seeds, and fruit. They scavenge on garbage and carrion.

AT A GLANCE

Food American Crows are omnivores, taking a vast array of plant and animal foods, including crop pests and aquatic animals such as fish, crayfish, and clams. A frequent nest predator on eggs and nestlings of many species, it also eats carrion and garbage.

Nesting Both members of a breeding pair help build the nest. Young birds from the previous year sometimes help as well. The nest is made largely of medium-sized twigs with an inner cup lined with pine needles, weeds, soft bark, or animal hair. Nest size is quite variable, typically 6–19 inches across, with an inner cup about 6–14 inches across and 4–15 inches deep.

Habitat Highly adaptable, crows live in open areas, from big cities to wilderness. They're common on farms, pastures, landfills, feedlots, and towns. They avoid deserts and unbroken forest, but show up on campgrounds and venture into forests along roads and rivers.

RANGE MAP

■ Breeding
■ Nonbreeding
■ Year-round

KEYS TO IDENTIFICATION

MEASUREMENTS (Both sexes)

Length	Wingspan	Weight
15.7–20.9 in	33.5–39.4 in	11.1–21.9 oz
40–53 cm	85–100 cm	316–620 g

SIZE & SHAPE. The American Crow is a long-legged, thick-necked, oversized songbird with a heavy, straight bill. In flight, the wings are fairly broad and rounded with the wingtip feathers spread like fingers. The short tail is rounded or squared off at the end.

COLOR PATTERN. American Crows are all black, including the legs and bill. As crows molt, the old feathers can appear brownish or scaly compared to the glossy new ones.

BEHAVIOR. American Crows are very social, usually seen hanging out with family members or large flocks. Inquisitive and sometimes mischievous, they often raid garbage cans and pick over discarded food containers. They often chase away larger birds including hawks, eagles, owls, and herons.

Cool Facts

American Crows don't breed until they are 2 years old and most wait until they are 4 or more. The offspring often help their parents raise young for a few years before setting out on their own.

Backyard Tips

Crows don't regularly visit feeders, but they may steal garbage or pet food if it's not well contained. Peanuts left in an open place are a good attractant if you want crows in your yard.

Not everyone realizes it, but there are two kinds of crows across much of the eastern United States. Fish Crows are almost identical to the ubiquitous American Crow, making them tough to identify until you learn their nasal calls. They're found mostly around bodies of water, usually in flocks, sometimes with American Crows. Fish Crows have expanded their range inland and northward along major river systems in recent decades.

AT A GLANCE

Food Fish Crows eat carrion, trash, berries, fruit, grain, and anything they can take from other birds. They eat a lot of crabs, marine invertebrates, and turtle eggs. They also prey on eggs and nestlings of other birds; some specialize on raiding the nests of colonial waterbirds.

Nesting The female gathers nest materials and builds the nest herself; her mate does not help. The bulky nest, about 19 inches across with a cup about 5 inches across, is made of sticks. The inner cup is lined with soil, bark, Spanish moss, palm fibers, hair, and pine needles.

Habitat Fish Crows live along beaches, marshes, estuaries, lakes, and rivers. In addition to waterfront habitats, look for them around agricultural fields, cities, towns, and golf courses. In winter, they gather near landfills, feedlots, estuaries, and other sources of food.

RANGE MAP

■ Year-round

KEYS TO IDENTIFICATION

MEASUREMENTS (Both sexes)

Length	Wingspan	Weight
14.2–15.7 in	33.1 in	6.9–11.6 oz
36–40 cm	84 cm	195–330 g

SIZE & SHAPE. Fish Crows fit the standard crow shape: hefty, well-proportioned, oversized songbirds with heavy bills, sturdy legs, and broad wings. At rest, Fish Crows' wings fall short of their medium-length, square tails.

COLOR PATTERN. Fish Crows are all black, virtually identical to American Crows. Immatures are less glossy and become more brownish as their feathers fade in their first year.

BEHAVIOR. Fish Crows are sociable, seen in pairs in the breeding season and in much larger groups during migration and winter. They often mix with American Crows. When giving their distinctive nasal calls, they puff out their neck and body feathers, making their throat appear ragged.

Cool Facts

When Fish Crows find a good source of food, they may stash the surplus for later. These hiding places (called caches) can be in grass, in clumps of Spanish moss, or in crevices in tree bark.

Backyard Tips

Fish Crows may visit backyards for peanuts and corn in areas where they associate with American Crows and can pick up the habit from them.

COMMON RAVEN *(Corvus corax)*

The Common Raven has accompanied people around the Northern Hemisphere for centuries, following their wagons, sleighs, and hunting parties in hopes of a quick meal. Ravens are among the smartest of all birds, solving complicated problems invented by scientists. These big, sooty birds thrive among humans, stretching across the sky on easy, flowing wingbeats and filling empty spaces with their resounding croaks.

AT A GLANCE

Food Common Ravens are omnivores. They prey on animals ranging from mice and baby tortoises up to pigeons and nestling herons. They also eat eggs, insects, fish, dung, carrion, and garbage.

Nesting The female builds the 5-foot-wide nest platform from large sticks she and her mate take from live trees and old nests. She weaves more sticks, bones, wire, etc. into a basket. The inner cup, 9–12 inches across and 5–6 inches deep, is lined with softer materials.

Habitat Common Ravens occur over most of the Northern Hemisphere, in nearly every wild habitat except the open Great Plains. Once driven from eastern forests, they've been reappearing in recent years. They gravitate to landfills and have adapted to city life in some places.

RANGE MAP

■ Year-round

KEYS TO IDENTIFICATION

MEASUREMENTS (Both sexes)

Length	Wingspan	Weight
22–27.2 in	45.7–46.5 in	24.3–57.3 oz
56–69 cm	116–118 cm	689–1625 g

SIZE & SHAPE. Significantly more massive than a crow, the Common Raven has a thick neck, shaggy throat feathers, and a Bowie knife of a beak. In flight, it has a long, wedge-shaped tail. Its wings are longer and more slender than a crow's, with longer, thinner "fingers" at the wingtips.

COLOR PATTERN. Common Ravens are entirely black, including the legs, eyes, and beak. Adult plumage can be beautifully glossy, especially in good light.

BEHAVIOR. Common Ravens are less sociable than crows, spending most days alone or in pairs except at food sources such as landfills. On the ground, they strut or occasionally bound forward with light, two-footed hops. In flight they are buoyant and graceful, interspersing soaring, gliding, and slow flaps.

Cool Facts

Common Ravens can mimic the calls of other bird species. When raised in captivity, they can even imitate human words; one Common Raven raised from birth was taught to say the word "nevermore."

Backyard Tips

Ravens can cause problems in yards where garbage or pet food is left out. Keeping these attractants under wraps is typically a good idea.

Look through any bare, brown field, especially in winter, and you may notice little brownish birds milling about. These Horned Larks are widespread songbirds of fields, deserts, and tundra, where they forage for seeds and insects, often in mixed flocks with pipits, longspurs, and Snow Buntings. They sing a high, tinkling song on the ground, from a perch, or in flight. Though still common, they have undergone a sharp decline in the last half-century.

AT A GLANCE

Food Adult Horned Larks eat seeds taken from the ground or pulled from seedheads. They also eat sprouted seedlings and insects such as grasshoppers, beetles, and caterpillars. They feed their young mostly insects and such invertebrates as sowbugs and earthworms.

Nesting The Horned Lark's nest, set in a 3–4-inch-wide depression on bare ground, is a basket woven of fine grasses, shredded corn stalks, and other plant material, lined with down, fur, fine rootlets, and other fine fibers. The inner cup is about 2.5 inches wide and 1.5 inches deep.

Habitat Horned Larks favor deserts, tundra, beaches, dunes, heavily grazed pastures, plowed fields, mowed expanses around airstrips, roadsides, and feedlots. They are drawn to fields spread with waste grain and manure. In winter, they mostly feed in areas free of snow.

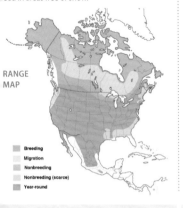

RANGE MAP

- ▉ Breeding
- ▉ Migration
- ▉ Nonbreeding
- ▉ Nonbreeding (scarce)
- ▉ Year-round

KEYS TO IDENTIFICATION

MEASUREMENTS (Both sexes)

Length	Wingspan	Weight
6.3–7.9 in	11.8–13.4 in	1.0–1.7 oz
16–20 cm	30–34 cm	28–48 g

SIZE & SHAPE. Horned Larks are small, long-bodied songbirds that usually adopt a horizontal posture. They have short, thin bills, short necks, and rounded heads, the shape sometimes broken by two small "horns" of feathers sticking up toward the back of the head.

COLOR PATTERN. Male Horned Larks are brown above and white beneath, with a black chest band, curving black mask, and head stripes that extend to the back of the head. These are sometimes raised into tiny "horns." The face and throat are yellow or white. Females have similar, less crisply defined markings.

BEHAVIOR. Horned Larks are social birds, usually found in flocks except during the breeding season. They creep along bare ground searching for small seeds and insects. They often join in winter flocks with other open-country species.

Cool Facts

Horned Larks inhabit an extensive elevation range, from sea level to altitudes of 13,000 feet. Linnaeus named this bird *Alauda alpestris*: "lark of the mountains."

Find This Bird

To find them, look for the barest ground around and scan carefully, watching for movement or for the birds to turn their black-and-yellow faces toward you.

PURPLE MARTIN *(Progne subis)*

Putting up a Purple Martin house in the East can be like installing a miniature neighborhood in your backyard. If you're lucky, you'll have martins peering from the entrances and chirping from the rooftops all summer. Our largest swallows, Purple Martins perform aerial acrobatics to snap up flying insects. At the end of the breeding season they gather in big flocks and make their way to South America.

AT A GLANCE

Food

A year-round insectivore, the Purple Martin eats a wide variety of flying insects high in the air. When it sees prey, it twists sideways or upward, speeds up, and flares its tail as it snatches the insect. It also picks up small bits of gravel to help it digest insect exoskeletons.

Nesting

In the East, Purple Martins nest mainly in birdhouses and hollowed gourds. In the West, they use holes in trees and cacti, cliff crevices, and, rarely, buildings. They build nests of twigs, plant stems, mud, and grass. Nest colonies can contain dozens of pairs.

Habitat

Purple Martins forage in the air over towns, parks, open fields, dunes, streams, and wetlands. During migration they can form very large roosts with tens of thousands of birds all sleeping in a stand of trees.

RANGE MAP

- Breeding
- Migration

KEYS TO IDENTIFICATION

MALE

FEMALE

MEASUREMENTS (Both sexes)

Length	Wingspan	Weight
7.5–7.9 in	15.4–16.1 in	1.6–2.1 oz
19–20 cm	39–41 cm	45–60 g

SIZE & SHAPE. Purple Martins, our largest swallows, are very broad-chested, with short, forked tails and long, tapered wings. They have a stout, slightly hooked bill, much shorter than the narrow bill of the European Starling; in flight they're more delicately built and more buoyant than starlings.

COLOR PATTERN. Adult males are iridescent, dark blue-purple overall with brown-black wings and tail. Females and immatures are duller, with variable amounts of gray on the head and chest and a whitish lower belly.

BEHAVIOR. Purple Martins fly rapidly, with a mix of flapping and gliding. They hunt in midair, catching large, aerial insects such as dragonflies. Martins feed and roost in flocks, often mixed with other species of swallows. They often feed higher in the air than other swallows, making them harder to spot.

Cool Facts

While he was traveling, famed bird artist John James Audubon used to choose which tavern to stay at by whether it had a Purple Martin box outside.

Backyard Tips

You can put out crushed eggshells to give the martins a source of grit for digesting insect exoskeletons.

TREE SWALLOW *(Tachycineta bicolor)*

Tree Swallows are a familiar sight in summer fields and wetlands across northern North America. They chase after flying insects with acrobatic twists and turns, their steely blue-green feathers flashing in the sunlight. Tree Swallows nest in tree cavities and also in nest boxes, which has allowed scientists to study their breeding biology in detail. Their beauty and insect-eating habits make them a great addition to backyards and everywhere else.

AT A GLANCE

Food Tree Swallows eat all kinds of flying insects, and, rarely, other small animals; They can eat plant foods when prey is scarce. They usually forage no more than 40 feet above the ground. They sometimes converge in large numbers where insects swarm.

Nesting The female collects grasses to construct the cup nest, about 2–3 inches across and 1–2 inches deep, inside a natural cavity, woodpecker hole, or bird box. She lines the nest with feathers of other bird species; the male gathers at least half of the feathers.

Habitat Tree Swallows breed in fields, marshes, and swamps, and around shorelines and beaver ponds, preferring bodies of water that produce multitudes of flying insects for food. Dead and old trees with cavities are used for nesting and sometimes roosting.

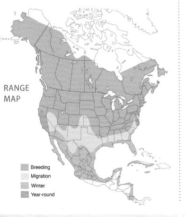

RANGE MAP

- Breeding
- Migration
- Winter
- Year-round

KEYS TO IDENTIFICATION

MALE

MEASUREMENTS (Both sexes)

Length	Wingspan	Weight
4.7–5.9 in	11.8–13.8 in	0.6–0.9 oz
12–15 cm	30–35 cm	16–25 g

SIZE & SHAPE. Tree Swallows are streamlined small songbirds with long, pointed wings and a short, squared or slightly notched tail. Their bills are very short and flat. They tend to perch with a vertical posture.

COLOR PATTERN. Adult males are blue-green above and white below with blackish flight feathers and a thin black eye mask. Females have more brown in their upperparts, and juveniles are completely brown above. Juveniles and some females can show a weak, blurry gray-brown breast band.

BEHAVIOR. Tree Swallows feed on small, aerial insects that they catch in their mouths during acrobatic flight. After breeding, they gather in large flocks to molt and migrate. In the nonbreeding season, they form huge communal roosts.

Cool Facts

The Tree Swallow—which is most often seen in open, treeless areas—gets its name from its habit of nesting in tree cavities. They also take readily to nest boxes.

Backyard Tips

Tree Swallows may supplement their insect diet with berries, such as bayberry and wax myrtle fruits. They often nest in birdhouses—find plans for making your own at *nestwatch.org/birdhouses*.

BARN SWALLOW (*Hirundo rustica*)

Barn Swallows dart gracefully over fields, barnyards, and open water in search of flying insect prey. Look for the long, deeply forked tail that streams out behind this agile flyer and sets it apart from all other North American swallows. Barn Swallows often cruise low, flying just a few inches above the ground or water. True to their name, they build their cup-shaped mud nests almost exclusively on human-made structures.

AT A GLANCE

Food

Barn Swallows mostly eat flies, along with beetles, bees, wasps, ants, butterflies, moths, and other flying insects. They usually take single insects rather than feeding on swarms of small ones. They eat grit and pebbles to help digest insects and get calcium.

Nesting

Barn Swallows plaster their heavy mud nests on eaves and rafters of buildings and beneath bridges, culverts, etc. They form mud and grasses into mouth-sized pellets to build the cup, and line it with grass and feathers. The inner cup is 3 inches wide and 2 inches deep.

Habitat

Barn Swallows forage in open areas throughout most of the continent, especially over fields or near water. Breeding habitat must include open areas for foraging, structures to build nests on, and a source of mud for building their nests.

RANGE MAP

- Breeding
- Migration
- Nonbreeding
- Year-round

KEYS TO IDENTIFICATION

MALE

MEASUREMENTS (Both sexes)

Length	Wingspan	Weight
5.9–7.5 in	11.4–12.6 in	0.6–0.7 oz
15–19 cm	29–32 cm	17–20 g

SIZE & SHAPE. When perched, this sparrow-sized swallow appears cone shaped, with flattened head, no visible neck, and broad shoulders that taper to long, pointed wings. The tail extends well beyond the wingtips and the long outer feathers give the tail a deep fork. In flight, the "swallow tail" is distinctive.

COLOR PATTERN. Barn Swallows have a steely blue back, wings, and tail with rufous to tawny underparts. The blue crown and face contrast with the cinnamon-colored forehead and throat. White spots under the tail can be difficult to see except in flight. Males are more boldly colored than females.

BEHAVIOR. Barn Swallows fly with fluid wingbeats in bursts of straight flight, and execute quick, tight turns and dives to feed on the wing. They catch insects from just above the ground or water to heights of 100 feet or more. They often join other swallows in mixed foraging flocks.

Cool Facts

Barn Swallow parents sometimes get help from other birds to feed their young. These "helpers at the nest" are usually older siblings from previous clutches, but unrelated juveniles may help as well.

Backyard Tips

Putting up a nest box may attract a breeding pair. Find plans for a Barn Swallow–specific nest box you can make yourself at *nestwatch.org/birdhouses*.

CAROLINA CHICKADEE *(Poecile carolinensis)*

The great bird artist John James Audubon was in South Carolina when he encountered this curious, intelligent little bird and gave it its name. The Carolina Chickadee is very similar to its northern cousin, the Black-capped Chickadee, but has plainer gray wings and sings a longer song of four clear whistles. Groups of these bold, social birds enliven feeders and forests all over the southeastern U.S.

AT A GLANCE

Food

In winter, the Carolina Chickadee's diet is about half plant, half animal—mostly insects and spiders. The rest of the year, 80%–90% of its diet is insects gleaned from foliage and bark. It holds seeds and insects in its feet, wedged against its perch, to peck into and eat.

Nesting

The male and female excavate or take over a cavity or nest box, usually 2–25 feet up in a tree. The female builds the nest base inside, using moss and sometimes strips of bark. Then she adds a thick lining of hair and plant fibers.

Habitat

Carolina Chickadees live in deciduous and coniferous forests, swamps, wet woods, open woods, parks, and urban and suburban yards.

RANGE MAP

■ Year-round

KEYS TO IDENTIFICATION

MEASUREMENTS (Both sexes)

Length	Wingspan	Weight
3.9–4.7 in	5.9–7.9 in	0.3–0.4 oz
10–12 cm	15–20 cm	8–12 g

SIZE & SHAPE. This tiny, approachable songbird has a short neck and large head, giving it a distinctive spherical body shape. Its tail is fairly long and narrow, its short bill thicker than a warbler's but thinner than a finch's.

COLOR PATTERN. Carolina Chickadees have a black cap and bib separated by stark white cheeks. The back, wings, and tail are soft gray. Compared to Black-capped Chickadees, their black bib is smaller and looks cleaner at the edge. The feather edges in the folded wing show very little white.

BEHAVIOR. Inquisitive and acrobatic, this sociable bird forms mixed feeding flocks with other small birds, roaming within a fairly large area except during the nesting season. When it finds a morsel, each chickadee separates from the group to eat, and then joins the group again to forage for the next tidbit.

Cool Facts

Where the two species' ranges come in contact, Carolina and Black-capped chickadees occasionally hybridize. Hybrids can sing the songs of either species, or might sing something intermediate.

Backyard Tips

Carolina Chickadees visit feeders for sunflower seeds, peanut chips, and suet. They often nest in birdhouses—find plans for a chickadee-sized nest box at *nestwatch.org/birdhouses*.

BLACK-CAPPED CHICKADEE *(Poecile atricapillus)*

The Black-capped Chickadee is a bird almost universally considered "cute" thanks to its oversized round head, tiny body, and unbounded curiosity. The chickadee's black cap and bib; white cheeks; gray back, wings, and tail; and whitish underside with buffy sides are distinctive. Its habit of investigating its home territory and its quickness to discover bird feeders make it one of the first birds most people learn.

AT A GLANCE

Food
In winter Black-capped Chickadees eat about half plant matter (seeds, berries, etc.) and half animal matter (insects, spiders, suet, etc.). The rest of the year, animal matter makes up 80%-90% of the diet. At feeders they take sunflower seeds, peanuts, suet, peanut butter, and mealworms.

Nesting
Chickadees nest in nest boxes, natural cavities, abandoned woodpecker cavities, or holes they excavate themselves, usually between 4 and 25 feet high. The female builds the cup-shaped nest of moss and other coarse material, lined with soft items such as rabbit fur.

Habitat
Chickadees are found in deciduous and mixed forests, open woods, parks, willow thickets, cottonwood groves, disturbed areas, and big cities as long as there are some trees and shrubs.

RANGE MAP

■ Year-round

KEYS TO IDENTIFICATION

MEASUREMENTS (Both sexes)

Length	Wingspan	Weight
4.7–5.9 in	6.3–8.3 in	0.3–0.5 oz
12–15 cm	16–21 cm	9–14 g

SIZE & SHAPE. This tiny songbird has a short neck and large head, giving it a distinctive, rather spherical body shape. It also has a long, narrow tail and a short bill a bit thicker than a warbler's but thinner than a finch's.

COLOR PATTERN. Black-capped Chickadees have black-and-white heads, soft gray backs, and buffy to white underparts. The wing feathers are strongly edged with white. The black cap extends down just beyond the black eyes, making the small eyes tricky to see.

BEHAVIOR. Black-capped Chickadees often visit feeders but seldom remain for long. They are acrobatic and associate in flocks—the sudden activity when a flock arrives is distinctive. They often fly across roads and open areas one at a time with a bouncy flight.

Cool Facts
Every autumn Black-capped Chickadees replace old brain neurons with new ones, allowing them to discard old information and adjust to new developments in their flocks and the environment.

Backyard Tips
Chickadees eat suet, sunflower seeds, and peanuts. They use hanging feeders and window feeders. They also use nest boxes—find plans for building a chickadee-sized box at *nestwatch.org/birdhouses*.

The Tufted Titmouse is common in eastern deciduous forests and a frequent visitor to feeders. The large black eyes, black forehead marking, small, round bill, and brushy crest give these birds a quiet but eager expression that matches the way they flit through canopies, hang from twig-ends, and visit feeders.

When a titmouse finds a large seed, it carries the prize to a perch where it cracks it with sharp whacks of its sturdy bill.

AT A GLANCE

Food
Tufted Titmice eat insects and spiders whenever available, along with seeds, berries, and nuts such as acorns and beech nuts. They always choose the largest seeds they can when foraging.

Nesting
Tufted Titmice nest in rotted cavities, woodpecker nest holes, and nest boxes. They build a cup-shaped nest of damp leaves, moss, grasses, and bark strips, lined with soft materials such as mammal fur.

Habitat
Tufted Titmice live in deciduous or mixed evergreen-deciduous woods with dense canopies, typically at elevations up to about 2,000 feet. They're also common in orchards, parks, and suburbs.

RANGE MAP

Year-round

KEYS TO IDENTIFICATION

MEASUREMENTS (Both sexes)

Length	Wingspan	Weight
5.5–6.3 in	7.9–10.2 in	0.6–0.9 oz
14–16 cm	20–26 cm	18–26 g

SIZE & SHAPE. Tufted Titmice look large among the small birds that come to feeders, an impression that comes from their big head and eye, thick neck, and full body. The pointed crest and stout bill help identify titmice even in silhouette.

COLOR PATTERN. Soft silvery or steel gray above and white below, with a rusty or peach-colored wash down the flanks. A black patch just above the bill makes the bird look snub-nosed. The large eyes and bill are black.

BEHAVIOR. Tufted Titmice are acrobatic foragers, a bit slower and more methodical than chickadees. They often join flocks of chickadees and other small birds as the group passes through the titmouse's territory. At feeders, they are assertive over smaller birds. Their flight tends to be fluttery but level.

Cool Facts
Most Tufted Titmice remain on their breeding territory all winter, often with one of their young from that year. Sometimes a young titmouse stays with its parents to help raise next year's brood.

Backyard Tips
Tufted Titmice visit feeders, especially in winter, for sunflower seeds, suet, and peanuts. They often use nest boxes. If you set one out, attach a predator guard to protect eggs and young.

RED-BREASTED NUTHATCH (Sitta canadensis)

An intense bundle of energy at your feeder, the Red-breasted Nuthatch is a tiny, active songbird of northern woods and western mountains. Long-billed and short-tailed, it travels through tree canopies with chickadees, kinglets, and woodpeckers but mostly sticks to tree trunks and branches, where it searches bark furrows and cones for hidden food items. Its excitable *yank-yank* call sounds like a tiny tin horn being honked in the treetops.

AT A GLANCE

Food
In summer, Red-breasted Nuthatches eat mainly insects and spiders. In fall and winter they switch to conifer seeds. During outbreaks of spruce budworm, they feast on the pests. They select the heaviest food item available, sometimes jamming it into bark to hammer it open.

Nesting
The female excavates a cavity with her mate in the soft wood of a dead tree, or finds an existing cavity. She builds a bed of grass, bark strips, and pine needles, then lines it with fur, feathers, fine grasses, or shredded bark. The pair applies sticky conifer resin to the entrance.

Habitat
Red-breasted Nuthatches live mainly in coniferous forests of spruce, fir, pine, hemlock, larch, and western red cedar. Eastern populations use some deciduous woods. During some winters they may "irrupt" or move far south of their normal range.

RANGE MAP

Nonbreeding
Year-round

KEYS TO IDENTIFICATION

MALE

MEASUREMENTS (Both sexes)

Length	Wingspan	Weight
4.3 in	7.1–7.9 in	0.3–0.5 oz
11 cm	18–20 cm	8–13 g

SIZE & SHAPE. Red-breasted Nuthatches are small, compact songbirds with slightly upturned, pointed bills; extremely short tails; and almost no neck. The body is plump or barrel chested, and the short wings are very broad.

COLOR PATTERN. The Red-breasted Nuthatch is blue-gray above. The male's underparts are rich rusty-cinnamon, the female's a softer peachy color. The male's head is strongly patterned with a black cap, white stripe above the eye, and black stripe through the eye. The female's head markings are softer gray.

BEHAVIOR. Red-breasted Nuthatches creep up, down, and sideways over trunks and branches, probing for food in crevices and under flakes of bark. They don't lean against their tail as woodpeckers do. Flight is short and bouncy.

Cool Facts

Red-breasted Nuthatches sometimes steal nest-lining material from the nests of other birds, including Pygmy Nuthatches and Mountain Chickadees.

Backyard Tips

Red-breasted Nuthatches visit feeders for sunflower seeds, suet, and peanuts. Make sure peanuts don't get wet or they'll mold. In their breeding range, Red-breasted Nuthatches sometimes use nest boxes.

WHITE-BREASTED NUTHATCH *(Sitta carolinensis)*

A common feeder bird with clean black, gray, and white markings, the White-breasted Nuthatch is an active, agile little bird with an appetite for insects and large, meaty seeds. It gets its common name from its habit of jamming large nuts and acorns into tree bark, then whacking them with its sharp bill to "hatch" out the seed from the inside. It may be small, but its voice is loud and carries well. The insistent nasal yammering can lead you right to one.

AT A GLANCE

Food White-breasted Nuthatches eat a wide variety of insects and spiders; also seeds and nuts including acorns, hawthorn fruits, sunflower seeds, and sometimes crops such as corn. At bird feeders they eat sunflower seeds, peanuts, suet, and peanut butter.

Nesting White-breasted Nuthatches nest in natural cavities or old woodpecker holes, but rarely excavate their own. They don't seem bothered by nest holes considerably larger than they are. They sometimes use nest boxes.

Habitat White-breasted Nuthatches are birds of mature deciduous woods. They're found more rarely in coniferous woods, where Red-breasted Nuthatches are more likely. They also occur in woodland edges and areas such as parks, wooded suburbs, and backyards.

RANGE MAP

Nonbreeding

Year-round

KEYS TO IDENTIFICATION

MALE

MEASUREMENTS (Both sexes)

Length	Wingspan	Weight
5.1–5.5 in	7.9–10.6 in	0.6–1.1 oz
13–14 cm	20–27 cm	18–30 g

SIZE & SHAPE. North America's largest nuthatch, the White-breasted Nuthatch is still fairly small, with a large head and almost no apparent neck. The tail is very short, and the long, narrow, sharp bill is straight or slightly upturned.

COLOR PATTERN. White-breasted Nuthatches are gray-blue on the back, with a frosty white face and underparts. The lower belly and under the tail are often chestnut. The black or gray cap and neck frame the face and make it look like this bird is wearing a hood.

BEHAVIOR. Like other nuthatches, white-breasteds creep along trunks and large branches, probing into bark furrows with their straight, pointed bills. They often turn sideways and upside down on vertical surfaces as they forage. They don't use their tails to brace against a vertical trunk as woodpeckers do.

Cool Facts

In winter, White-breasted Nuthatches join foraging flocks led by chickadees or titmice, perhaps partly because it makes food easier to find and partly because more birds can keep an eye out for predators.

Backyard Tips

White-breasted Nuthatches take suet, sunflower, and peanuts at feeders. Make sure the peanuts are fresh and dry to protect the birds from mold. Nuthatches sometimes nest in nest boxes.

BROWN-HEADED NUTHATCH *(Sitta pusilla)*

When the squeaky sound of rubber duckies drifts down out of a pine forest canopy in the South, look for Brown-headed Nuthatches. These tiny, blue-gray songbirds travel up, down, and sideways along pine tree trunks and branches, poking and hammering the bark for insects. They travel in noisy family groups, and young from previous years often stick around to help their parents raise a new set of siblings.

AT A GLANCE

Food Brown-headed Nuthatches pick, pry, and hammer at bark and pine needle clusters looking for beetles, spiders, weevils, egg cases, and larvae. During colder months, they pry seeds out of pine cones and often hide them away for later.

Nesting Brown-headed Nuthatches nest in cavities and nest boxes. Males, females, and sometimes young birds help excavate cavities in dead and decaying trees, especially pines. They make the nest primarily of pine seed wings, adding bark shreds, Spanish moss, fur, feathers, and other soft material.

Habitat Brown-headed Nuthatches live in or around pine forests of the southeastern U.S., especially in open, mature forests of loblolly, shortleaf, slash, and longleaf pine where natural fire patterns have been maintained.

RANGE MAP

■ Year-round

KEYS TO IDENTIFICATION

MEASUREMENTS (Both sexes)

Length	Wingspan	Weight
3.9–4.3 in	6.3–7.1 in	0.4 oz
10–11 cm	16–18 cm	10 g

SIZE & SHAPE. Like other nuthatches, this tiny songbird has a large head, short legs, and a very short tail. They also have a long and sharp-tipped bill.

COLOR PATTERN. This is a bluish-gray bird with a clean brown cap neatly set off from the whitish face and throat. The underparts are pale grayish-white.

BEHAVIOR. Brown-headed Nuthatches climb head first in a zigzag pattern up and down trunks and branches, often high in the trees. They forage in family groups and fly with shallow dips between trees. Brown-headed Nuthatches also join winter foraging flocks with other species.

Cool Facts

Brown-headed Nuthatches sometimes use a rudimentary tool to find food: they use a piece of bark to pry off additional layers of bark to get at the tasty morsel inside.

Backyard Tips

If you live in or near mature pine forests in the Southeast, Brown-headed Nuthatches may come to a nest box or visit feeders for suet or sunflower seeds.

Brown Creepers are tiny woodland birds with an affinity for the biggest trees they can find. Look for these long-tailed scraps of brown and white spiraling up stout trunks and main branches, sometimes passing downward-facing nuthatches along the way. They probe into crevices and pick at loose bark with their slender, curved bills. Listening for their thin but piercing calls can make it easier to find this well-camouflaged species.

AT A GLANCE

Food

Brown Creepers forage for insects and larvae in the furrowed bark of large, live trees. In winter they supplement this diet with small amounts of seeds. They occasionally visit suet feeders.

Nesting

The female builds the hammock-shaped nest behind peeling flakes of bark using twigs, strips of bark, bits of leaves, and lichens, using cocoons and spider egg cases as adhesives. The nest cup is about 2.5 inches deep and 6 inches across.

Habitat

Look for Brown Creepers in deciduous or coniferous forests with large, live trees. In summer they are often among evergreens such as hemlock, pine, fir, redwood, and cypress. In winter they use a wider variety of wooded habitats, parks, and yards.

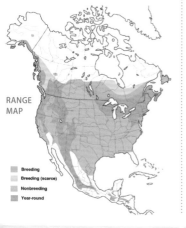

RANGE MAP

- Breeding
- Breeding (scarce)
- Nonbreeding
- Year-round

KEYS TO IDENTIFICATION

MEASUREMENTS (Both sexes)

Length	Wingspan	Weight
4.7–5.5 in	6.7–7.9 in	0.2–0.4 oz
12–14 cm	17–20 cm	5–10 g

SIZE & SHAPE. Brown Creepers are tiny, slender songbirds. They have a long, spine-tipped tail that curves slightly downward, a slim body, and a thin, curved bill.

COLOR PATTERN. Streaked brown and buff above, with the white underparts usually in shadow and hidden against a tree trunk, Brown Creepers blend easily into bark. Their brownish heads show a broad, buffy stripe over the eye.

BEHAVIOR. Brown Creepers hunt for insects by hitching upward in a spiral around tree trunks and limbs, using their stiff tails for support. Then they fly weakly to the base of another tree and resume climbing up. They sing a high, warbling song and give a high, wavering call note.

Cool Facts

Tiny Brown Creepers burn only an estimated 4 to 10 calories per day.

Backyard Tips

Though they eat mostly insects, in winter Brown Creepers will visit backyard feeders, especially to eat suet and peanut butter.

HOUSE WREN (Troglodytes aedon)

A plain brown bird with an exuberant voice, the House Wren is a common backyard bird over nearly the entire Western Hemisphere. Listen for its rush-and-jumble song in summer and you'll find this species zipping through shrubs and low tree branches, snatching at insects. House Wrens readily use nest boxes, and you may find their twig-filled nests in old cans, boots, or boxes lying around in your garage.

AT A GLANCE

Food House Wrens eat a wide variety of insects and spiders, including both sluggish and quick species. They also eat snail shells, probably for the calcium they contain and to provide grit for digestion.

Nesting House Wrens nest in all kinds of cavities and crevices within 100 feet of woody vegetation. The male piles twigs into several cavities. When he attracts a female, she chooses one, and builds a nest cup into a depression in the twigs, lined with softer materials.

Habitat House Wrens have a huge geographic range and live in many habitats featuring trees, shrubs, and tangles interspersed with clearings. They thrive around human habitations, often exploring the nooks and crannies in houses, garages, and play spaces.

RANGE MAP

- Breeding
- Migration
- Nonbreeding
- Year-round

KEYS TO IDENTIFICATION

MEASUREMENTS (Both sexes)

Length	Wingspan	Weight
4.3–5.1 in	5.9 in	0.4 oz
11–13 cm	15 cm	10–12 g

SIZE & SHAPE. The House Wren is small and compact, with a flat head and fairly long, thin, curved bill. It has short wings and a longish tail that it keeps either cocked above the line of the body or slightly drooped.

COLOR PATTERN. The House Wren is subdued brown overall with darker barring on the wings and tail. The pale eyebrow that is characteristic of so many wren species is much fainter in House Wrens.

BEHAVIOR. Bubbly and energetic, just like their songs, House Wrens hop or flit quickly through tangles and low branches. They call attention to themselves year-round with harsh scolding chatter and, in spring and summer, frequent singing.

Cool Facts

The House Wren has an enormous range—from Canada to the tip of South America. The map above shows only the range of the North American subspecies.

Backyard Tips

Wrens use brush piles for cover, protection, and a source of insects. If you prune trees or cut brush in your yard, consider heaping the cuttings into a pile for them.

CAROLINA WREN *(Thryothorus ludovicianus)*

In summer, many patches of woods in the eastern United States ring with the rolling song of the Carolina Wren. This shy bird can be hard to see, but it delivers an amazing number of decibels for its size. Follow its *teakettle-teakettle* and other piercing exclamations through backyard or forest, and you may be rewarded with glimpses of this bird's rich cinnamon plumage and long, upward-cocked tail.

AT A GLANCE

Food
Insects and spiders make up the bulk of this wren's diet. It also eats small amounts of plant matter, such as fruit pulp and seeds from bayberry, sweetgum, or poison ivy.

Nesting
Carolina Wrens nest in open cavities near the ground, and in trees, overhangs, stumps, and all kinds of human items. The bulky nest, made of a great variety of materials, is 3–9 inches long and 3–6 inches wide; it's usually domed with a side entrance and a woven "porch."

Habitat
Carolina Wrens frequent vegetated habitats such as lowland cypress swamps, bottomland woods, and ravines choked with hemlock and rhododendron. They're drawn to shrubby, wooded residential areas and overgrown farmland.

RANGE MAP

■ Year-round

KEYS TO IDENTIFICATION

MEASUREMENTS (Both sexes)

Length	Wingspan	Weight
4.7–5.5 in	11.4 in	0.6–0.8 oz
12–14 cm	29 cm	18–22 g

SIZE & SHAPE. The Carolina Wren is a small but chunky bird with a round body and a long tail that it often cocks upward. The head is large with very little apparent neck, and the distinctive bill marks it as a wren: long, slender, and downcurved.

COLOR PATTERN. Both males and females are a bright, unpatterned reddish-brown above and warm buffy-orange below, with a long white eyebrow stripe, dark bill, and white chin and throat.

BEHAVIOR. The Carolina Wren creeps around, scooting up and down tree trunks in search of insects and fruit. It explores yards, garages, and woodpiles, sometimes nesting there. It's a weak flier that usually makes only short aerial forays. It defends its territory by singing, scolding and chasing intruders.

Cool Facts

One captive male Carolina Wren sang nearly 3,000 times in a single day.

Backyard Tips

Carolina Wrens visit suet feeders during winter. In the cold north, they sometimes take shelter in nest boxes containing dried grasses.

BLUE-GRAY GNATCATCHER *(Polioptila caerulea)*

A tiny, lithe, long-tailed bird of broadleaf forests and scrublands, the Blue-gray Gnatcatcher makes itself known by its soft but insistent calls and its constant motion. It hops and sidles about in dense outer foliage, foraging for insects and spiders. As it moves, this steely blue-gray bird conspicuously flicks its white-edged tail from side to side, scaring up insects and chasing after them.

AT A GLANCE

Food

Gnatcatchers eat small insects, spiders, and other invertebrates. They swallow small prey alive and tear apart larger prey, sometimes beating their bodies on a perch before eating them. Parents feed hatchlings tiny prey, giving them larger items as the nestlings grow.

Nesting

The pair builds the 2–3-inch-wide nest high in a live broadleaf tree. The nest cup, made of fine plant materials and lichen, is held together and attached to its branch with spider silk. After the brood fledges, the male may build a second nest as the female tends to the fleglings.

Habitat

Blue-gray Gnatcatchers live in deciduous and mixed wooded habitats, especially in moist areas near edges.

RANGE
MAP

- ■ Breeding
- ■ Migration
- ■ Nonbreeding
- ■ Year-round

KEYS TO IDENTIFICATION

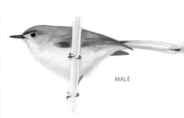

MALE

MEASUREMENTS (Both sexes)

Length	Wingspan	Weight
3.9–4.3 in	6.3 in	0.2–0.3 oz
10–11 cm	16 cm	5–9 g

SIZE & SHAPE. Blue-gray Gnatcatchers are tiny, slim songbirds with long legs, long tails, and thin, straight bills.

COLOR PATTERN. Blue-gray Gnatcatchers are pale blue-gray birds with white underparts and a mostly black tail with white edges. The underside of the tail is mostly white. The face is highlighted by a white eyering. In summer, males sport a black "V" on their foreheads extending above their eyes.

BEHAVIOR. This energetic little bird rarely slows down, fluttering after small insects among shrubs and trees with its tail cocked at a jaunty angle. It often takes food from spiderwebs, and also takes strands of webbing for its tiny nest, which is shaped like a tree knot.

Cool Facts

In spite of their name, gnats do not form a significant part of the Blue-gray Gnatcatcher's diet.

Find This Bird

These tiny birds can be hard to see in tree canopies, so listen for their insistent, nasal-sounding squeaks to clue you in to their presence.

RUBY-CROWNED KINGLET *(Regulus calendula)*

A tiny songbird overflowing with energy, the Ruby-crowned Kinglet forages almost frantically through lower branches of shrubs and trees, often at or below eye level. Its restless habit of constantly flicking its wings is a key identification clue. The male's brilliant ruby crown patch stays hidden unless he's agitated. Your best chance of seeing the crown is to track down a singing male.

AT A GLANCE

Food
Ruby-crowned Kinglets prey on spiders, insects, and other tiny invertebrates, taken at any height in trees and shrubs. They hover and peck to glean this prey from leaves and branches. They also eat some seeds and fruit, including poison-oak berries and dogwood berries.

Nesting
Ruby-crowned Kinglets nest high in trees. The female builds the compact structure using grasses, feathers, mosses, spiderwebs, and cocoon silk for the outer structure, and fine plant material and fur for the inner lining. The nest is elastic, stretching as the brood grows.

Habitat
Ruby-crowned Kinglets breed in spruce-fir forests, mixed woodlands, and shrubby meadows in northern North America. During migration and winter they occur in woods and thickets.

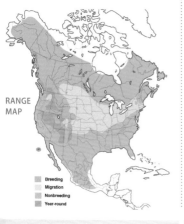

RANGE MAP

- Breeding
- Migration
- Nonbreeding
- Year-round

KEYS TO IDENTIFICATION

MALE

MEASUREMENTS (Both sexes)

Length	Wingspan	Weight
3.5–4.3 in	6.3–7.1 in	0.2–0.4 oz
9–11 cm	16–18 cm	5–10 g

SIZE & SHAPE. Kinglets are tiny songbirds with relatively large heads, almost no apparent neck, and thin tails. They have a very small, thin, straight bill.

COLOR PATTERN. Ruby-crowned Kinglets are olive-green songbirds with a prominent white eyering and white wingbar. This wingbar contrasts with an adjacent blackish bar on the wing. The "ruby crown" of the male is only occasionally visible.

BEHAVIOR. Ruby-crowned Kinglets are restless, acrobatic birds that move quickly through foliage, typically at lower and middle levels. They flick their wings almost constantly as they go.

Cool Facts

Metabolic studies on Ruby-crowned Kinglets suggest that these tiny birds use only about 10 calories per day.

Find This Bird

These are fast-moving but quiet little birds, best seen in winter in much of the U.S. Watch for their near-constant activity and habit of flicking their wings.

EASTERN BLUEBIRD *(Sialia sialis)*

A drive through open country almost anywhere in the East in summer may turn up an Eastern Bluebird. These small thrushes sit on telephone wires or nest boxes, calling out in a short, wavering voice or abruptly dropping to the ground after an insect. The bright male displays at his nest cavity to attract the more muted female. Bluebirds have long been associated with happiness.

AT A GLANCE

Food In spring and summer, bluebirds mostly eat insects caught on the ground. In fall and winter they eat fruit, especially various berries. They have also been recorded eating salamanders, shrews, snakes, lizards, and tree frogs.

Nesting Eastern Bluebirds nest in nest boxes or natural cavities, especially old woodpecker holes in dead pine or oak trees. The female weaves grasses and pine needles into a cup, then lines it with more grass and occasionally horsehair or turkey feathers.

Habitat Eastern Bluebirds live in open country with scattered trees but little understory and sparse ground cover, such as frequently burned pine savannas, forest openings, pastures, agricultural fields, suburban parks, spacious backyards, and golf courses.

RANGE MAP

Breeding
Winter
Year-round

KEYS TO IDENTIFICATION

MALE

MEASUREMENTS (Both sexes)

Length	Wingspan	Weight
6.3–8.3 in	9.8–12.6 in	1–1.1 oz
16–21 cm	25–32 cm	28–32 g

SIZE & SHAPE. The Eastern Bluebird is a small thrush with a big, rounded head, large eye, plump body, and alert posture. The wings are long, but the tail and legs are fairly short. The bill is short and straight.

COLOR PATTERN. Male Eastern Bluebirds are vivid, deep blue above with a rusty or brick-red throat and breast and a white belly. The blue is more vivid in good light; males often look grayish from a distance. Females are grayish above with an orange-brown breast and blue tinges to the wings.

BEHAVIOR. Eastern Bluebirds perch erect on wires, posts, and low branches in open country, scanning the ground for prey. They feed by dropping to the ground onto insects or, in fall and winter, by perching on fruiting trees to gulp down berries.

Cool Facts

Eastern Bluebirds usually raise more than one brood each year. Young produced in early nests leave their parents in summer, but many from later nests stay with their parents through winter.

Backyard Tips

Eastern Bluebirds sometimes visit feeders that provide mealworms. They famously use nest boxes, but not in typical backyards—they require more open habitat.

HERMIT THRUSH *(Catharus guttatus)*

An unassuming bird with a lovely, melancholy song, the Hermit Thrush spends summer lurking in the understories of forests in the mountains and far north. They winter in the southern states and along the Pacific Coast. The first brown thrush to return to northern forests in spring, it's the last to leave in fall. It forages for insects on the forest floor. To identify this small thrush, look for its distinctive rusty tail.

AT A GLANCE

Food
In spring, the Hermit Thrush eats mainly insects such as beetles, caterpillars, bees, ants, wasps, and flies. It also occasionally eats small amphibians and reptiles. In winter, it eats far more fruit, including wild berries.

Nesting
In the East, most Hermit Thrushes nest on the ground; in the West they build fairly low in shrubs or trees. Made of grass, leaves, pine needles, and bits of wood, the nest is lined with finer fibers inside and mud and lichen around the outside. The nest measures 4–6 inches across.

Habitat
Hermit Thrushes breed in open areas inside boreal forests, deciduous woods, and mountain forests. In winter, they often occupy lower-elevation forests with dense understory and berry bushes, including pine, evergreen, and deciduous woods.

RANGE MAP

Breeding
Migration
Nonbreeding
Year-round

KEYS TO IDENTIFICATION

MEASUREMENTS (Both sexes)

Length	Wingspan	Weight
5.5–7.1 in	9.8–11.4 in	0.8–1.3 oz
14–18 cm	25–29 cm	23–37 g

SIZE & SHAPE. Hermit Thrushes have a chunky shape similar to an American Robin, but smaller. They stand upright, often with the slender, straight bill slightly raised. Like other thrushes, the head is round and the tail fairly long.

COLOR PATTERN. The Hermit Thrush is soft brown on the head and back, with a distinctly warm, reddish tail. The underparts are pale with distinct spots on the throat and smudged spots on the breast. With a close look you may see a thin pale eyering (not a bold one).

BEHAVIOR. Hermit Thrushes hop and scrape in leaf litter while foraging. They perch low to the ground on fallen logs and shrubs, often wandering into open areas such as forest clearings or trails. Hermit Thrushes have a distinctive habit of raising the tail and then lowering it slowly.

Cool Facts

Hermit Thrushes usually make their nests in and around trees and shrubs, but they can also get more creative. Nests have been found on a cemetery grave, on a golf course, and in a mine shaft.

Find This Bird

Look for Hermit Thrushes in forest openings or along trails, and check the range map to know whether to search during summer or winter. In winter, look for them around shrubs and vines with berries.

WOOD THRUSH *(Hylocichla mustelina)*

The Wood Thrush's loud, flutelike *ee-oh-lay* song rings through the deciduous forests of the eastern United States in summer. This reclusive bird's cinnamon-brown upperparts provide camouflage as it scrabbles for invertebrates in the leaf litter deep in the forest. Though still numerous, its numbers are rapidly declining.

AT A GLANCE

Food

In spring and summer, Wood Thrushes feed mostly on leaf-litter invertebrates. As summer fades into fall and winter, they eat more fruits and berries. When fueling up for migration, they choose berries high in fat.

Nesting

The nest, usually in the lower branches of a sapling or shrub, is made of grass, leaves, stems, and sometimes paper or plastic. The female weaves walls 2–6 inches high to create a cup 4–6 inches across with a 3-inch inner cup lined with mud and a covering of soft rootlets.

Habitat

The Wood Thrush breeds in deciduous and mixed forests in the eastern U.S. where there are large trees, moderate understory, shade, and abundant leaf litter for foraging. It winters in lowland tropical forests in Central America.

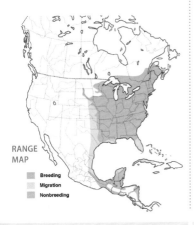

RANGE MAP

- Breeding
- Migration
- Nonbreeding

KEYS TO IDENTIFICATION

MEASUREMENTS (Both sexes)

Length	Wingspan	Weight
7.5–8.3 in	11.8–13.4 in	1.4–1.8 oz
19–21 cm	30–34 cm	40–50 g

SIZE & SHAPE. The Wood Thrush's plump body, medium-length tail, straight bill, big head, and upright posture give it the profile of a scaled-down American Robin.

COLOR PATTERN. Wood Thrushes are warm reddish-brown above and white with bold black spots on their underparts. Juveniles show a somewhat muted version of the same pattern. All have a bold, white eyering.

BEHAVIOR. The reclusive Wood Thrush hops through leaf litter on the forest floor, probing for insects and then bobbing upright again. The male's clear, flutelike song echoes through the forest in spring and early summer. Both sexes make distinctive, machine-gun-like alarm notes.

Cool Facts

The Wood Thrush is a consummate songster. Its syrinx, or voice box, allows it to sing two separate notes or melodies at the same time. The bird's beautiful song actually harmonizes with itself.

Find This Bird

Wood Thrushes are good at staying hidden, but they are very vocal. Learn their flutelike song or rapid call note to key in on where they are.

The quintessential early bird, American Robins are common sights on lawns across North America, where you often see them tugging earthworms out of the ground. Robins are popular birds for their warm orange breast, cheery song, and early appearance at the end of winter. Though they're familiar town and city birds, American Robins are at home in wilder areas, too, including mountain forests and Alaskan wilderness.

AT A GLANCE

Food

American Robins eat worms, snails, and other invertebrates, as well as fruit and berries. One study suggested that robins may try to round out their diet by selectively eating fruits that have bugs in them.

Nesting

Robins build their sturdy grass-and-mud nests on thick branches, horizontal structures on buildings, or the ground. The finished nest is 6–8 inches across and 3–6 inches high. They usually choose an evergreen rather than a deciduous tree for the first nest of spring.

Habitat

American Robins are common across the continent in gardens, parks, yards, golf courses, fields, pastures, and tundra, as well as deciduous woodlands, pine forests, shrublands, and forests regenerating after fires or logging.

RANGE MAP

- Breeding
- Year-round
- Winter

KEYS TO IDENTIFICATION

MALE

MEASUREMENTS (Both sexes)

Length	Wingspan	Weight
7.9–11 in	12.2–15.7 in	2.7–3 oz
20–28 cm	31–40 cm	77–85 g

SIZE & SHAPE. American Robins are the largest North American thrush, with a large, plump body, long legs, and fairly long tail. Their profile offers a good chance to learn the basic shape of most thrushes, and they make a good reference point for comparing the size and shape of other birds, too.

COLOR PATTERN. American Robins are gray-brown birds with warm-orange underparts and dark heads. In flight, a white patch on the lower belly and under the tail can be conspicuous. Compared with males, females have paler heads that contrast less with the gray back.

BEHAVIOR. American Robins are industrious birds that run or hop across lawns or stand erect, beak tilted upward, to survey their environs. When alighting they habitually flick their tails downward several times. In fall and winter they form large flocks and gather in trees to roost or eat berries.

Cool Facts

Winter robin roosts can sometimes number a quarter-million birds. In summer, adult females sleep at or near the nest; adult males and fledged young gather at roosts to sleep.

Backyard Tips

Robins visit fruit trees and lawns much more than feeders. Pesticides kill the invertebrates they eat and can be toxic to the birds. Robins often use nest platforms on houses and often visit birdbaths.

GRAY CATBIRD *(Dumetella carolinensis)*

If you think you'll never be able to learn bird calls, start with the Gray Catbird. Its catlike *mew* is easy to recognize. Follow the sound into a thicket or vine tangle and you may see an elegant gray bird with a black cap and bright rusty feathers under the tail. The catbird, related to the mockingbird, shares its vocal abilities, copying the sounds of other species and stringing them together to make its own song, punctuated with that distinctive *mew*.

AT A GLANCE

Food

In early summer, Gray Catbirds eat mostly insects such as beetles, grasshoppers, midges, caterpillars, and moths. When fruits are available they eat holly berries, cherries, elderberries, poison ivy, greenbrier, bay, blackberries, and many domestic fruits.

Nesting

Catbirds nest on horizontal branches hidden in the middle of dense shrubs, small trees, or vines. Nests may be on the ground or up to 60 feet high. The nest is a bulky, open cup made of twigs, straw, bark, mud, etc., with a finely woven inner lining of grass, hair, rootlets, and pine needles.

Habitat

Look for Gray Catbirds in dense tangles of shrubs, small trees, and vines, along forest edges, streamside thickets, old fields, and fence rows. They are often found in backyards that have planted shrubs or tangled thickets.

RANGE MAP

- Breeding
- Nonbreeding
- Year-round

KEYS TO IDENTIFICATION

MEASUREMENTS (Both sexes)

Length	Wingspan	Weight
8.3–9.4 in	8.7–11.8 in	0.8–2 oz
21–24 cm	22–30 cm	23.2–56.5 g

SIZE & SHAPE. The Gray Catbird is a medium-sized, slender songbird with a long, round-tipped black tail and a narrow, straight bill. Catbirds are fairly long legged and have broad, rounded wings.

COLOR PATTERN. Catbirds give the impression of being entirely slaty gray. Looking closer, you may see the small black cap, blackish tail, and rich rufous-brown patch under the tail.

BEHAVIOR. Catbirds are secretive but energetic, hopping and fluttering from branch to branch through tangles of vegetation. Singing males sit atop shrubs and small trees. They are usually reluctant to fly across open areas, preferring quick, low flights over vegetation.

Cool Facts

The Gray Catbird's song may last for 10 minutes. The male sings a loud song to proclaim his territory, and a softer version near the nest. The female may sing the quiet song back to him.

Backyard Tips

Planting dense native shrubs and native fruit-bearing trees such as dogwood, winterberry, and serviceberry can attract catbirds. They sometimes visit feeders for grape jelly.

BROWN THRASHER (*Toxostoma rufum*)

CATBIRDS · THRASHERS · MOCKINGBIRDS

It can be tricky to see a Brown Thrasher in a tangled mass of shrubbery, but once you do you may wonder how such a boldly patterned, gangly bird could stay so hidden. Brown Thrashers wear a somewhat severe expression thanks to their heavy, slightly curved bill and staring yellow eyes. They are the only thrasher species east of Texas. Brown Thrashers are exuberant singers, with one of the largest repertoires of any North American songbird.

AT A GLANCE

Food Brown Thrashers eat insects and other arthropods, fruits, seeds, and nuts. They sweep their bills through leaf litter and soil with quick, sideways motions. They also forage in trees and bushes, and catch some insects in the air.

Nesting Brown Thrashers usually nest low in a tree or thorny shrub, or sometimes on the ground. The nest is a bulky cup made of twigs, dead leaves, thin bark, grass stems, and well-cleaned rootlets. The inner cup is about 2 inches deep and 3.5 inches across..

Habitat Scrubby fields, dense regenerating woods, and forest edges are the primary habitats of Brown Thrashers. They rarely venture far from thick undergrowth into which they can easily retreat.

RANGE MAP

- Breeding
- Breeding (scarce)
- Winter
- Year-round

KEYS TO IDENTIFICATION

MEASUREMENTS (Both sexes)

Length	Wingspan	Weight
9.1–11.8 in	11.4–12.6 in	2.2–3.1 oz
23–30 cm	29–32 cm	61–89 g

SIZE & SHAPE. Brown Thrashers are fairly large, slender songbirds with long proportions. The legs are long and sturdy, the bill long and slightly downcurved. The long tail is often cocked upward.

COLOR PATTERN. Brown Thrashers are foxy brown birds with heavy, dark streaking on their whitish underparts. The face is gray-brown and the wings show two black-and-white wingbars. They have bright-yellow eyes.

BEHAVIOR. Brown Thrashers skulk in shrubby tangles or on the ground below dense cover, but often sing from treetops. The song is a string of musical phrases, many copied from other birds' songs, each phrase usually sung twice. They also make a harsh *tsuck* note.

Cool Facts

Brown Thrashers are prolific singers and mimics. In 1981, a Brown Thrasher featured in *Ripley's Believe It or Not!* was credited with having a repertoire of 2,400 distinctly different songs.

Backyard Tips

Brown Thrashers may come to feeders on or near the ground with dense cover close by. You can also attract them by planting shrubs that produce berries.

NORTHERN MOCKINGBIRD *(Mimus polyglottos)*

If you've been hearing an endless string of 10 or 15 different birds singing in your yard, it might have been just one Northern Mockingbird. This gray bird apparently pours all its color into its songs, sometimes singing all night long. By day it harasses birds, cats, and other intruders in its territory, flying slowly around them or prancing toward them, legs extended, flaunting the white patches in its wings.

AT A GLANCE

Food
Northern Mockingbirds eat mainly small animal prey such as beetles, earthworms, moths, and grasshoppers in summer. They switch to mostly fruit and berries in fall and winter.

Nesting
Northern Mockingbirds nest in shrubs and trees, usually 3–10 feet up but sometimes as high as 60 feet. The nest is made of dead twigs shaped into an open cup, lined with grasses, rootlets, leaves, and sometimes shreds of trash.

Habitat
Year-round the Northern Mockingbird is found in parkland, cultivated land, suburban areas, and regenerating habitat at low elevations. It prefers grassy areas rather than bare spots for foraging.

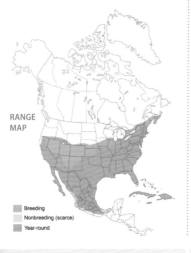

RANGE MAP

■ Breeding
□ Nonbreeding (scarce)
■ Year-round

KEYS TO IDENTIFICATION

MEASUREMENTS (Both sexes)

Length	Wingspan	Weight
8.3–10.2 in	12.2–13.8 in	1.6–2 oz
21–26 cm	31–35 cm	45–58 g

SIZE & SHAPE. The Northern Mockingbird is a medium-sized songbird, a bit more slender than a thrush and with a longer tail. It has a small head, long, thin bill with a hint of a downward curve, and long legs. The wings are short, rounded, and broad, making the tail seem particularly long in flight.

COLOR PATTERN. The Northern Mockingbird is overall gray-brown, paler on the breast and belly, with two white wingbars on each wing. A white patch in each wing is often visible when the bird is perched, and in flight these become large white flashes. The white outer tail feathers are also flashy in flight.

BEHAVIOR. The Northern Mockingbird usually sits conspicuously on high vegetation, fences, eaves, or telephone wires, or runs and hops along the ground. Found alone or in pairs throughout the year, it aggressively chases off intruders on its territory.

Cool Facts

People once kept mockingbirds as pets, endangering some populations. In New York in 1828, good singers could cost $50. President Jefferson had a pet mocker in the White House.

Backyard Tips

Northern Mockingbirds are common in backyards, but don't often visit feeders. They're attracted to open lawns with fruiting trees and brambles.

EUROPEAN STARLING *(Sturnus vulgaris)*

First brought to North America by Shakespeare enthusiasts in the nineteenth century, European Starlings are now among the continent's most numerous songbirds. These stocky brown birds with triangular wings are sometimes disliked for their abundance and aggressiveness. For much of the year, they wheel through the sky and mob lawns in big, noisy flocks. They're excellent mimics and are related to mynas.

AT A GLANCE

Food

Starlings are omnivores but focus on small invertebrates such as grasshoppers, beetles, caterpillars, snails, earthworms, millipedes, and spiders. They also eat fruits and berries, seeds, nectar, livestock feed, and garbage.

Nesting

Starlings nest in cavities, nest boxes, and nooks and crannies of human-made structures including streetlights and traffic-signal supports. The male fills the cavity with grass, pine needles, feathers, trash, cloth, and string. The nest cup is lined with soft material.

Habitat

Starlings are common in towns, suburbs, farms, and countryside near human settlements. They feed on the ground on lawns, fields, sidewalks, and parking lots. They perch and roost high on wires, trees, and buildings.

RANGE MAP

Nonbreeding
Year-round

KEYS TO IDENTIFICATION

MEASUREMENTS (Both sexes)

Length	Wingspan	Weight
7.9–9.1 in	12.2–15.7 in	2.1–3.4 oz
20–23 cm	31–40 cm	60–96 g

SIZE & SHAPE. Starlings are chunky and blackbird-sized, but with short tails and long, slender bills. In flight their wings are short and pointed, creating the starlike silhouette that gives them their name.

COLOR PATTERN. At a distance, starlings look black. In summer they are an iridescent purplish-green with a yellow beak; in fresh winter plumage they are brown, covered in bright white spots.

BEHAVIOR. Starlings are boisterous and loud, and they travel in large groups, sometimes with blackbirds. They shuffle across fields with beak down, probing the grass for food; or they sit high on wires or trees making a constant stream of rattles, whirs, and whistles.

Cool Facts

Every European Starling in North America is descended from 100 birds released in New York in the early 1890s. Genetically, those in Virginia are almost identical to those in California.

Backyard Tips

Starlings often come to bird feeders and nest in nest boxes—often driving away native species in the process. See *nestwatch.org/birdhouses* for ways to help with this problem.

CEDAR WAXWING (Bombycilla cedrorun

Cedar Waxwings have plumage so silky it hardly looks real. Sociable year-round, waxwings are rarely seen alone. In spring and summer, flocks are small, but several pairs may nest in a small stand of trees, seldom squabbling except when one steals another's nesting materials. In fall, they gather by the hundreds to eat berries or perch in dead trees, sallying out to capture flying insects. Winter flocks are mainly found in fruit trees.

AT A GLANCE

Food Cedar Waxwings feed on insects, many caught on the wing, but also eat fruit year-round, even feeding their nestlings more fruit than insects, unlike most songbirds. Cowbirds seldom survive in a waxwing nest because of the relatively low-protein diet.

Nesting Cedar Waxwings nest in the fork of a tree, anywhere from 3 to 50 feet up. The female weaves twigs, grasses, cattail down, etc., into a bulky cup about 5 inches across and 3 inches high, lined with fine fibers. She often takes these materials from other birds' nests.

Habitat Cedar Waxwings live in deciduous or coniferous woodlands, old fields, and sagebrush, especially near water. They're increasingly common in towns and suburbs, where ornamental fruit trees flourish.

RANGE MAP

▇ Breeding
▇ Nonbreeding
▇ Year-round

KEYS TO IDENTIFICATION

MEASUREMENTS (Both sexes)

Length	Wingspan	Weight
5.5–6.7 in	8.7–11.8 in	1.1 oz
14–17 cm	22–30 cm	32 g

SIZE & SHAPE. The Cedar Waxwing is a medium-sized, sleek bird with a large head, short neck, and short, wide bill. Waxwings have a crest that often lies flat and droops over the back of the head. The wings are broad and pointed, like a starling's. The tail is fairly short and square-tipped.

COLOR PATTERN. Cedar Waxwings are pale brown on the head and chest fading to soft gray on the wings. The belly is pale yellow, and the tail is gray with a bright-yellow tip. The face has a narrow black mask neatly outlined in white. The red waxy tips to the wing feathers are not always easy to see.

BEHAVIOR. Cedar Waxwings are social birds that associate in flocks year-round. They sit in fruiting trees swallowing berries whole, or pluck them from outer twigs with a brief fluttering hover. They also course over water for insects, flying like tubby, slightly clumsy swallows.

Cool Facts

The name "waxwing" comes from waxy red secretions found on the tips of the secondary feathers in the wings.

Backyard Tips

Cedar Waxwings feed primarily on fruit. To attract them to your yard, plant native trees and shrubs that bear small fruits, such as dogwood, serviceberry, cedar, juniper, and others.

The Ovenbird's rapid-fire *teacher-teacher-teacher* song rings out in summer hardwood forests from the Mid-Atlantic states to northeastern British Columbia. It's very loud for such an inconspicuous warbler. It struts like a tiny chicken across the dim forest floor, gleaning invertebrates from the leaf litter. Its nest, a leaf-covered dome resembling an old-fashioned outdoor oven, gives the Ovenbird its name.

AT A GLANCE

Food

Ovenbirds eat mainly forest insects and other invertebrates found in leaf litter, leaves, and bark. They also take advantage of temporary food sources, such as an outbreak of spruce budworms. In winter they also eat seeds.

Nesting

The Ovenbird's domed nest, of dead leaves, grasses, stems, etc., is set in thick leaf litter on the open forest floor 60 or more feet from the forest edge. The side entrance is hidden from above and faces downhill if the nest is built on a slope. The inner cup is 3 inches across and 2 inches deep.

Habitat

Ovenbirds breed in closed-canopy deciduous and mixed deciduous-coniferous woods. Look for them in most forest types, from rich oak or maple woods to dry pine forest, although they avoid wet or swampy areas.

RANGE MAP

- Breeding
- Migration
- Nonbreeding

KEYS TO IDENTIFICATION

MEASUREMENTS (Both sexes)

Length	Wingspan	Weight
4.3–5.5 in	7.5–10.2 in	0.6–1 oz
11–14 cm	19–26 cm	16–28 g

SIZE & SHAPE. The Ovenbird is a chunky, larger-than-average warbler, smaller than a Song Sparrow, with a round head and fairly thick bill. It often cocks its jaunty tail upward.

COLOR PATTERN. Ovenbirds are olive-green above and spotted below, with bold black-and-orange crown stripes. A white eyering gives them a somewhat surprised expression. Like several other terrestrial or near-terrestrial warblers, Ovenbirds have pink legs.

BEHAVIOR. Ovenbirds spend much of their time foraging on the ground, walking with a herky-jerky, wandering stroll unlike most songbirds. Males sing from tree branches, occasionally high up. They frequently sing even in the heat of midafternoon.

Cool Facts

Robert Frost paid tribute to this bird's high-volume song in a poem: "There is a singer everyone has heard, / Loud, a mid-summer and a mid-wood bird, / Who makes the solid tree trunks sound again."

Find This Bird

Ovenbirds sing loudly and often, so listen for their high-volume *tea-cher, tea-cher, tea-cher* song in rich woods. Then look on the forest floor or low in the understory for these small, streaky warblers.

BLACK-AND-WHITE WARBLER (Mniotilta vari...

The Black-and-white Warbler's thin, squeaky song is one of the first signs that spring birding has sprung. This crisply striped bundle of black and white feathers creeps along tree trunks and branches like a nimble nuthatch, probing the bark for insects with its slightly curved bill. Though usually seen in trees, they build their little cup-shaped nests on the forest floor amid the leaf litter.

AT A GLANCE

Food

Black-and-white Warblers eat mostly insects and other small arthropods, especially caterpillars but also ants, flies, spiders, beetles, and leafhoppers. They sometimes visit sap wells made by Yellow-bellied Sapsuckers to eat insects caught in the sticky flow.

Nesting

Black-and-white Warbler nests are usually hidden on the ground at the base of a tree, rock, stump, or fallen log. The round, cup-shaped nest is made from dry leaves, bark strips, grass, and pine needles and lined with moss, animal hair, and dried grasses.

Habitat

Black-and-white Warblers breed in deciduous and mixed forest, usually with trees of mixed ages. During migration, look for them in any forest or woodlot. They winter in forests and forest edges in Florida, the Caribbean, and Central America.

RANGE MAP

- Breeding
- Migration
- Nonbreeding

KEYS TO IDENTIFICATION

MALE

MEASUREMENTS (Both sexes)

Length	Wingspan	Weight
4.3–5.1 in	7.1–8.7 in	0.3–0.5 oz
11–13 cm	18–22 cm	8–15 g

SIZE & SHAPE. Black-and-white Warblers are medium-sized warblers (small songbirds). They have a fairly long, slightly downcurved bill. The head often appears somewhat flat and streamlined, with a short neck. The wings are long and the tail is short.

COLOR PATTERN. These birds are entirely black and white. Their black wings are highlighted by two wide, white wingbars. Adult males have more obvious black streaking on the underparts and cheek. Females (especially immatures) have less streaking and usually a wash of buff on the flanks. The undertail coverts have distinctive large black spots.

BEHAVIOR. Black-and-white Warblers act more like nuthatches than warblers, foraging for hidden insects in the bark of trees by creeping up, down, and around branches and trunks.

Cool Facts

Black-and-white Warblers have an extra-long hind claw and heavier legs than other warblers, which help them hold onto and move around on bark.

Find This Bird

Black-and-white Warblers are among the earliest warblers to return in spring—they're often around before trees have leafed out, making them easier to spot as they work trunks and main branches.

COMMON YELLOWTHROAT *(Geothlypis trichas)*

A broad black mask lends a touch of highwayman's mystique to the male Common Yellowthroat. The female lacks the mask and is much browner, though it usually shows a hint of warm yellow at the throat. One of our most numerous warblers, the yellowthroat skulks through tangled vegetation, often at the edges of marshes and wetlands. Both the *witchety-witchety-witchety* songs and distinctive call notes help reveal its presence.

AT A GLANCE

Food Common Yellowthroats forage on or near the ground, eating insects and spiders in low vegetation, sometimes sallying out from a perch to catch prey. They also eat grit, which helps them digest food and may also add minerals to their diet.

Nesting The well-concealed, bulky nest is usually set on or near the ground and supported by sedges, cattails, or other low plants. Nests in marshes are usually higher off the ground, to be safer from flooding. Some nests are roofed, like the nest of an Ovenbird.

Habitat Yellowthroats live in open areas with thick, low vegetation, ranging from marsh to grassland to open pine forest. During migration, they use an even broader suite of habitats including backyards and forests.

RANGE MAP

- Breeding
- Breeding (scarce)
- Migration
- Nonbreeding
- Year-round

KEYS TO IDENTIFICATION

MALE

MEASUREMENTS (Both sexes)

Length	Wingspan	Weight
4.3–5.1 in	5.9–7.5 in	0.3–0.4 oz
11–13 cm	15–19 cm	9–10 g

SIZE & SHAPE. Common Yellowthroats are small songbirds with chunky, rounded heads and medium-length, slightly rounded tails.

COLOR PATTERN. Adult males are bright yellow below, with a sharp black mask and olive upperparts. Immature males show traces of the mask. Females are olive-brown, usually with yellow brightening the throat and under the tail. They lack the black mask.

BEHAVIOR. Common Yellowthroats skulk low to the ground in dense thickets and fields, searching for small insects and spiders. Males sing a rolling *wichety-wichety-wichety* song, and both sexes give a full-sounding *chuck* note. During migration, this is often the most common warbler found in fields and edges.

Cool Facts

The Common Yellowthroat was one of the first bird species to be catalogued from the New World, when a specimen from Maryland was described by Linnaeus in 1766.

Find This Bird

Look for yellowthroats in reeds, rushes, brambles, and shrubs around wet areas. Though they live deep in tangles, they are inquisitive and often pop up to take a look if you pish or squeak at them.

AMERICAN REDSTART *(Setophaga ruticilla)*

A lively warbler that hops among tree branches in search of insects, the male American Redstart is coal-black with vivid orange patches on the sides, wings, and tail. It seems to startle its prey out of the foliage by flashing its strikingly patterned tail and wing feathers. Females and immature males have more subdued yellow flashes on a gray background. These sweet-singing warblers nest in open woodlands across much of North America.

AT A GLANCE

Food American Redstarts eat mostly insects. In late summer they also eat small berries and fruits. They forage everywhere between the ground and the top of the canopy. They take more flying prey than most warbler species, competing with flycatchers for prey.

Nesting The nest is supported by the main trunk of a tree or shrub and some vertical stems, and is well camouflaged by foliage. It is a tightly woven cup of small fibers such as birch-bark strips, milkweed seed hairs, and feathers, measuring 2–3 inches across and 2–3 inches high with a smaller inner cup.

Habitat American Redstarts breed in open deciduous woods. In migration, the species can be found in nearly any habitats with trees. Their tropical winter habitat is in woodlands and open forest at lower and middle elevations.

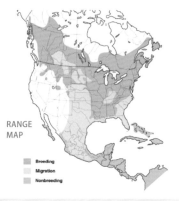

RANGE MAP

- Breeding
- Migration
- Nonbreeding

KEYS TO IDENTIFICATION

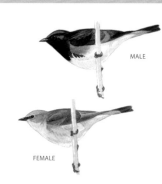

MALE

FEMALE

MEASUREMENTS (Both sexes)

Length	Wingspan	Weight
4.3–5.1 in	6.3–7.5 in	0.2–0.3 oz
11–13 cm	16–19 cm	6–9 g

SIZE & SHAPE. This medium-sized warbler has a relatively wide, flat bill and fairly long, expressive tail. In flight it has a deep chest, slim belly, and long, somewhat club-shaped tail.

COLOR PATTERN. Adult male American Redstarts are mostly black with bright orange patches on the sides, wings, and tail. The belly is white. Females and immature males replace the orange with yellow or yellow-orange. They have a gray head and underparts, with an olive back and wings and a dark gray tail.

BEHAVIOR. American Redstarts are active insectivores that seem never to stand still. They rapidly spread their cocked tails, exposing the orange or yellow in quick flashes. This often startles insect prey into flushing, whereupon the redstart darts after it, attempting to catch it in the air.

Cool Facts

Yearling males look like females but act like adult males, singing vigorously to defend a territory and attract a mate. Few succeed until they are in the full black-and-orange plumage of an adult male.

Find This Bird

Redstarts nest in open woods, so they may show up in yards or parks that include small patches of trees, even if you don't have true forest. In late summer they may come to berry bushes.

YELLOW WARBLER *(Setophaga petechia)*

North America has more than 50 species of warblers, but few combine brilliant color and easy viewing quite like the Yellow Warbler. In summer, males sing their sweet whistled song from willows, wet thickets, and roadsides across almost all of North America. The females and immatures aren't as bright, and lack the male's rich chestnut streaking, but their overall warm yellow tones, unmarked faces, and prominent black eyes help distinguish them.

AT A GLANCE

Food
Yellow Warblers eat mostly insects that they pick from foliage or capture on short flights. Typical prey include midges, caterpillars, beetles, leafhoppers and other bugs, and wasps.

Nesting
Yellow Warblers nest in the vertical fork of a bush or small tree, often within about 10 feet of the ground. The female builds a cup of grasses, bark strips, etc. She places plant fibers, spiderwebs, and plant down around the outside, and lines the inner cup with fine soft fibers.

Habitat
Yellow Warblers breed in shrubby thickets and woods, especially near water. Favorite trees include willows, alders, and cottonwoods. In winter they mainly occur in mangrove forests of Central and South America.

RANGE MAP

- ▉ Breeding
- ▉ Breeding (scarce)
- ▉ Migration
- ▉ Nonbreeding
- ▉ Year-round

KEYS TO IDENTIFICATION

BREEDING MALE

MEASUREMENTS (Both sexes)

Length	Wingspan	Weight
4.7–5.1 in	6.3–7.9 in	0.3–0.4 oz
12–13 cm	16–20 cm	9–11 g

SIZE & SHAPE. Yellow Warblers are small, evenly proportioned songbirds with medium-length tails and rounded heads. For a warbler, the straight, thin bill is relatively large.

COLOR PATTERN. Yellow Warblers are yellow from head to tail. Males are a bright, egg-yolk yellow with reddish streaks on the underparts. Both sexes flash yellow patches in the tail. The face is unmarked, accentuating the large black eye.

BEHAVIOR. Look for Yellow Warblers near the tops of tall shrubs and small trees. They forage restlessly, with quick hops along small branches and twigs to glean caterpillars and other insects. Males sing their sweet, whistled songs from high perches.

Cool Facts

Yellow Warblers have to watch out for strange eggs that appear in their nests, laid by Brown-headed Cowbirds. The warbler responds by building a new nest directly on top of the previous one.

Find This Bird

Yellow Warblers don't visit feeders. Keep an eye out for them in shrubs and trees along streams, where the males often sing a sweet, whistled song from outer branches.

PALM WARBLER *(Setophaga palmarum)*

Most warblers can test a viewer's patience by hiding behind leaves at the limits of vision—but the helpful Palm Warbler sticks closer to ground level and even wags its tail to make sure you notice it. It's a rusty-capped bird with bright lemon-yellow on the face and under the tail. It breeds in northern Canada, but large numbers sweep through eastern North America during migration, heading to Florida and the Caribbean for winter.

AT A GLANCE

Food Palm Warblers feed on open ground much more than other warblers, focusing almost entirely on insects such as grasshoppers, beetles, and caterpillars in summer. They add seeds and berries to the mix in fall and winter.

Nesting Palm Warblers build a cup-shaped nest of weed stalks, grass, sedges, bark shreds, rootlets, and ferns, lined with fine grasses, mosses, and occasionally hair and feathers. They place the nest in sphagnum moss at the base of a short tree.

Habitat The Palm Warbler breeds in bogs and boreal coniferous forest, usually near water. During migration and winter it uses woodlands, thickets, savannas, open fields, and mangroves.

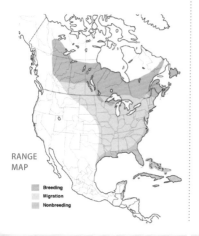
RANGE MAP
Breeding
Migration
Nonbreeding

KEYS TO IDENTIFICATION

BREEDING ADULT

MEASUREMENTS (Both sexes)

Length	Wingspan	Weight
4.7–5.5 in	7.9–8.3 in	0.2–0.5 oz
12–14 cm	20–21 cm	7–13 g

SIZE & SHAPE. This small songbird, an average-sized warbler, has a thin, straight bill and medium-length tail.

COLOR PATTERN. Palm Warblers are brownish above with a chestnut cap, yellow face, and bright yellow under the tail. The underside varies from bright yellow in birds from the Eastern population to a softer, duller yellowish in those from the Western population.

BEHAVIOR. Palm Warblers are most easily distinguished by the way they wag their tail up and down, drawing attention to the bright yellow feathers beneath the tail. They spend most of their time on the ground, and aren't particularly shy, so can be easy to see as they pass through on migration or in winter anywhere in Florida or along the Gulf Coast.

Cool Facts

Despite its tropical-sounding name, the Palm Warbler is one of the most northerly breeding warblers. It was named from a specimen found on the bird's wintering grounds in the Caribbean.

Find This Bird

Palm Warblers breed in forests of the far north, so most people see them on migration and in winter. Look for this warbler in open country or on low branches, and watch for its habit of wagging its tail.

A bird true to its name, the Pine Warbler is common in many eastern pine forests and is rarely seen away from pines. These yellowish warblers are hard to spot as they move along high branches to prod clumps of needles with their sturdy bills. If you don't see them, listen for their steady, musical trill, which sounds very much like a Chipping Sparrow or Dark-eyed Junco, which are also common piney-woods sounds through much of the year.

AT A GLANCE

KEYS TO IDENTIFICATION

Food

Pine Warblers eat mostly insects and spiders, but also fruits and seeds, especially during colder months. They move more slowly than most warblers, picking food from bark and needles. They sometimes catch insects in the air.

Nesting

Pine Warblers build their nests high in a pine, concealed among needles and cones. The female uses grass, twigs, and other plant fibers to construct the 1.5-inch-deep cup, bound together with spider or caterpillar silk and lined with feathers, hair, and plant down.

Habitat

Pine Warblers are well named—they spend most of their time in pine trees, in pine forests or in deciduous woods with pine mixed in. They live in similar habitats in winter, but also visit backyards and come to bird feeders to eat seeds and suet.

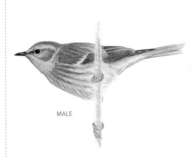

MALE

MEASUREMENTS (Both sexes)

Length	Wingspan	Weight
5.1–5.5 in	7.5–9.1 in	0.3–0.5 oz
13–14 cm	19–23 cm	9–15 g

SIZE & SHAPE. Pine Warblers are small songbirds but are hefty for a warbler, with long tails and stout bills. The tip of the tail usually appears to have a central notch.

COLOR PATTERN. Pine Warblers are yellowish—brightest in adult males—with an olive back, whitish belly, and two prominent white wingbars on gray wings. The pale eyerings connect in front of the eye.

BEHAVIOR. Pine Warblers are usually hard to see high in pines, where they feed on insects and pine seeds. They also eat fruits and seeds, especially during migration and winter, when they sometimes visit feeders. Males sing their even, rich trill from the tops of pines.

RANGE MAP

- Breeding
- Migration
- Nonbreeding
- Year-round

Cool Facts

The Pine Warbler is the only warbler that eats large quantities of seeds—primarily pine seeds pulled out of cones. This ability to go vegetarian may be one reason why they don't leave the U.S. in winter.

Backyard Tips

The only warbler that regularly eats seeds and suet, the Pine Warbler sometimes visits feeders in winter. Planting native berry bushes and vines may also attract them.

YELLOW-RUMPED WARBLER *(Setophaga coronata)*

Scads of these abundant warblers flood the continent each fall. Shrubs and trees fill with the streaky birds giving their distinctive, sharp chips. Their colors are subdued all winter, but spring molt brings a transformation, leaving them a dazzling mix of bright yellow, charcoal gray and black, and bold white. The "Audubon's" form of this species is common in the West and has a yellow throat. In the East look for the white throat of the "myrtle" form.

AT A GLANCE

Food
In summer, Yellow-rumped Warblers eat mainly insects, including spruce budworm. On migration and in winter they eat secretions from scale insects, fruits such as bayberry, wax myrtle, juniper berries, and poison ivy, and some wild seeds. They sometimes visit feeders.

Nesting
Yellow-rumped Warblers nest on horizontal branches of conifers. The nest is a cup of twigs, pine needles, etc., sometimes with moose, horse, or deer hair, moss, and lichens, lined with feathers that may curl up and over the eggs.

Habitat
In summer, Yellow-rumped Warblers live in open coniferous forests and edges, and to a lesser extent in deciduous forests. In fall and winter they move to open woods and shrubby habitats, including coastal vegetation, parks, and residential areas.

RANGE MAP

- Breeding
- Migration
- Winter
- Winter (scarce)
- Year-round

KEYS TO IDENTIFICATION

BREEDING MALE (MYRTLE)

FEMALE (AUDUBON'S)

BREEDING MALE (AUDUBON'S)

MEASUREMENTS (Both sexes)

Length	Wingspan	Weight
4.7–5.5 in	7.5–9.1 in	0.4–0.5 oz
12–14 cm	19–23 cm	12–13 g

SIZE & SHAPE. The Yellow-rumped Warbler is a small songbird, fairly large and full bodied for a warbler, with a large head, sturdy but slender bill, and fairly long, narrow tail.

COLOR PATTERN. In summer, both sexes are a smart gray or black with yellow on the crown, sides, and rump. Males are bright; females are duller and may show some brown. Winter birds are paler brown and streaky, with bright yellow rumps and usually some yellow on the sides.

BEHAVIOR. Yellow-rumped Warblers forage in the outer tree branches at middle heights. They're active, often sallying out to catch insects in midair, sometimes on long flights. In winter they spend lots of time eating berries from shrubs, and they often travel in large flocks.

Cool Facts

Yellow-rumped Warblers can digest the waxes found in bayberries and wax myrtles, so they can winter farther north than other warblers. They're also the most versatile at catching insects.

Backyard Tips

During migration and winter, Yellow-rumped Warblers sometimes come to bird feeders for suet and peanut butter. They and other warblers are very vulnerable to window collisions.

EASTERN TOWHEE *(Pipilo erythrophthalmus)*

A strikingly marked, oversized sparrow of the East, feathered in bold black and warm reddish-browns—if you can get a clear look at it. Eastern Towhees are birds of the undergrowth, where their rummaging makes far more noise than you would expect for their size. Their *chewink* calls let you know how common they are, but many sightings are mere glimpses through tangles of little stems.

AT A GLANCE

Food — Towhees eat many foods: seeds, fruits, insects, spiders, millipedes, centipedes, and snails, as well as soft leaf and flower buds in spring. Common plant foods include ragweed, smartweed, grasses, acorns, blackberries, blueberries, wheat, corn, and oats.

Nesting — Eastern Towhees usually nest on the ground, with the nest cup sunk into the fallen leaves up to the level of the rim. They sometimes build their nests in shrubs or grape, honeysuckle, or greenbrier tangles, up to about 4 feet off the ground.

Habitat — Eastern Towhees are characteristic birds of forest edges, overgrown fields, woodlands, and scrubby backyards or thickets. The most important habitat qualities seem to be dense shrub cover with plenty of leaf litter for the towhees to scratch around in.

RANGE MAP

- ▇ Breeding
- ▇ Migration
- ▇ Nonbreeding
- ▇ Nonbreeding (scarce)
- ▇ Year-round

KEYS TO IDENTIFICATION

MALE

MEASUREMENTS (Both sexes)

Length	Wingspan	Weight
6.8–8.2 in 17.3–20.8 cm	7.9–11 in 20–28 cm	1.1–1.8 oz 32–52 g

SIZE & SHAPE. Towhees are a kind of large sparrow. Look for their thick, triangular, seed-cracking bill as a tip-off they're in the sparrow family. Also notice the chunky body and long, rounded tail.

COLOR PATTERN. Males are striking: bold sooty black above and on the breast, with warm rufous sides and white on the belly. Females have the same pattern, but are rich brown where the males are black.

BEHAVIOR. Eastern Towhees spend most of their time on the ground, scratching at leaves using both feet at the same time, in a kind of backwards hop. They spend lots of time concealed beneath thick underbrush. You may see this bird more often when it climbs into shrubs and low trees to sing.

Cool Facts

Older bird watchers may remember the "Rufous-sided Towhee"—that's the old name for this species and the closely related Spotted Towhee of the West.

Backyard Tips

Eastern Towhees are likely to visit–or perhaps live in–your yard if you've got brushy, shrubby, or overgrown borders.

AMERICAN TREE SPARROW (Spizelloides arborea)

American Tree Sparrows are busy visitors in winter backyards and weedy, snow-covered fields across southern Canada and the northern United States. Hopping up at bent weeds or even beating their wings to dislodge seeds from grass heads, they scratch and peck the ground in small flocks, trading soft, musical twitters. Come snowmelt, these small sparrows begin their long migrations to breeding grounds in the tundra of the far North.

AT A GLANCE

Food American Tree Sparrows eat seeds, berries, and insects. The relative proportions of these foods in their diet change radically from winter to summer months.

Nesting American Tree Sparrows nest on or near the ground, often in a tussock of grass at the base of a shrub, occasionally as high as about 4 feet on a limb of a willow or spruce. In open tundra with no trees in sight, the nest may sit on a mossy hummock.

Habitat Look for small flocks of American Tree Sparrows in winter in weedy fields with hedgerows or shrubs, along forest edges, or near marshes. They readily visit backyards, especially if there's a seed feeder. American Tree Sparrows breed in the far north and are rarely seen south of northern Canada in summer.

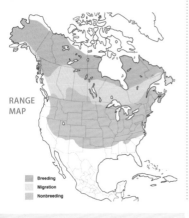

RANGE MAP

- Breeding
- Migration
- Nonbreeding

KEYS TO IDENTIFICATION

MEASUREMENTS (Both sexes)

Length	Wingspan	Weight
5.5 in	9.4 in	0.5–1 oz
14 cm	24 cm	13–28 g

SIZE & SHAPE. American Tree Sparrows are small, round-headed birds that often fluff out their feathers, making their plump bodies look even chubbier. Among sparrows, they have fairly small bills and long, thin tails.

COLOR PATTERN. American Tree Sparrows are reddish-brown and gray birds. They have rusty caps and rusty (not black) eyelines on a gray head, with a smooth gray to buff breast. A dark smudge in the center of the unstreaked breast is common.

BEHAVIOR. Small flocks of American Tree Sparrows hop about on the ground, scrabbling for grass and weed seeds, calling back and forth with a soft, musical twitter. Individuals may perch in the open on goldenrod stalks or shrubs, or on low tree branches.

Cool Facts

American Tree Sparrows need to consume about 30% of their body weight in food and a similar amount in water each day to survive.

Backyard Tips

If you live in northern North America, you may have American Tree Sparrows at your feeders all winter, only to be replaced by the similar Chipping Sparrow when spring and summer come around.

CHIPPING SPARROW *(Spizella passerina)*

This is a crisp, pretty sparrow whose bright reddish cap and black eyeline provide a splash of color and make adults fairly easy to identify. Chipping Sparrows are common across North America wherever trees are interspersed with grassy openings. Their loud, trilling songs are one of the most common sounds of spring woodlands and suburbs.

AT A GLANCE

Food Chipping Sparrows eat seeds of a great variety of grasses and herbs. During the breeding season they also hunt for protein-rich insects, and these form a large part of their summer diet. Sometimes they eat small fruits such as cherries.

Nesting Females typically build their nests between 3 and 10 feet off the ground, hidden in foliage at the tip of a branch. They gravitate toward evergreen trees, but also nest in crabapples, honeysuckle tangles, ornamental shrubs, and other deciduous species. Females can be finicky about placement, often beginning to build a nest, then leaving to begin in another spot.

Habitat Look for Chipping Sparrows in open woodlands and forests with grassy clearings across North America, all the way up to the highest elevations. You'll also see them in parks, along roadsides, and in your backyard, particularly if you have feeders and trees.

RANGE MAP

- Breeding
- Migration
- Nonbreeding
- Year-round

KEYS TO IDENTIFICATION

BREEDING

NONBREEDING

MEASUREMENTS (Both sexes)

Length	Wingspan	Weight
4.7–5.9 in	8.3 in	0.4–0.6 oz
12–15 cm	21 cm	11–16 g

SIZE & SHAPE. The Chipping Sparrow is a slender, fairly long-tailed sparrow with a medium-sized bill that is a bit small compared to those of other sparrows.

COLOR PATTERN. Summer Chipping Sparrows look clean and crisp, with frosty underparts, pale face, and black line through the eye, topped off with a bright rusty crown. In winter, Chipping Sparrows are subdued, buff brown, with darkly streaked upperparts. The black line through the eye is still visible, and the cap is a warm but more subdued reddish brown.

BEHAVIOR. Chipping Sparrows feed on the ground, take cover in shrubs, and sing from the tops of small trees (often evergreens). You'll often see loose groups of them flitting up from open ground. When singing, they cling to high outer limbs.

Cool Facts

A naturalist in 1929 memorably described the Chipping Sparrow as "the little brown-capped pensioner of the dooryard and lawn."

Backyard Tips

Chipping Sparrows will eat many kinds of birdseed, particularly black oil sunflower seeds from feeders, but also seed mixes scattered on the ground.

FIELD SPARROW *(Spizella pusilla)*

The clear, "bouncing-ball" trill of the Field Sparrow is a familiar summer sound in brushy fields and roadsides of the East and Midwest. The singer is a small, warm-toned sparrow with a rusty cap. Though still common, Field Sparrows have declined sharply in the last half-century, partly because of the expansion of suburbs. Populations in the prairies have remained strong thanks in part to measures such as the Conservation Reserve Program.

AT A GLANCE

Food Field sparrows eat mainly grass seeds in winter, adding insect prey as the weather warms. Their small bill limits them to small seeds. Insects, spiders, and snails make up about half the summer diet. Parents feed nestlings a high-protein diet of spiders and insects.

Nesting Nests are built on or near the ground in a clump of grass or at the base of a shrub, away from human habitation. Within a framework of crisscrossed grass stems, the open cup is made of coarse and fine grasses lined with grass, rootlets, and hair, 3.3–8.3 inches across and 1.9–4.3 inches high.

Habitat Field Sparrows are so-called "old-field" specialists; look for them in areas of tall grass and brush that are growing up into small trees and shrubs, especially near thorny shrubs such as roses and briars.

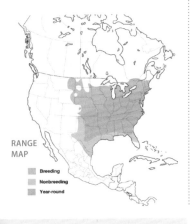

RANGE MAP

- Breeding
- Nonbreeding
- Year-round

KEYS TO IDENTIFICATION

MEASUREMENTS (Both sexes)

Length	Wingspan	Weight
4.7–5.9 in	7.9 in	0.4–0.5 oz
12–15 cm	20 cm	11–15 g

SIZE & SHAPE. Field Sparrows are small, slender sparrows with relatively short, conical bills, rounded heads, and somewhat long tails.

COLOR PATTERN. These are warm-colored birds with a distinct white eyering, a pink bill, and pale grayish underparts with buff-orange highlights. The head is pale gray with a bright rufous crown and a wide rufous line behind the eye. The whitish throat is bordered by soft brown throat stripes. The back is brown with black streaks, contrasting with the gray rump and tail. The wings have two weak wingbars.

BEHAVIOR. Field Sparrows can be easily overlooked except for the distinctive song of breeding males. On spring and summer mornings they sing this sweet, accelerating song from exposed perches. Individuals and small flocks quietly feed on weed and grass seeds on or near the ground, flushing into shrubby cover when disturbed.

Cool Facts

Male Field Sparrows usually return to breed in the same territory each year. Females are less likely to return to the same territory, and young ones only rarely return to where they hatched.

Backyard Tips

Field Sparrows usually avoid human habitation but do often visit feeders near fields, especially for millet and black oil sunflower seed. Delaying mowing old fields until late July helps them.

SAVANNAH SPARROW *(Passerculus sandwichensis)*

Some streaky brown birds are easier to identify than others. Savannah Sparrows are understated but distinctive, with a short tail, small head, and telltale yellow spot before the eye. They're one of the most abundant songbirds in North American grasslands and fields, despite sometimes being overlooked. In summer, their soft but distinctive insectlike song drifts lazily over farm fields and grasslands.

AT A GLANCE

Food During the breeding season, these sparrows eat mostly insects and spiders, foraging on the ground and hopping onto weeds to devour foods such as spittlebug nymphs. In winter they eat seeds. In coastal areas, they take tiny crustaceans.

Nesting Savannah Sparrows hide their nests in a thatch of dead grasses on or near the ground. The nest exterior is about 3 inches across and made of coarse grasses. Inside is a finely woven, tiny cup of thin grass about 2 inches across and 1 inch deep.

Habitat Savannah Sparrows breed on tundra, grasslands, marshes, and farmland. On their winter range, they stick to the ground or in low vegetation in open areas; look for them along the edges of roads adjacent to farms.

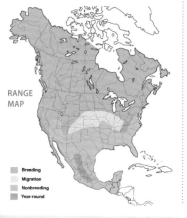

RANGE MAP

- Breeding
- Migration
- Nonbreeding
- Year-round

KEYS TO IDENTIFICATION

MEASUREMENTS (Both sexes)

Length	Wingspan	Weight
4.3–5.9 in	7.9–8.7 in	0.5–1 oz
11–15 cm	20–22 cm	15–28 g

SIZE & SHAPE. Savannah Sparrows are medium-sized sparrows with short, notched tails. The head appears small for the plump body, and the crown feathers often flare up to give the bird's head a small peak. The thick-based, seed-eating bill is small for a sparrow.

COLOR PATTERN. Savannah Sparrows are brown above with dark streaks. They are white below with thin brown or black streaks on the breast and flanks. They usually show a small yellow mark above and in front of the eye.

BEHAVIOR. Savannah Sparrows forage on or near the ground. When flushed, they usually fly up, flare their short tails, and circle before landing a few yards away. Males sing from exposed, low perches such as fence posts.

Cool Facts

Savannah Sparrows have a strong tendency to return each year to the area where they hatched. This is called "natal philopatry" and has led to several distinct Savannah Sparrow subspecies.

Backyard Tips

Savannah Sparrows are not feeder birds, though they may visit backyards adjoining fields. A brush pile may lure them to swoop in and take cover during migration or over the winter.

FOX SPARROW (Passerella iliaca)

Typically seen sending up a spray of leaf litter as they kick around in search of food, Fox Sparrows are dark, splotchy birds of dense thickets. Named for their rich red hues, this species is one of our most variable birds, with four main forms that can range from foxy red to gray to dark brown. Most breed in remote areas, so many people see them only during migration and in winter, when the birds move into backyard thickets or visit feeders.

AT A GLANCE

Food Fox Sparrows forage for insects and seeds in leaf litter and bare ground, often under dense cover. They find their prey with a characteristic "double-scratch" involving a hop forward and an immediate hop back, during which they simultaneously scratch both feet backwards through the leaf litter.

Nesting Fox Sparrows nest on or near the ground. Nests vary a lot in size. The outer wall is made of twigs, strips of bark, shredded or rotting wood, moss, coarse dry grass, and lichens. The inner cup is often lined with fine grass, rootlets, mammal hair, or feathers.

Habitat Fox Sparrows breed in coniferous forest and dense mountain scrub. They spend winters in scrubby habitat and forest, when they are most likely to be seen kicking around under backyard bird feeders.

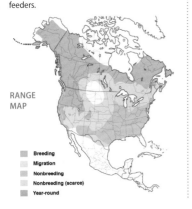

RANGE MAP

- Breeding
- Migration
- Nonbreeding
- Nonbreeding (scarce)
- Year-round

KEYS TO IDENTIFICATION

ADULT
(RED FORM)

MEASUREMENTS (Both sexes)

Length	Wingspan	Weight
6–7.5 in	10.5–11.5 in	0.9–1.5 oz
15–19 cm	26.7–29 cm	26–44 g

SIZE & SHAPE. Fox Sparrows are large, round-bodied sparrows with stout bills and medium-length tails.

COLOR PATTERN. Fox Sparrows are generally rust-brown above with a mix of rust and gray on the head and heavy brownish splotches on the flanks and the center of the chest. Those of interior mountains are dull gray above with brownish splotches below, and those along the Pacific Coast are very dark brown above. The bill can range from yellowish to dark gray.

BEHAVIOR. Fox Sparrows spend a lot of time on the ground, using their sturdy legs to kick away leaf litter in search of insects and seeds. They rarely venture far from cover and frequently associate with other sparrows. In spring and summer, listen for Fox Sparrows' sweet, whistled song from scrub or forest, and also for a sharp *smack* call.

Cool Facts

People have spotted Fox Sparrows in Greenland, Iceland, Ireland, Germany, and Italy. Some of these vagrant birds probably went part of the way on a ship after landing on one to rest.

Backyard Tips

Fox Sparrows feed on the ground close to dense vegetation. To attract them, scatter millet and sunflower seeds close to a brush pile, and plant native berry bushes.

SONG SPARROW *(Melospiza melodia)*

A rich, russet-and-gray bird with bold streaks down its white chest, the Song Sparrow is one of the most familiar North American sparrows. Don't let its bewildering variety of regional plumage differences deter you: this is one of the first species you should suspect if you see a streaky sparrow in an open, shrubby, or wet area. If it perches on a low shrub, leans back, and sings a stuttering, clattering song, so much the better.

AT A GLANCE

Food

Song Sparrows eat mainly seeds and fruits, adding invertebrates in summer. Food types vary greatly depending on what's most available. In British Columbia, Song Sparrows have even been observed picking at the droppings of Glaucous-winged Gulls.

Nesting

Song Sparrows nest in grasses or weeds, often near water, from ground level up to 15 feet. The female builds a simple, sturdy cup of grasses, weeds, and bark lined with finer material. The finished nest is 4–8 inches across and 2.5–4 inches deep.

Habitat

Look for Song Sparrows in nearly any open habitat, including marsh edges, overgrown fields, backyards, desert washes, and forest edges. Song Sparrows commonly visit bird feeders and build nests in residential areas.

RANGE MAP

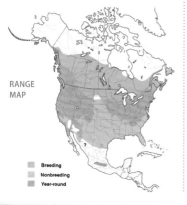

■ Breeding
■ Nonbreeding
■ Year-round

KEYS TO IDENTIFICATION

MEASUREMENTS (Both sexes)

Length	Wingspan	Weight
4.7–6.7 in	7.1–9.4 in	0.4–1.9 oz
12–17 cm	18–24 cm	12–53 g

SIZE & SHAPE. Song Sparrows are medium-sized and fairly bulky sparrows. For a sparrow, the bill is stout and the head fairly rounded. The tail is long and rounded and the wings are broad.

COLOR PATTERN. Song Sparrows are streaky and brown with thick streaks on a white chest and flanks. The breast streaks usually coalesce in a dark central spot. The head is strongly striped with russet on gray, with conspicuous dark, triangular "malar" stripes bordering the throat.

BEHAVIOR. Song Sparrows flit through dense, low vegetation or low branches, occasionally moving onto open ground to feed. Flights are short and fluttering, with a characteristic downward pumping of the tail. Male Song Sparrows sing from exposed perches such as small trees.

Cool Facts

Song Sparrows of coastal areas have more dark pigment (melanin) in their feathers. The melanin toughens the feathers, reducing damage caused by mites that flourish in humid climates.

Backyard Tips

Song Sparrows visit feeding stations, or more often the ground beneath feeders, for many seeds, especially sunflower and white millet. They often nest in shrubs, flower beds, and woodpiles.

WHITE-THROATED SPARROW *(Zonotrichia albicollis)*

Crisp facial markings make the White-throated Sparrow attractive as well as a hopping, flying anatomy lesson. Look for its black eyestripe, yellow lores, and white throat bordered by a black whisker. It's also a great entrée into the world of birdsong, with its pretty, wavering whistle of *oh-sweet-Canada*. This forest sparrow breeds mostly across Canada, but is a familiar winter bird across eastern and southern North America and California.

AT A GLANCE

Food

White-throated Sparrows eat seeds and fruits. In spring they add tender buds, blossoms, and young seeds of oak, apple, maple, beech, and elm. In summer they take insects from the forest floor and occasionally in quick flights. Parents feed insects to their nestlings.

Nesting

The cup nest is set on or just above the ground under shrubs, grasses, or ferns, in roots of an upturned tree or a brush pile, or in a coniferous tree. It's made of grass, twigs, wood chips, and pine needles and is 3–5.5 inches across on the outside, with an inner cup 1.7–4 inches across and 1–2.5 inches deep.

Habitat

White-throated Sparrows live in woods, forest edges, recently logged or burned areas, pond and bog edges, and copses near the treeline. In winter they live in thickets, overgrown fields, parks, woodsy suburbs, and backyard feeding stations.

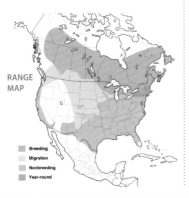

RANGE MAP

- ■ Breeding
- ■ Migration
- ■ Nonbreeding
- ■ Year-round

KEYS TO IDENTIFICATION

MEASUREMENTS (Both sexes)

Length	Wingspan	Weight
6.3–7.1 in	7.9–9.1 in	0.8–1.1 oz
16–18 cm	20–23 cm	22–32 g

SIZE & SHAPE. The White-throated Sparrow is a large, full-bodied sparrow with a fairly prominent bill, rounded head, long legs, and long, narrow tail.

COLOR PATTERN. White-throated Sparrows are brown above and gray below. One form has a striking head pattern: a black-and-white-striped crown, bright white throat, and yellow between the eye and the gray bill. A second form, called "tan-striped," has a buff-on-brown face pattern rather than white-on-black.

BEHAVIOR. White-throated Sparrows stay near the ground, scratching through leaves in search of food, often in flocks. You may see them low in bushes as well, particularly in spring when they eat fresh buds. White-throated Sparrows sing their distinctive songs frequently, even in winter.

Cool Facts

White-striped and tan-striped forms (see Color Pattern) tend to mate with the opposite form. White-striped birds are more aggressive; white-striped females outcompete tan-striped for mates.

Backyard Tips

White-throated Sparrows visit feeders and peck at seeds on the ground, preferring millet and sunflower seeds. Brush piles provide cover and resting places.

The striking Harris's Sparrow is rarely found far east or west of the middle of North America. The only bird species that breeds in Canada and nowhere else in the world, it nests along the edge of boreal forest and tundra, and winters in the very center of the United States, where it's a beloved backyard visitor. Its remote breeding habitat and secretive nesting behavior made it one of the last songbirds in North America to have its nest and eggs described.

AT A GLANCE

Food Harris's Sparrows eat a variety of seeds and some fruits, especially during migration and winter. They focus on insects and other arthropods mainly in the nesting season. They sometimes eat young conifer needles.

Nesting Harris's Sparrows place their nest on the ground, sunken into moss and lichens. The open cup nest is constructed of mosses, small twigs, and lichens, lined with dried grass and often some caribou hair.

Habitat Harris's Sparrows breed at the edge of boreal forest and tundra. They winter along hedgerows, shelterbelts, agricultural fields, weed patches, and pastures, often visiting feeders, especially near brush piles or other low hiding places.

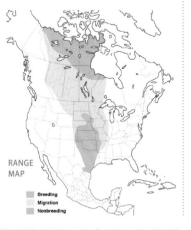

RANGE MAP

- Breeding
- Migration
- Nonbreeding

KEYS TO IDENTIFICATION

MEASUREMENTS (Both sexes)

Length	Wingspan	Weight
6.7–7.9 in	10.6 in	0.9–1.7 oz
17–20 cm	27 cm	26–49 g

SIZE & SHAPE. This medium-sized songbird is fairly large for a sparrow. It has a rounded head and a moderately long tail.

COLOR PATTERN. Spring adults have a striking black hood covering the crown, nape, throat, and upper breast that contrasts with the gray face and white underparts. In fall and winter, brown obscures some of the black hood. Immatures have very little black on the face or crown.

BEHAVIOR. Harris's Sparrows feed on the ground, picking up seeds and occasionally insects. They often scratch in litter with both feet to reveal food. They also visit feeding stations, concentrating on the ground beneath feeders near cover.

Cool Facts

Winter flocks of Harris's Sparrows have a pecking order that's based on who's got the largest black bib marking. That usually means older birds, but younger birds with large bibs also rank highly.

Backyard Tips

Harris's Sparrows visit bird feeders or, more often, the ground beneath them. Scatter white millet and black oil sunflower seeds near shrubs or a brush pile to attract them.

WHITE-CROWNED SPARROW *(Zonotrichia leucophrys)*

White-crowned Sparrows appear in droves each winter over much of North America, gracing gardens and trails. The smart black-and-white head, pale beak, and crisp gray breast give them a dashing look and make identification fairly simple. Flocks scurry through brushy borders, overgrown fields, and backyards. As spring approaches, they start singing their thin, sweet whistle before and during migration.

AT A GLANCE

Food White-crowned Sparrows eat mainly seeds of weeds and grasses. In summer they also eat considerable numbers of caterpillars, wasps, beetles, and other insects. They also eat grains such as oats, wheat, barley, and corn, and fruit including elderberries and blackberries.

Nesting White-crowned Sparrows nest fairly low in shrubs or on the ground, hiding the cup nest among mats of mosses, lichens, and ground-hugging shrubs. The nest, about 5 inches across and 2 inches deep, is built from twigs, grasses, pine needles, moss, bark, and dead leaves, lined with grasses and hairs.

Habitat White-crowned Sparrows live where safe tangles of brush mix with open or grassy ground for foraging. In much of the United States, they're most common in winter; they're found year-round in parts of the West.

RANGE MAP

- Breeding
- Migration
- Nonbreeding
- Nonbreeding (scarce)
- Year-round

KEYS TO IDENTIFICATION

MEASUREMENTS (Both sexes)

Length	Wingspan	Weight
5.9–6.3 in	8.3–9.4 in	0.9–1 oz
15–16 cm	21–24 cm	25–28 g

SIZE & SHAPE. The White-crowned Sparrow is a large sparrow with a small bill and a long tail. The head can look either distinctly peaked or smooth and flat, depending on the bird's posture and activity.

COLOR PATTERN. White-crowned Sparrows are gray-and-brown birds with large, bold black-and-white stripes on the head. The bill can be pale pink or yellow. Young birds have brown, not black, markings on the head.

BEHAVIOR. White-crowned Sparrows usually stay low at the edges of brushy habitat, hopping on the ground or on branches, usually below waist height. They're also found on open ground, usually with shrubs or trees nearby for when they need to retreat quickly to a hiding place.

Cool Facts

A migrating White-crowned Sparrow was tracked flying 300 miles in a single night. In the lab they've been tracked running on a treadmill at about a third of a mile per hour without tiring.

Backyard Tips

White-crowned Sparrows visit feeders or the ground beneath them for millet and sunflower and other seeds. A brush pile encourages them to spend more time in your yard.

Dark-eyed Juncos are neat, even flashy little sparrows that flit about forest floors of the western mountains and Canada, then flood the rest of North America for winter. They're easy to recognize by their simple (though extremely variable) markings and the bright white tail feathers they flash in flight. One of the most abundant forest birds of North America, you'll see juncos on woodland walks as well as in flocks at your feeders or on the ground beneath them.

AT A GLANCE

Food
Seeds make up about 75% of the Dark-eyed Junco's year-round diet. At feeders it seems to prefer millet over sunflower seeds. During the breeding season, it also preys on insects including beetles, moths, butterflies, caterpillars, ants, wasps, and flies.

Nesting
Juncos usually build nests on the ground, sheltered by tree roots, rocks, or sloping ground. Nests are made of grasses, pine needles, and other plant material. The nest is 3–5.5 inches across and up to 3 inches deep.

Habitat
Dark-eyed Juncos breed in coniferous or mixed-coniferous forests across Canada, the western U.S., and the Appalachians. During winter you'll find them in open woodlands, fields, parks, roadsides, and backyards.

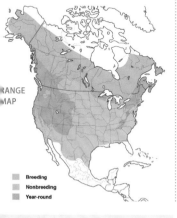

RANGE MAP

- Breeding
- Nonbreeding
- Year-round

KEYS TO IDENTIFICATION

MALE
(SLATE-COLORED FORM)

MEASUREMENTS (Both sexes)

Length	Wingspan	Weight
5.5–6.3 in	7.1–9.8 in	0.6–1.1 oz
14–16 cm	18–25 cm	18–30 g

SIZE & SHAPE. The Dark-eyed Junco is a medium-sized sparrow with a rounded head, a short, stout bill, and a fairly long tail.

COLOR PATTERN. Juncos vary across the country but in general are dark gray or brown with a white belly, pink bill, and white outer tail feathers that flash when the bird spreads its tail, particularly in flight.

BEHAVIOR. Dark-eyed Juncos hop around the bases of trees and shrubs in forests or venture out onto lawns looking for fallen seeds. They give high chip notes almost absent-mindedly while foraging, or more insistently as they take short, low flights through cover.

Cool Facts

Some juncos live in the Appalachian mountains year-round. These residents have shorter wings than migrants that join them each winter. Longer wings are better suited to flying long distances.

Backyard Tips

Dark-eyed Juncos visit feeders, the ground beneath feeders, and wood or brush piles. They have a preference for white millet and sunflower seed. They also visit birdbaths.

SUMMER TANAGER *(Piranga rubra)*

The only completely red bird in North America, the strawberry-colored male Summer Tanager is an eye-catching sight against the green leaves of the forest canopy. The mustard-yellow female is harder to spot, though both sexes have a distinctive chuckling call note. Fairly common during the summer, they migrate to Central and South America each winter. Year-round, they catch bees and wasps on the wing, somehow avoiding being stung by their prey.

AT A GLANCE

Food Summer Tanagers specialize on bees and wasps on both their breeding and wintering ranges. They also eat other insects and fruits. They capture flying insects during short sallies and glean terrestrial insects from the leaves and bark of trees and shrubs.

Nesting The nest, usually within a cluster of leaves or a fork of branches overhanging a road, creekbed, or treefall gap in the forest, is a crude cup of grasses and other plant matter measuring about 3.5 inches across and 2 inches high, with an inner cavity about 1 inch deep and 3 inches across.

Habitat Summer Tanagers breed near gaps and edges of open forests, especially deciduous or mixed pine-oak woodlands. In the Southwest, look for them along streams among willows, cottonwoods, mesquite, or saltcedar.

RANGE MAP

Breeding
Migration
Nonbreeding

KEYS TO IDENTIFICATION

MALE

FEMALE

MEASUREMENTS (Both sexes)

Length	Wingspan	Weight
6.7 in	12 in	1.1 oz
17 cm	30 cm	30 g

SIZE & SHAPE. Summer Tanagers are medium-sized, chunky songbirds with a big body, large head, and fairly long tail. They have a large, thick, blunt-tipped bill.

COLOR PATTERN. Adult male Summer Tanagers are entirely bright red, year-round. Females and immature males are bright yellow-green—yellower on the head and underparts and slightly greener on the back and wings. The bill is pale. Molting immature males can be patchy yellow and red.

BEHAVIOR. Summer Tanagers tend to stay fairly high in the forest canopy, where they sit still between sallying out to catch flying insects in midair, or they move slowly along tree branches to glean food. Males have a sweet, whistling song similar to an American Robin; both sexes give a distinctive *pit-ti-tuck* call note.

Cool Facts

This tanager specializes in catching bees and wasps in flight with its oversized bill. After catching one, it beats it against a branch and then rubs it on the branch to remove the stinger.

Backyard Tips

Although Summer Tanagers mostly eat bees and wasps, they may forage on backyard berry bushes and fruit trees near their forest habitat. They sometimes visit feeders, especially in fall.

SCARLET TANAGER *(Piranga olivacea)*

CARDINALS · GROSBEAKS · BUNTINGS

Male Scarlet Tanagers are among the most blindingly gorgeous birds in Eastern deciduous forests in summer, with blood-red bodies and jet-black wings and tail. They're also hard to find as they stay high in the forest canopy singing rich, burry songs. The yellowish-green, dark-winged females can be even harder to spot until you key in on their *chick-burr* call. In fall, males change their red feathers to yellow-green and the species heads to South America.

AT A GLANCE

Food
In North America, Scarlet Tanagers eat insects along with some fruit and tender buds. They usually find food by walking along branches high in the canopy, but can hover with fast wingbeats to grab insects from leaves, bark, and flowers, or snatch flying insects in midair.

Nesting
The flimsy nest, usually fairly high on a nearly horizontal branch well away from the trunk, has an unobstructed view of the ground and open flight paths from nearby trees. The saucer of twigs, bark strips, rootlets, etc., has a shallow, asymmetrical center for the eggs.

Habitat
Scarlet Tanagers breed in deciduous and mixed forests in eastern North America, especially in large, undisturbed tracts of forest. During migration, they move through a broader variety of forest and shrubby habitats, as well as backyards.

RANGE MAP

- ■ Breeding
- ■ Breeding (scarce)
- ■ Migration

KEYS TO IDENTIFICATION

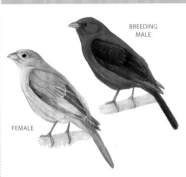

BREEDING MALE

FEMALE

MEASUREMENTS (Both sexes)

Length	Wingspan	Weight
6.3–6.7 in	9.8–11.4 in	0.8–1.3 oz
16–17 cm	25–29 cm	23–38 g

SIZE & SHAPE. Scarlet Tanagers are medium-sized songbirds with fairly stocky proportions. They have thick, rounded bills suitable both for catching insects and eating fruit. The head is fairly large and the tail is somewhat short and broad.

COLOR PATTERN. In spring and summer, adult males are an unmistakable, brilliant red with shiny black wings and tail. Females and fall immatures are olive-yellow with darker olive wings and tail. After breeding, adult males molt to female-like plumage, but with black wings and tail.

BEHAVIOR. Scarlet Tanagers can be difficult to see as they skulk among the wide leaves of deciduous trees in the forest canopy. The best way to zero in on them is to listen for their distinctive, harsh *chick-burr* call and, in spring, their burry, rambling song.

Cool Facts

The female Scarlet Tanager sings a song similar to the male's, but softer, shorter, and less harsh. She sings while she is gathering nesting material, and also in answer to her mate's song.

Backyard Tips

Scarlet Tanagers don't visit feeders, but during late summer and fall they may come to berry bushes planted in backyards.

NORTHERN CARDINAL *(Cardinalis cardinalis)*

The male Northern Cardinal is perhaps responsible for getting more people to open up a field guide than any other bird. The male is a conspicuous red; the female is brown with a sharp crest and red accents. Cardinals don't migrate and the male doesn't molt into a dull plumage, so it's still breathtaking in winter's backyards. In summer, the sweet whistled song is one of the first sounds of morning.

AT A GLANCE

Food Northern Cardinals eat mainly seeds and fruit, supplemented with insects. Cardinals eat many kinds of birdseed, particularly black oil sunflower seed and, in some areas, safflower. They feed their young almost entirely insects.

Nesting Nests are usually wedged into a fork of small branches in dense vegetation, up to about 15 feet high. The female builds the cup, about 2–3 inches tall and 4 inches across, of coarse twigs covered in a leafy mat, lined with grapevine bark and finer fibers.

Habitat Northern Cardinals live in open or fragmented habitat such as backyards, parks, woodlots, and shrubby forest edges, nesting in dense tangles of shrubs and vines. They're virtually never found in large forest interiors.

RANGE MAP

■ Year-round

KEYS TO IDENTIFICATION

MALE

FEMALE

MEASUREMENTS (Both sexes)

Length	Wingspan	Weight
8.3–9.1 in	9.8–12.2 in	1.5–1.7 oz
21–23 cm	25–31 cm	42–48 g

SIZE & SHAPE. The Northern Cardinal is a fairly large, long-tailed songbird with a short, very thick bill and a prominent pointed crest. Cardinals often sit with a hunched-over posture and with the tail pointed straight down.

COLOR PATTERN. Male cardinals are brilliant red all over, with a reddish bill and a solid black area around the bill. Adult females are pale brown overall with warm reddish tinges in the wings, tail, and crest, with black around the red-orange bill. Fledglings lack the black face and red bill.

BEHAVIOR. Northern Cardinals tend to sit low in shrubs and trees and forage on or near the ground, often in pairs. They are common at bird feeders but may be inconspicuous away from them, at least until you learn their loud, metallic chip note.

Cool Facts

Unlike most songbirds, female Northern Cardinals sing, sometimes even from the nest. A pair shares song phrases, but the female's song may be longer and slightly more complex than the male's.

Backyard Tips

Cardinals come to feeders with sunflower or safflower seeds. In spring they sometimes fight their reflections in windows. If this happens, cover the window with paper on the outside for a few days.

Bursting with black, white, and rose-red, the male Rose-breasted Grosbeak is like an exclamation mark at feeders. Females and immatures are streaked brown and white with a bold face pattern and enormous bill. Look for these birds in forest edges and woodlands. Their songs are similar to those of American Robins, but more hurried and richer, as if they had operatic training. They also make a sharp *chink* like the squeak of a sneaker.

AT A GLANCE

Food Rose-breasted Grosbeaks eat insects, fruits, and seeds. They usually glean their food from dense foliage and branches, but can also snag food while hovering, and by flying out to hawk for insects in midair. They visit feeders during migration, but seldom while nesting.

Nesting Rose-breasted Grosbeaks nest in a vertical fork or crotch of a sapling. The male and female construct the loose, open cup lined with fine fibers. The nest, 3.5–9 inches across and 1.5–5 inches high, may be so flimsy that you can see the outline of the eggs through it.

Habitat Rose-breasted Grosbeaks breed in eastern forests among both deciduous trees and conifers. They are most common in regenerating woodlands and often concentrate along forest edges and in parks. During migration, they gravitate to fruiting trees.

RANGE MAP

- Breeding
- Migration
- Nonbreeding

KEYS TO IDENTIFICATION

BREEDING MALE

FEMALE

MEASUREMENTS (Both sexes)

Length	Wingspan	Weight
7.1–8.3 in	11.4–13 in	1.4–1.7 oz
18–21 cm	29–33 cm	39–49 g

SIZE & SHAPE. Rose-breasted Grosbeaks are stocky, medium-sized songbirds with oversized triangular bills. They are broad-chested, with a short neck and a medium-length, squared tail.

COLOR PATTERN. Adult males are black and white with brilliant red from the throat to the center of the breast. Females and young are brown and streaked, with a bold whitish stripe over the eye. Males flash pink-red under the wings; females yellowish. Both sexes have white patches in the wings and tail.

BEHAVIOR. These chunky birds tend to sing from high in trees and may remain on the same perch for long periods. The sweet, rambling song, given by both sexes, is a familiar voice of eastern forests; the sharp *chink* calls are also very distinctive.

Cool Facts

The male Rose-breasted Grosbeak takes a turn incubating the eggs for several hours during the day, while the female incubates the rest of the day and all night long.

Backyard Tips

Rose-breasted Grosbeaks often visit bird feeders for sunflower seeds as well as safflower seeds, raw peanuts, and occasionally oranges.

BLUE GROSBEAK (Passerina caerulea)

A large, vibrantly blue bunting with an oversized silver bill and chestnut wingbars, the male Blue Grosbeak sings a rich, warbling song from trees and roadside wires. He and his cinnamon-colored mate often raise two broods in a single breeding season. These birds of shrubby habitats can be hard to spot unless you hear them singing or calling first. The species is widespread but not abundant across the southern U.S., and is expanding its range.

AT A GLANCE

Food Blue Grosbeaks feed mostly on insects, especially grasshoppers and crickets, and also seeds of wild and cultivated grains. Before feeding an insect to their nestlings, they remove the head, wings, and most of the legs.

Nesting Blue Grosbeaks build their nests low in small trees, shrubs, and tangles, often near open areas. The compact, cup-shaped nest is woven from twigs, bark strips, rootlets, snakeskin, and sometimes trash. It's lined with rootlets, hair, and fine grasses.

Habitat Look for Blue Grosbeaks in old fields beginning to grow back into woodland. They breed in areas covered with grass, forbs, and shrubs, with a few taller trees. In dry areas, they often concentrate in the shrubby growth along watercourses.

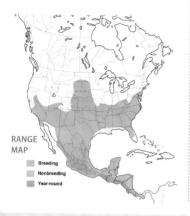

RANGE MAP

- Breeding
- Nonbreeding
- Year-round

KEYS TO IDENTIFICATION

MALE

FEMALE

MEASUREMENTS (Both sexes)

Length	Wingspan	Weight
5.9–6.3 in	11 in	0.9–1.1 oz
15–16 cm	28 cm	26–31 g

SIZE & SHAPE. The Blue Grosbeak is a stocky songbird with a very large, triangular bill that seems to cover the entire front of its face, from throat to forehead.

COLOR PATTERN. Adult males are deep, rich blue with a tiny black mask in front of the eyes, chestnut wingbars, and a black-and-silver beak. Females are rich cinnamon-brown, richer on the head and paler on the underparts; the tail is bluish. Both sexes have two wingbars, the upper chestnut and the lower grayish to buffy. Immature Blue Grosbeaks are a rich, dark chestnut brown, with chestnut wingbars.

BEHAVIOR. Blue Grosbeaks are unobtrusive despite their bright colors and frequent rich, warbling songs. They sing while perched on high points in shrubs and small trees of their open habitats. Listen for their loud, almost metallic *chink* call. Also watch for their odd habit of twitching the tail sideways.

Cool Facts

For such a widespread bird with a conspicuous song, very little field research has been done on the Blue Grosbeak. According to genetic evidence, its closest relative is the Lazuli Bunting.

Backyard Tips

Blue Grosbeaks are sometimes attracted to grains and seeds at feeders in shrubby backyards.

The all-blue male Indigo Bunting sings with cheerful gusto and looks like a scrap of sky with wings. Sometimes nicknamed "blue canaries," these brilliantly colored yet common and widespread birds whistle their bouncy songs through the late spring and summer all over eastern North America. Look for them in weedy fields and shrubby areas near trees, singing from dawn to dusk atop the tallest perch in sight and foraging for seeds and insects in low vegetation.

AT A GLANCE

Food
Indigo Buntings eat mainly insects during summer and then turn to seeds, berries, and buds the remainder of the year. Commonly eaten seeds include thistle, dandelion, and goldenrod.

Nesting
Indigo Buntings nest near the ground in fields, edges of woods, and roadsides. The nest is an open cup woven of leaves, grasses, stems, and bark, wrapped with spider silk. The inner cup is lined with slender grasses, tiny roots, bark strips, thistledown, and sometimes deer hair.

Habitat
Indigo Buntings live in weedy or brushy areas, forest edges, hedgerows, and brushy roadsides. They forage in shrubs and grasses. Males sing from the tallest perches around, including telephone lines.

RANGE MAP

Breeding
Migration
Nonbreeding

KEYS TO IDENTIFICATION

BREEDING MALE

FEMALE

MEASUREMENTS (Both sexes)

Length	Wingspan	Weight
4.7–5.1 in	7.5–8.7 in	0.4–0.6 oz
12–13 cm	19–22 cm	12–18 g

SIZE & SHAPE. Indigo Buntings are small (roughly sparrow-sized), stocky birds with short tails and short, thick, conical bills. In flight, they appear plump with short, rounded tails.

COLOR PATTERN. Breeding males are all blue, richest on the head, with a silver-gray bill. Females are brown with faint streaking on the breast and sometimes a touch of blue on the wings, tail, or rump. Immature and winter males are patchy blue and brown.

BEHAVIOR. Male Indigo Buntings sing from treetops, shrubs, and telephone lines all summer. While perching, they often swish their tails from side to side. Fairly solitary during breeding season, they form large flocks during migration and on their wintering grounds.

Cool Facts

Indigo Buntings migrate by night, orienting by the North Star, like sailors of old. Studies done in planetariums suggest the birds learn the position of this star when they're young.

Backyard Tips

Indigo Buntings visit feeders, especially during spring migration. They usually take small seeds such as thistle or nyjer. Live mealworms may attract them as well.

PAINTED BUNTING (*Passerina ciris*)

With their vivid fusion of blue, green, yellow, and red, male Painted Buntings seem to have flown straight out of a child's coloring book. Females and immatures are a distinctive bright green with a pale eyering. These fairly common finches breed in the coastal Southeast and in the south-central U.S., where they often come to feeders. They are often sold illegally as cage birds, a practice that puts pressure on their breeding populations.

AT A GLANCE

Food Painted Buntings eat seeds, usually on the ground, most of the year, switching to insects in the breeding season. They often pull invertebrates from spiderwebs, or even dive straight through a web to grab a spider's prey.

Nesting Painted Buntings nest near the ground if there is ground cover, or as high as 50 feet up if there isn't. The female builds the sturdy nest, firmly attached to a supporting plant, with an inner cup 2 inches wide and 1.5 inches deep, bound with cobwebs and lined with horsehair.

Habitat Painted Buntings breed in dense brush, often adjacent to thick, grassy areas or woodland edges. During migration and winter they favor dense, weedy habitats as well as the understory of semiopen forest.

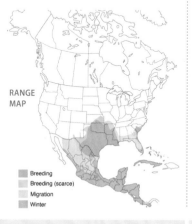

RANGE MAP

- Breeding
- Breeding (scarce)
- Migration
- Winter

KEYS TO IDENTIFICATION

MALE

FEMALE

MEASUREMENTS (Both sexes)

Length	Wingspan	Weight
4.7–5.1 in	8.5 in	0.5–0.7 oz
12–13 cm	22 cm	13–19 g

SIZE & SHAPE. Painted Buntings are medium-sized finches with thick, seed-eating bills.

COLOR PATTERN. Males are stunningly colored with a blue head, red underparts, and green back. Females and immatures are a uniform, bright yellow-green, with a pale eyering. Though they are basically unpatterned, their overall color is greener and brighter than similar songbirds.

BEHAVIOR. Painted Buntings forage on the ground in dense cover, among grasses, or at seed feeders. Sometimes they venture into grass to forage on seeds. On migration they form loose flocks with other seed-eating birds. Breeding males often perch in the open to sing their jumbled, sweet songs.

Cool Facts

The French name of the Painted Bunting, *nonpareil*, means "without equal," referring to the bird's dazzling plumage.

Backyard Tips

Painted Buntings eat seeds, including sunflower and white millet, during migration and winter. They're more likely to visit feeders in a yard with low, dense vegetation.

RED-WINGED BLACKBIRD *(Agelaius phoeniceus)* BLACKBIRDS · GRACKLES · ORIOLES

One of the most abundant birds in North America, the Red-winged Blackbird is a familiar sight atop cattails, along roadsides, and on telephone wires. Glossy-black males have scarlet-and-yellowish shoulder patches they can puff up or hide almost completely. Females are a subdued, streaky brown, almost like a large, dark sparrow. In the North, their early arrival and tumbling song are happy indications of the return of spring.

AT A GLANCE

Food
Red-winged Blackbirds eat mainly insects in the summer and a wide variety of seeds and grains in the winter. They probe the bases of aquatic plants with their slender bills, prying them open to get at insects hidden inside.

Nesting
Red-winged Blackbirds build their nests low among shrubs, trees, and vertical shoots of marsh vegetation. The female winds stringy plant material around several upright stems, weaves a platform of coarse, wet vegetation, and plasters the inside with mud to form the cup.

Habitat
Red-winged Blackbirds breed in wetlands, salt marshes, along streams, water hazards on golf courses, wet roadsides, and old fields. In winter, look for them in crop fields, feedlots, and pastures.

RANGE MAP

- Breeding
- Nonbreeding
- Year-round

KEYS TO IDENTIFICATION

FEMALE

MALE

MEASUREMENTS (Both sexes)

Length	Wingspan	Weight
6.7–9.1 in	12.2–15.7 in	1.1–2.7 oz
17–23 cm	31–40 cm	32–77 g

SIZE & SHAPE. This stocky, broad-shouldered blackbird has a slender, conical bill and a medium-length tail. It often shows a humpbacked silhouette while perched; males often sit with tail slightly flared.

COLOR PATTERN. Male Red-winged Blackbirds are hard to mistake. They're glossy black with red-and-yellow shoulder badges. Females are streaked and dark brownish overall, paler on the breast, with a whitish or buffy eyebrow.

BEHAVIOR. In spring, male Red-winged Blackbirds sit conspicuously on high perches to belt out their *conk-la-ree* song. Females skulk through vegetation for food and quietly attend to nesting. In winter they all gather in huge flocks to eat grains with other blackbirds.

Cool Facts

Male Red-winged Blackbirds typically defend territories big enough for several females to nest in. The technical term for this system of one male mating with multiple females is "polygyny."

Backyard Tips

Red-winged Blackbirds may come to your yard for mixed grains and seeds, particularly during migration. Spread some grain or seed on the ground where they prefer to feed.

EASTERN MEADOWLARK (Sturnella magna,

The sweet, simple whistles of Eastern Meadowlarks waft over grasslands and farms in eastern North America in spring and summer. The birds sing from fence posts and telephone lines. They stalk through the grass, probing the ground for insects with their long, sharp bills. On the ground, their brown-and-black dappled upperparts camouflage them against dirt clods and dry grasses.

AT A GLANCE

Food

Eastern Meadowlarks eat mostly insects such as crickets, grasshoppers, and grubs. In winter they also eat weed seeds, spilled corn, and wild fruits. They probe the ground with their bill, opening the mandibles to expose grubs and worms in a typical blackbird feeding tactic called "gaping."

Nesting

Eastern Meadowlarks nest on the ground, in a small depression or hoofprint, well concealed by dense grassy vegetation. The cup nest, woven with dead grasses, plant stems, and strips of bark, is about 6–9 inches wide and 2–3 inches deep. Some nests have overhead roofs and tunnel entrances.

Habitat

Eastern Meadowlarks live in farm fields, native grasslands, and wet fields. They will breed in many kinds of grassy areas as long as they can find about 6 acres in which to create a territory.

RANGE MAP

- ■ Breeding
- ■ Nonbreeding
- ■ Year-round

Cool Facts

As simple as the meadowlark's song sounds, each male sings many variations. When the songs of one individual in New York were analyzed, researchers found more than 100 different patterns.

KEYS TO IDENTIFICATION

MEASUREMENTS (Both sexes)

Length	Wingspan	Weight
7.5–10.2 in	13.8–15.7 in	3.2–5.3 oz
19–26 cm	35–40 cm	90–150 g

SIZE & SHAPE. Eastern Meadowlarks are chunky, medium-sized songbirds with short tails and long, spear-shaped bills. In flight, their rounded wings, short tails, and long bills are distinctive.

COLOR PATTERN. Eastern Meadowlarks are pale brown marked with black, with bright-yellow underparts and a bold black V across the chest. Though most of the tail is brown with blackish barring, the outer feathers are white and are conspicuous during flight.

BEHAVIOR. Eastern Meadowlarks are hard to see as they walk on the ground concealed by grasses or crops. In summer males sing their beautiful, flutelike songs from exposed perches, especially fence posts. Their flight is also conspicuous: a sequence of rapid fluttering and short glides, usually just above the vegetation. In winter you may see flocks of meadowlarks hunting insects in fields.

Find This Bird

In summer, meadowlarks sing till late in the day, so listen for their flutelike songs. When they're silent, their low, fluttering flight can help you find them.

A bird to be seen in the full sun, the male Brewer's Blackbird is a glossy, almost liquid combination of black, midnight blue, and metallic green. Females are a staid brown, without the male's bright eye or the female Red-winged Blackbird's streaks. Common in towns and open habitats within their range, these long-legged birds forage on sidewalks and city parks, and gather in flocks atop shrubs, trees, and reeds.

AT A GLANCE

Food Brewer's Blackbirds eat mostly seeds and grains, and also, when available, insects, small frogs, young voles, and some nestling birds. Around marshes, you may see them walk on lily pads to hunt aquatic insects.

Nesting Brewer's Blackbirds nest in colonies of a few to more than 100 pairs in shrubs, trees, reeds or cattails, on the ground, or sometimes even in tree cavities. The nest cup of plant stems and twigs is lined with fine dried grasses, sometimes cemented with mud or manure.

Habitat Look for Brewer's Blackbirds in open habitats such as coastal scrub, grasslands, riversides, meadows, and city parks and streets. Where they overlap with Common Grackles, Brewer's Blackbirds stick to fields and grasslands.

RANGE MAP

■ Breeding
■ Migration
■ Nonbreeding
■ Year-round

KEYS TO IDENTIFICATION

MALE

MEASUREMENTS (Both sexes)

Length	Wingspan	Weight
7.9–9.8 in	14.6 in	1.8–3 oz
20–25 cm	37 cm	50–86 g

SIZE & SHAPE. Brewer's Blackbirds are medium-sized, fairly long-legged songbirds. The fairly long tail is balanced by a full body, round head, and long, thick-based beak. The tail often appears widened and rounded toward the tip.

COLOR PATTERN. Males are glossy black with a blue sheen on the head and greenish sheen on the body; their eyes are yellow. Females are brown with darker wings and tail and a dark eye. Immatures look like pale females.

BEHAVIOR. Brewer's Blackbirds feed on open ground or underfoot in parks and busy streets. Their long legs give them a halting walk, head jerking with each step like a chicken's. Flying flocks seem to rise and fall; they often circle in slow fluttering flight before landing.

Cool Facts

Most birds fly south for the winter, but a small number of Brewer's Blackbirds fly west–leaving the frigid Canadian prairies for the milder coastal regions of British Columbia and Washington.

Backyard Tips

Brewer's Blackbirds visit feeders, though they're a bit clumsy when perching. Scattering seed on the ground or using an open platform feeder usually is most effective at attracting them.

COMMON GRACKLE *(Quiscalus quiscula)*

Common Grackles are blackbirds that look like they've been stretched and shined. They strut on lawns and fields on their long legs or gather in noisy groups high in trees, especially evergreens. They eat many crops (notably corn) and nearly anything else as well, including garbage. Gardeners appreciate that they feed voraciously on slugs. In flight their long tails trail behind them, sometimes folded down the middle into a shallow V shape.

AT A GLANCE

Food Common Grackles eat mostly seeds, including agricultural grains such as corn and rice. They also take acorns, fruits, and garbage. In summer, one-quarter or more of their diet is animal, including insects, fish, salamanders, mice, and birds.

Nesting The nest is usually set high in a conifer but may be just off the ground. Sites can include cattails, nest boxes, woodpecker holes, crevices, or in an Osprey or Great Blue Heron nest. The bulky cup is made of twigs, leaves, and grasses along with bits of debris, reinforced with mud and lined with mammal hair.

Habitat Common Grackles thrive around agricultural fields, feedlots, city parks, and suburban lawns. They're also common in open habitats including woodland, forest edges, meadows, and marshes.

RANGE MAP

Breeding
Nonbreeding
Year-round

KEYS TO IDENTIFICATION

MEASUREMENTS (Both sexes)

Length	Wingspan	Weight
11–13.4 in	14.2–18.1 in	2.6–5 oz
28–34 cm	36–46 cm	74–142 g

SIZE & SHAPE. Common Grackles are large, lanky blackbirds with long legs and long tails. The head is flat and the bill is longer than in most blackbirds, with the hint of a downward curve. In flight, the wings appear short in comparison to the tail. Males are slightly larger than females.

COLOR PATTERN. Common Grackles appear black from a distance, but up close their glossy purple heads contrast with bronzy-iridescent bodies. A bright golden eye gives grackles an intent expression. Females are slightly less glossy than males. Young birds are dark brown with a dark eye.

BEHAVIOR. Common Grackles form large flocks, flying or foraging on lawns and in agricultural fields. They peck for food rather than scratching. At feeders they dominate smaller birds. When resting they sit atop trees or on telephone lines, keeping up a raucous chattering. Flight is direct, with stiff wingbeats.

Cool Facts

Common Grackles are versatile eaters: they follow plows to catch invertebrates and mice, wade into water to catch small fish, pick leeches off the legs of turtles, and steal worms from American Robins.

Backyard Tips

Where slugs are a problem, grackles are welcome visitors in backyards. They can be aggressive to other birds at feeders, but switching to feeders with small perches can keep these big birds at bay.

A big, brash blackbird, the male Great-tailed Grackle shimmers in iridescent black and purple, trailing a tail that will make you look twice. The rich brown female is about half the male's size. Flocks of these long-legged, social birds strut and hop on suburban lawns, golf courses, fields, and marshes. In the evening, raucous flocks pack neighborhood trees, filling the sky with their amazing and, some might say, ear-splitting voices.

AT A GLANCE

Food
Great-tailed Grackles eat grains, fruits, insects, spiders, slugs, amphibians, reptiles, fish, small mammals, bird eggs, and nestlings. In summer and early fall, about 80% of the female's diet and half of the male's is animal.

Nesting
The bulky nest is placed as high as possible in a tree or shrub, rushes or other marsh vegetation, or a structure such as a duck blind or telephone pole. Nest material can include plastic strips and bags, ribbons, feathers, and string. The nest is lined with mud or cow dung and fine grasses.

Habitat
Great-tailed Grackles forage in agricultural fields and feedlots, golf courses, cemeteries, parks, and neighborhood lawns. Large trees and vegetation edging marshes, lakes, and lagoons provide roosting and breeding sites.

RANGE MAP

■ Breeding
■ Year-round

KEYS TO IDENTIFICATION

MALE

MEASUREMENTS (Both sexes)

Length	Wingspan	Weight
15–18.1 in	18.9–22.8 in	3.7–6.7 oz
38–46 cm	48–58 cm	105–190 g

SIZE & SHAPE. Males are big, long-legged, slender blackbirds with a flat-headed profile and stout, straight bill. The tapered tail, nearly as long as the body, folds into a distinctive V or keel shape. Females are half the size of males and have long, slender tails.

COLOR PATTERN. Adult males are iridescent black with yellow eyes and black bills and legs. Adult females are dark brown above, paler below. Juveniles have the female colors, but with streaked underparts and a dark eye.

BEHAVIOR. Great-tailed Grackles hang out in flocks, pecking for food on lawns, fields, and at marsh edges, vying for trash in urban settings, or crowding in trees and on telephone lines in noisy roosts.

Cool Facts

Boat-tailed Grackles are very similar, but their eyes are dark instead of yellow. They live almost exclusively in salt marshes along the East and Gulf coasts, while Great-tailed is more widespread.

Backyard Tips

Great-tailed Grackles take cracked corn, milo, and other seed from beneath feeders, often chasing off smaller birds. Using feeders with small perches can give the littler birds a chance.

BROWN-HEADED COWBIRD *(Molothrus ater)*

The Brown-headed Cowbird is a stocky blackbird with a fascinating approach to raising its young. Females lay their eggs in the nests of other birds, which raise the cowbird chick, usually at the expense of its own. Once confined to the open grasslands of middle North America and associated with bison, cowbirds have surged in numbers and range as humans built towns and cleared woods. They have become a conservation problem for some native birds.

AT A GLANCE

Food
Brown-headed Cowbirds feed mostly on seeds from grasses and weeds, with some crop grains. Insects make up about a quarter of their diet. Females eat snail shells and sometimes eggs taken from nests. This helps provide the calcium needed for so much egg production.

Nesting
Cowbirds lay eggs in the nests of over 140 host species, from tiny kinglets to meadowlarks. Cowbirds prefer the nests of larger species. Common hosts include the Yellow Warbler, Song and Chipping sparrows, Red-eyed Vireo, Eastern and Spotted towhees, and Red-winged Blackbird.

Habitat
Brown-headed Cowbirds live in many open habitats, such as fields, pastures, meadows, forest edges, and lawns. When not displaying or feeding on the ground, they often perch high on prominent tree branches.

RANGE MAP

- Breeding
- Nonbreeding
- Year-round

KEYS TO IDENTIFICATION

MALE

MEASUREMENTS (Both sexes)

Length	Wingspan	Weight
7.5–8.7 in	14.2 in	1.5–1.8 oz
19–22 cm	36 cm	42–50 g

SIZE & SHAPE. Brown-headed Cowbirds are smallish blackbirds, with a shorter tail and thicker head than most other blackbirds. The bill has a distinctive shape: it's shorter and thicker-based than other blackbirds', almost finchlike at first glance. In flight, look for the shorter tail.

COLOR PATTERN. Male Brown-headed Cowbirds have glossy black plumage and a rich brown head that often looks black in poor lighting or at distance. Female Brown-headed Cowbirds are plain grayish-brown birds, lightest on the head and underparts, with fine streaking on the belly.

BEHAVIOR. Brown-headed Cowbirds feed on the ground in mixed-species flocks of blackbirds and starlings. Males gather on lawns to strut and display; females prowl woodlands and edges in search of nests. Brown-headed Cowbirds are noisy, making a multitude of clicks, whistles, and chatterlike calls in addition to a gurgling song.

Cool Facts

A female cowbird spends no energy raising her young each year, so she pours everything into creating eggs—sometimes three dozen in a single summer.

Backyard Tips

This species often comes to backyards, eating sunflower seeds, corn, and other foods from tube and hopper feeders, as well as from the ground.

BALTIMORE ORIOLE *(Icterus galbula)*

The rich, whistling song of the Baltimore Oriole, echoing from treetops near homes and parks, is a sweet herald of spring in eastern North America. Look way up to find the male's orange plumage blazing from high branches. You might also spot the female weaving her remarkable hanging nest from slender fibers. Drawn to fruit and nectar as well as insects, Baltimore Orioles are easily lured to backyard feeders, especially during spring migration.

AT A GLANCE

Food
Baltimore Orioles eat insects, fruit, and nectar, the proportion of each food varying by season and availability. In summer, while breeding and feeding their young, much of the diet consists of insects, which are rich in the proteins needed for growth.

Nesting
The female anchors her remarkable, sock-shaped hanging nest firmly to a fork in the slender upper branches of an American elm, maple, cottonwood, or similar tree. The distinctive nest usually hangs below a branch, but is sometimes anchored along a vertical tree trunk.

Habitat
Look for Baltimore Orioles high in leafy deciduous trees, but not in deep forests: they're found in open woodlands, forest edges, orchards, parks, backyards, and along rivers.

RANGE MAP

- Breeding
- Migration
- Nonbreeding

KEYS TO IDENTIFICATION

MALE

MEASUREMENTS (Both sexes)

Length	Wingspan	Weight
6.7–7.5 in	9.1–11.8 in	1.1–1.4 oz
17–19 cm	23–30 cm	30–40 g

SIZE & SHAPE. Smaller and more slender than a robin, Baltimore Orioles are medium-sized, sturdy-bodied songbirds with thick necks and long legs. Look for their long, thick-based, pointed bills, a hallmark of the blackbird family they belong to.

COLOR PATTERN. Adult males are flame-orange and black, with a solid-black head and one white bar on their black wings. Females and immature males are yellow-orange on the breast, grayish on the head and back, with two bold white wing bars.

BEHAVIOR. Baltimore Orioles are more often heard than seen as they feed high in trees, searching leaves and small branches for insects, flowers, and fruit. They also feed on fruit in vines and bushes and at feeders. Their flight between tree tops is fluttering; they make a characteristic *wink* or chatter call in flight.

Cool Facts

Baltimore Orioles use their slender bills to feed by "gaping." They stab the bill into fruit, then open their mouth, drinking the juice with their brushy-tipped tongues.

Backyard Tips

Cut oranges in half and hang them from trees to invite orioles into your yard, especially during spring migration. They also visit hummingbird feeders and may eat jelly from small dishes.

HOUSE FINCH (Haemorhous mexicanus)

The House Finch is a recent arrival to much of North America (and Hawaii)—it originally hails from the southwestern U.S. This now-common bird has received a warmer reception than other arrivals such as the European Starling and House Sparrow. That's partly due to the cheerful red head and breast of males, and to the bird's long, twittering song, which can be heard in most of the neighborhoods of the continent.

AT A GLANCE

Food
House Finches eat seeds, buds, and fruits—cultivated and wild—and very few insects or other animal foods. At feeders they prefer black oil sunflower over the larger, striped sunflower seeds.

Nesting
House Finches nest in trees, cactus, and rock ledges, and also in or on buildings, lights, ivy, and hanging planters. The nest is a cup made of fine stems, leaves, rootlets, thin twigs, string, wool, and feathers, with similar, but finer materials for the lining. The inner cup is 1–3 inches across and up to 2 inches deep.

Habitat
House Finches frequent city parks, backyards, urban centers, farms, and forest edges across the continent. In the western U.S., you'll also find them in their native habitats of deserts, grassland, chaparral, and open woods.

RANGE MAP

Year-round

KEYS TO IDENTIFICATION

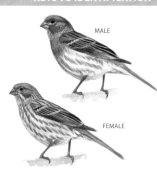

MALE

FEMALE

MEASUREMENTS (Both sexes)

Length	Wingspan	Weight
5.1–5.5 in	7.9–9.8 in	0.6–1 oz
13–14 cm	20–25 cm	16–27 g

SIZE & SHAPE. House Finches are small-bodied finches with fairly large beaks and somewhat long, flat heads. The wings are short, making the tail seem long by comparison. Many finches have distinctly notched tails, but the House Finch has a relatively shallow notch in its tail.

COLOR PATTERN. Adult males are rosy red around the face and upper breast, with streaky brown back, belly, and tail. In flight, the red rump is conspicuous. Adult females aren't red; they are plain grayish-brown with thick, blurry streaks.

BEHAVIOR. House Finches are gregarious birds that collect at feeders or perch high in nearby trees. When they're not at feeders, they eat on the ground, on weed stalks, or in trees. They move fairly slowly and sit still as they shell seeds by crushing them with rapid bites. Their flight is bouncy, like that of many finches.

Cool Facts

The male's red coloration comes from pigments in its food during the time it molts. The more pigment in the food, the redder the male. Females choose the brightest male available.

Backyard Tips

Fill your backyard feeders with black oil sunflower seed, which House Finches prefer over the thicker striped sunflower. They sometimes visit feeders in flocks of 50 or more.

PURPLE FINCH *(Haemorhous purpureus)*

The Purple Finch was famously described by Roger Tory Peterson as a "sparrow dipped in raspberry juice." In much of the U.S., it's an irregular winter visitor to feeders. Separating it from the more widespread House Finch requires a careful look, but the reward is a delicately colored, cleaner version of that red finch. In spring, the male sings his rich warbling song from the highest parts of trees, especially conifers.

AT A GLANCE

Food Purple Finches eat seeds from coniferous and deciduous trees and ground plants. They also take soft buds, nectar (extracted by biting the bases off flowers), berries, fruits, and some insects.

Nesting Purple Finches nest far out on a limb of a tree (usually coniferous), shrub, or vine tangle. Nests are often built under an overhanging branch for shelter, and made from twigs, sticks, and roots, lined with fine grasses and animal hair. The nests are about 7 inches wide and 4 inches tall.

Habitat Purple Finches breed mainly in coniferous forests or mixed deciduous and coniferous woods. During winter you can find them in a wider variety of habitats, including shrublands, old fields, forest edges, and backyards.

RANGE MAP

- Breeding
- Breeding (scarce)
- Migration
- Nonbreeding
- Nonbreeding (scarce)
- Year-round

KEYS TO IDENTIFICATION

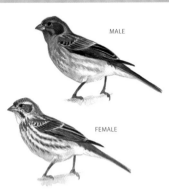

MALE

FEMALE

MEASUREMENTS (Both sexes)

Length	Wingspan	Weight
4.7–6.3 in	8.7–10.2 in	0.6–1.1 oz
12–16 cm	22–26 cm	18–32 g

SIZE & SHAPE. Purple Finches are larger and chunkier than the chickadees, kinglets, and nuthatches they live near. Their powerful, conical beak is larger than a sparrow's. The tail seems short and is clearly notched at the tip.

COLOR PATTERN. Male Purple Finches have a pink-red head and breast blending with brown on the face, head, and back. Females are crisply streaked brown and white, with a neat white eyebrow stripe on a brown face. In both sexes, the chest streaks give way to a whitish belly.

BEHAVIOR. In forests in spring, Purple Finches can be noisy but hard to see as they forage high in trees. In winter they may descend to eat seeds from plants and stalks in weedy fields and at feeders. Their flight is undulating.

Cool Facts

The Purple Finch uses its thick bill and muscular tongue to crush shells and fruits to extract the seed within, or to get at nectar without eating the whole flower.

Backyard Tips

Purple Finches prefer black oil sunflower seeds, selecting thinner over wider ones. Coniferous trees in your backyard may encourage them to visit and discover your feeders.

COMMON REDPOLL (Acanthis flammea)

Energetic as their electric zapping call notes would suggest, Common Redpolls are active foragers that travel in busy flocks. They feed on birch catkins as well as at feeders. These small finches of the arctic tundra and boreal forest migrate erratically, and they occasionally show up in large numbers as far south as the central U.S. During such irruption years, redpolls often congregate at bird feeders, especially for nyjer seed, allowing delightfully close looks.

AT A GLANCE

Food Common Redpolls eat small seeds of trees such as birch, willow, alder, spruce, and pine. They also eat seeds of grasses, sedges, and wildflowers, and some berries. During summer they also eat spiders and insects. At feeders they eat millet and nyjer (thistle) seed.

Nesting Redpolls nest low in spruces, alders, and willows or, on the tundra, on driftwood, rock ledges, or other ground cover. The nest of grasses, fine twigs, moss, etc., rests on a foundation of small twigs, and is lined with ptarmigan or Spruce Grouse feathers and other insulating material.

Habitat Common Redpolls frequent tundra and associated habitats such as willow flats, open conifer forest, and open, weedy fields. They visit backyard bird feeders as well, especially during winter and early spring.

RANGE MAP

- Breeding
- Winter
- Winter (scarce)
- Year-round
- Irruptive

KEYS TO IDENTIFICATION

MALE

MEASUREMENTS (Both sexes)

Length	Wingspan	Weight
4.7–5.5 in	7.5–8.7 in	0.4–0.7 oz
12–14 cm	19–22 cm	11–20 g

SIZE & SHAPE. Common Redpolls are very small songbirds with small heads and short, pointed, seed-eating bills. The tail is short with a small notch at the tip.

COLOR PATTERN. Common Redpolls are brown-and-white finches with heavily streaked sides and two white wingbars. The small red forehead patch and black feathering around the yellow bill distinguish them from Pine Siskins. Males have varying amounts of pink or red on the chest and upper flanks.

BEHAVIOR. Redpolls travel in flocks of up to several hundred individuals. They move frenetically, foraging on seeds in weedy fields or small trees one minute and swirling away in a mass of chattering birds the next. Their buzzy *zap* and rising *dreeee* calls are distinctive.

Cool Facts

Common Redpolls can survive temperatures of –65 degrees Fahrenheit. A study in Alaska found that Redpolls molted into winter plumages about 31% heavier than their summer set of feathers.

Backyard Tips

Common Redpolls are drawn to thistle or nyjer feeders, and also take black oil sunflower and spilled seeds opened by larger-billed birds. Wet and moldy seeds can make them sick.

PINE SISKIN *(Spinus pinus)*

Huge flocks of tiny Pine Siskins may monopolize your thistle feeder one winter and be entirely absent the next. These nomadic finches wander widely and erratically across the continent in response to seed crops. Adapted to clinging to branch tips rather than hopping along the ground, these brown-streaked acrobats flash yellow wing markings as they flutter while feeding or as they explode into flight.

AT A GLANCE

Food Pine Siskins eat seeds of conifers and deciduous trees, soft buds of willows, emerging seedlings of many small plants, and tiny seeds of grasses, dandelions, etc. They also take some insects or feed at sap wells drilled by sapsuckers.

Nesting The small cup nest, composed of twigs, grasses, leaves, weed stems, rootlets, bark strips, and lichens, lined by softer fibers, is loosely attached toward the end of a horizontal branch in the middle heights of a conifer. Neighboring nests can be just a few trees away.

Habitat Pine Siskins prefer coniferous or mixed coniferous and deciduous forests with open canopies, but are opportunistic and adaptable. They forage in weedy fields, scrubby thickets, and backyards. They flock around feeders in woodlands and suburbs.

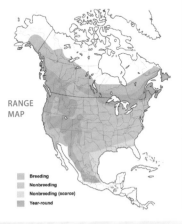

RANGE MAP

- ▇ Breeding
- ▇ Nonbreeding
- ▇ Nonbreeding (scarce)
- ▇ Year-round

KEYS TO IDENTIFICATION

MEASUREMENTS (Both sexes)

Length	Wingspan	Weight
4.3–5.5 in	7.1–8.7 in	0.4–0.6 oz
11–14 cm	18–22 cm	12–18 g

SIZE & SHAPE. Pine Siskins are very small songbirds with sharp, pointed bills and short, notched tails. Their conical bill is more slender than most finches' bills. In flight, look for their sharply notched tail and pointed wingtips.

COLOR PATTERN. Pine siskins are brown and very streaky finches with subtle yellow edgings on wings and tails. Flashes of yellow can erupt as they take flight, flutter at branch tips, or display during mating.

BEHAVIOR. Pine Siskins visit feeders in winter (particularly for nyjer seed) and cling to branch tips of pines and other conifers, sometimes hanging upside down to pick at seeds below them. They forage in tight flocks and twitter incessantly, even during their undulating flight.

Cool Facts

Pine Siskins can store seeds totaling as much as 10% of their body mass in a part of their esophagus called the crop, sustaining them for 5–6 nighttime hours of subzero temperatures.

Backyard Tips

Pine Siskins flock to feeders and the ground below for nyjer, millet, and black oil sunflower seeds. If your yard has plants or weeds with hardy seed heads, such as dandelion, these may also attract siskins.

AMERICAN GOLDFINCH (Spinus tristis)

This handsome little finch, the state bird of New Jersey, Iowa, and Washington, is welcome and common at feeders where it takes primarily sunflower and nyjer seeds. Goldfinches often flock with Pine Siskins and Common Redpolls. Spring males are brilliant yellow and shiny black with a bit of white. Females and all winter birds are duller but identifiable by their conical bill, dark wings, wingbars, and lack of streaking.

AT A GLANCE

Food Goldfinches eat seeds almost exclusively, especially seeds from composite plants (in the family Asteraceae: sunflowers, thistle, asters, etc.), grasses, and trees such as alder, birch, western red cedar, and elm. At feeders they prefer nyjer (thistle) and sunflower seeds.

Nesting The female builds the nest, an open cup of rootlets and plant fibers lined with plant down, usually in a shrub or sapling in open habitat. The nest, often woven so tightly that it can hold water, is about 3 inches across and 2–4.5 inches high.

Habitat The goldfinch's main natural habitats are weedy fields and floodplains where thistles and asters are common. They're also found in cultivated areas, roadsides, orchards, and backyards. They visit feeders any time of year, but most abundantly during winter.

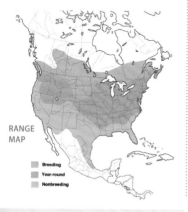

RANGE MAP

- Breeding
- Year-round
- Nonbreeding

KEYS TO IDENTIFICATION

BREEDING MALE

NONBREEDING MALE

MEASUREMENTS (Both sexes)

Length	Wingspan	Weight
4.3–5.1 in	7.5–8.7 in	0.4–0.7 oz
11–13 cm	19–22 cm	11–20 g

SIZE & SHAPE. This is a tiny finch with a short, conical bill, a small head, long wings, and a short, notched tail.

COLOR PATTERN. Adult males in spring and summer are brilliant yellow with a black forehead, black wings with white markings, and white patches above and beneath the tail. Adult females are dull yellow beneath, olive above. Winter birds are unstreaked brownish, with dark wings and two pale wingbars.

BEHAVIOR. American Goldfinches are active and acrobatic little finches that cling to weeds and seed socks, and sometimes mill about in large numbers at feeders or on the ground beneath them. They fly with a bouncy, undulating pattern and often call in flight, drawing attention to themselves.

Cool Facts

Goldfinches are among the strictest vegetarians in the bird world. They are even known to feed their baby chicks regurgitated seeds rather than insects.

Backyard Tips

Native thistles and milkweed attract goldfinches. At feeders they prefer nyjer and sunflower. They often eat on the ground in areas where there's little leaf litter.

HOUSE SPARROW *(Passer domesticus)*

Along with two other introduced species, the European Starling and the Rock Pigeon, House Sparrows are some of our most abundant birds. Their constant presence outside our doors makes them easy to take for granted, and their tendency to displace native birds from nest boxes makes their large numbers a genuine problem. But House Sparrows, with their capacity to live so intimately with humans, are just beneficiaries of our own species' success.

AT A GLANCE

Food House Sparrows eat grains and seeds, livestock feed, and discarded food. In summer, they catch insects by pouncing on them, following lawnmowers, picking them out of car grilles, or plucking them from lights at dusk.

Nesting House Sparrows nest in holes of buildings, streetlights, signs, etc., or in vines climbing the walls of buildings. They displace bluebirds and Tree Swallows from nest boxes. They make bulky nests using coarse materials that often fill the entire hole, adding finer material for the lining.

Habitat House Sparrows have lived around humans for millennia. Look for them in urban, suburban, and rural areas, from big cities to farms and pastures. They're absent from undisturbed forests and natural grasslands.

RANGE MAP

■ Year-round
■ Year-round (scarce)

KEYS TO IDENTIFICATION

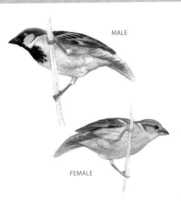

MALE

FEMALE

MEASUREMENTS (Both sexes)

Length	Wingspan	Weight
5.9–6.7 in	7.5–9.8 in	1.0–1.1 oz
15–17 cm	19–25 cm	27–30 g

SIZE & SHAPE. Compared to most native American sparrows, House Sparrows are chunkier, fuller in the chest, with a larger, rounded head, shorter tail, and stouter bill.

COLOR PATTERN. Male House Sparrows are brightly colored with a gray head, whitish cheeks, black bib, and rufous neck. Females are buffy-brown with dingy underparts. The backs of both are striped with buff, black, and brown.

BEHAVIOR. House Sparrows flutter from eaves and fence rows, fly in and out of nest holes hidden behind shop signs or in traffic lights, and hang around parking lots and outdoor cafés waiting for crumbs. Their noisy, sociable *cheep cheep* calls are familiar wherever they are found.

Cool Facts

House Sparrows take frequent dust baths, throwing loose soil and dust over their feathers as if bathing with water. Each one may defend a good dust-bathing spot against other sparrows.

Backyard Tips

House Sparrows are not native and can be a problem when they take over the nest sites of native species. They are frequent visitors to backyard feeders, where they eat most kinds of birdseed.

The Cornell Lab of Ornithology is a world leader in advancing the understanding and protection of birds. Every day, the Cornell Lab shares the joy and science of birds—bringing people of all walks of life together to learn about birds and contribute to scientific discovery and conservation.

SCIENCE. In the quest to understand nature, scientists and students at the Cornell Lab reveal new insights about birds, wildlife, and the ecosystems we all depend on for a healthy planet.

LIFELONG LEARNING. The Cornell Lab inspires people of all ages to explore the world of birds—and trains the next generation of conservation leaders. Tell a teacher about the BirdSleuth K–12 curriculum, delve into the online Cornell Lab Bird Academy, or become a field biologist in your own living room with live Bird Cams.

CITIZEN SCIENCE. More than 400,000 citizen-science participants help the Cornell Lab illuminate where birds are, how they migrate, and how birds are faring through time across the globe.

TECHNOLOGY. The Lab's engineers, computer scientists, and biologists invent new ways to use digital technologies to study the natural world—whether to forecast bird migrations, reveal the movements of birds across the hemisphere, or listen to night skies filled with the sounds of birds.

CONSERVATION. Communities, nonprofits, industries, and governments trust the Cornell Lab to provide the best scientific information for conservation decisions and action.

If you love birds and want to help, join more than 100,000 people who support the nonprofit Cornell Lab of Ornithology. As a member, you'll receive the Lab's beautiful and insightful quarterly magazine, *Living Bird*. Visit *birds.cornell.edu.*

EDITORS

Hugh Powell is the senior science editor at the Cornell Lab of Ornithology, where he writes and edits for *Living Bird* magazine and the Lab's All About Birds website and species guide. He has written about ecology, evolution, conservation, and ocean science in Hawaii, Peru, Iceland, Australia, and Antarctica for outlets including Smithsonian, Slate, and the Woods Hole Oceanographic Institution. For many years he was a field researcher in Georgia, Idaho, Montana, and Panama. Hugh lives in Williamstown, Massachusetts.

Brian Scott Sockin has authored eight books, including the Cornell Lab Publishing Group's children's picture book *Am I Like You?* and the Storytelling World Awards honor book, *C.A.R.E. Treasury of Children's Folklore*. Brian has a B.A. in psychology from Binghamton University and an M.B.A. from the Wharton School of Business. He is CEO of the Cornell Lab Publishing Group, which has afforded him a rare opportunity to pair his passion for nature and writing with his business career. Brian has worked intimately with the Cornell Lab of Ornithology for many years on numerous education and publishing initiatives, including the *wildbirdclub.com* family website. Brian is a native of upstate New York and now lives in Cary, North Carolina, with his family.

Laura Erickson has been a scientist, teacher, writer, wildlife rehabilitator, blogger, public speaker, photographer, and science editor at the Cornell Lab of Ornithology. She has written eight books about birds, including the Cornell Lab Publishing Group's children's picture book *Am I Like You?*, *The Bird Watching Answer Book*, and the *National Geographic Pocket Guide to Birds of North America*. Laura is a National Outdoor Book Award winner and a columnist and contributing editor for *BirdWatching* magazine. In 2014, she was awarded the prestigious Roger Tory Peterson Award for lifetime achievement in promoting the cause of birding by the American Birding Association. Laura also writes and produces a daily radio segment about birds. Laura lives in Duluth, Minnesota.

ILLUSTRATOR

Pedro Fernandes is a freelance wildlife illustrator. Born in Lisbon, Portugal, Pedro earned a degree in earth sciences and later studied science illustration at the University of California, Santa Cruz, and at the Cornell Lab of Ornithology, where he was a

Bartels Science Illustration Intern. As a child, Pedro wanted to be a condor when he grew up. Having failed at that, he settled for becoming a wildlife illustrator. He loves watching birds, drawing birds, and going places to see birds—his pretext to explore the natural world and an endless source of amazement and discovery. Pedro lives in Morocco.

DESIGNER

Patricia Mitter is the creative director of the Cornell Lab Publishing Group. After earning her graphic design degree in Caracas, Venezuela, she moved to the United States with her husband. She then began a new career path in the world of editorial design and soon learned that her passion for nature and animals was a perfect fit. Patricia is also a photographer and lives in Durham, North Carolina.

ASSISTANT EDITORS

Kathi Borgmann, Diane Tessaglia-Hymes, and Francesca Chu.

WRITERS

Gustave Axelson, Ben Barkley, Jessie Barry, Kathi Borgmann, Martha Brown, Alice Cascorbi, Victoria Campbell, Miyoko Chu, Laura Erickson, Rusten Hogness, Andrew Johnson, Tom Johnson, Roberta Kwok, Pat Leonard, Tony Leukering, Abby McBride, Kevin McGowan, Hugh Powell, Matt Savoca, Carolyn Sedgwick, Sarah Rabkin, Marie Read, Erik Vance, and Nathaniel Young.

ACKNOWLEDGMENTS

We owe our gratitude to the photographers who generously granted permission to include their photos in this book, including members of the Cornell Lab of Ornithology's Birdshare Flickr site. Special thanks to B. N. Singh, Brian Kushner, and Ken Phenicie, Jr., for their numerous selections and/or cover shots. Many thanks to all of the photographers (see pages 192–193).

We thank the Cornell Lab of Ornithology's Birds of North America team for the use of maps in this book, as well as the content at *birdsna.org*, which provided much of the information presented on each species.

The Cornell Lab's Macaulay Library provided sounds that you can hear using the Bird QR companion app for this book.

We thank Jessie Barry, Miyoko Chu, and Mary Guthrie for their guidance throughout the preparation of this book. Special thanks to Jill Leichter and Dan Otis for their editorial help, and Bartels Science Illustration Intern Virginia Greene for the illustrations on pages 44–45.

Development of the All About Birds website was supported by the National Science Foundation under grants DRL-9618945 and DRL-0087760. The opinions expressed on the site are those of the authors and do not necessarily reflect the views of the National Science Foundation.

113 Gary Fairhead
114 Eric Lu
115 DeeDee Gollwitzer
116 Kelly Colgan Azar
117 Raymond M. K. Lee
118 B. N. Singh flickr.com/photos/bnsingh
119 B. N. Singh flickr.com/photos/bnsingh
120 Jon Corcoran
121 Linda Petersen
122 Brian E. Kushner
123 Kurt Hasselman
124 Doug Sonerholm
125 Eric Lu
126 Malcolm Gold
127 Raymond M. K. Lee
128 Ray Hennessy
129 B. N. Singh flickr.com/photos/bnsingh
130 Linda Petersen
131 B. N. Singh flickr.com/photos/bnsingh
132 Yves Déry
133 Matt MacGillivray
134 Richard Williams
135 Miguel de la Bastide
136 Bob Gunderson
137 B. N. Singh flickr.com/photos/bnsingh
138 Ken Phenicie, Jr.
139 Conrad Tan
140 Alan Gutsell
141 Corey Hayes
142 michaelmuchmore on Flickr
143 Keith Richardson
144 B. N. Singh flickr.com/photos/bnsingh
145 Andrew Jordan
146 Brian E. Kushner
147 Nick Dean
148 Olivier Levasseur
149 Corey Hayes
150 Bryan Hix
151 Stephen Parsons
152 Linda Petersen
153 B. N. Singh flickr.com/photos/bnsingh
154 Daniel Behm
155 B. N. Singh flickr.com/photos/bnsingh
156 Laura Meyers
157 Ellen DeCarlo
158 Prem Raja

159 Bob Vuxinic
160 B. N. Singh flickr.com/photos/bnsingh
161 Brian E. Kushner
162 Ryan Schain
163 Bob Vuxinic
164 Brian E. Kushner
165 Linda Petersen
166 Beth Hamel
167 ©bryanjsmith
168 Alan Gutsell
169 Ronald Zigler
170 B. N. Singh flickr.com/photos/bnsingh
171 Gary Tyson
172 www.GregGard.com
173 Cory McIvor
174 Danny Bales
175 Team Hymas
176 Joshua Clark www.momentsinature.com
177 Earthling Photos
178 Bryan Hix
179 Gerald McGee
180 Jon Corcoran
181 Jessica L. Botzan
182 Matt Cuda
183 Ken Phenicie, Jr.
184 Corey Hayes
185 Ross Taylor
186 Keith Bowers
187 Sterling Moore

Red-tailed Hawk

WEBSITES

All About Birds
AllAboutBirds.org

Bird Academy
Academy.AllAboutBirds.org

Birds of North America
Birdsna.org

eBird
eBird.org

Great Backyard Bird Count
BirdCount.org

Project FeederWatch
FeederWatch.org

NestWatch
NestWatch.org

Celebrate Urban Birds
CelebrateUrbanBirds.org

Habitat Network
www.Habitat.Network

Merlin Bird ID App
Merlin.AllAboutBirds.org